AN INQUIRY INTO THE GENERAL PRINCIPLES OF
SCRIPTURE-INTERPRETATION,

IN

EIGHT SERMONS

PREACHED BEFORE

THE UNIVERSITY OF OXFORD,

IN THE YEAR MDCCCXIV.

AT THE

LECTURE

FOUNDED BY

THE LATE REV. JOHN BAMPTON, M. A.

CANON OF SALISBURY.

BY

WILLIAM VAN MILDERT, D. D.

REGIUS PROFESSOR OF DIVINITY, AND CANON OF CHRIST CHURCH,
NOW BISHOP OF DURHAM.

THIRD EDITION.

WIPF & STOCK · Eugene, Oregon

Wipf and Stock Publishers
199 W 8th Ave, Suite 3
Eugene, OR 97401

The Battle for the Keys
Revelation 1:18 and Christ's Descent into the Underworld
By Bass, Justin
Copyright©2014 Paternoster
ISBN 13: 978-1-62564-839-6
Publication date 4/15/2014
Previously published by Paternoster, 2014

TO

THE RIGHT REVEREND

AND REVEREND

THE HEADS OF COLLEGES

IN THE

UNIVERSITY OF OXFORD,

THE

FOLLOWING SERMONS,

PREACHED BY THEIR APPOINTMENT,

ARE RESPECTFULLY

INSCRIBED.

Jan. 9, 1815.

CONTENTS.

SERMON I.

Introductory Observations on Religious Controversy. Necessity of adhering to some general Principles of Scripture-Interpretation. Plan of the ensuing Discourses.

TITUS i. 9.

Holding fast the faithful word, as he hath been taught, that he may be able, by sound doctrine, both to exhort and to convince the gainsayers.

SERMON II.

Dispositions and Qualifications previously requisite in the Interpreter of Scripture.

JOHN vii. 17.

If any man will do His will, he shall know of the doctrine, whether it be of God.

SERMON III.

Authority of Scripture as the Rule of Faith and the Interpreter of its own Doctrines.

1 PETER iv. 11.

If any man speak, let him speak as the oracles of God.

SERMON IV.

Continuation of the same Subject, with reference to other means necessary for the Interpretation of Scripture, in subordination to Scripture itself.

1 Peter iv. 11.

If any man speak, let him speak as the oracles of God.

SERMON V.

Analysis of Scripture. Fundamental Truths. Distinctions respecting the several Dispensations of Revealed Religion. Various Subject-matter of the Sacred Writings. Different Occasions and Purposes for which they were composed.

2 Timothy ii. 15.

Rightly dividing the word of truth.

SERMON VI.

Analogy of Faith. Systematic Arrangements of Scripture-Truth. Attention to Verbal, Historical, and Doctrinal Analogies indispensably necessary. Errors arising from the neglect of them.

1 Corinthians ii. 13.

Comparing spiritual things with spiritual.

SERMON VII.

Figurative and mystical Interpretation of Scripture. Its proper use explained and illustrated. Parables, Types, and Allegories. Cautions against its Misapplication, and the danger of carrying it to Excess.

2 CORINTHIANS iii. 6.

Who also hath made us able ministers of the new testament; not of the letter, but of the spirit: for the letter killeth, but the spirit giveth life.

SERMON VIII.

Preservation of Scripture-Truth a sacred Charge committed to the Church. Inquiry how far it has hitherto fulfilled that Trust. Conduct of the Church of England in this respect. Her principles of Scripture-Interpretation. Her Purity and Moderation. Importance of maintaining her Ascendancy, for the general interests of Christianity.

1 TIMOTHY iii. 15.

Which is the Church of the living God, the pillar and ground of the Truth.

EXTRACT

EXTRACT

FROM

THE LAST WILL AND TESTAMENT

OF THE

REV. JOHN BAMPTON,

CANON OF SALISBURY.

—— " I give and bequeath my Lands and Estates to
" the Chancellor, Masters, and Scholars of the University
" of Oxford for ever, to have and to hold all and sin-
" gular the said Lands or Estates upon trust, and to the
" intents and purposes hereinafter mentioned; that is to
" say, I will and appoint that the Vice-Chancellor of the
" University of Oxford for the time being shall take and
" receive all the rents, issues, and profits thereof, and
" (after all taxes, reparations, and necessary deductions
" made) that he pay all the remainder to the endowment
" of eight Divinity Lecture Sermons, to be established for
" ever in the said University, and to be performed in the
" manner following:

" I direct and appoint, that, upon the first Tuesday in
" Easter Term, a Lecturer be yearly chosen by the Heads
" of Colleges only, and by no others, in the room adjoin-
" ing to the Printing-House, between the hours of ten in
" the morning and two in the afternoon, to preach eight
" Divinity Lecture Sermons, the year following, at St.
" Mary's in Oxford, between the commencement of the
" last month in Lent Term, and the end of the third week
" in Act Term.

EXTRACT FROM CANON BAMPTON'S WILL.

"Also I direct and appoint, that the eight Divinity Lecture Sermons shall be preached upon either of the following Subjects—to confirm and establish the Christian Faith, and to confute all heretics and schismatics—upon the divine authority of the holy Scriptures—upon the authority of the writings of the primitive Fathers, as to the faith and practice of the primitive Church—upon the Divinity of our Lord and Saviour Jesus Christ—upon the Divinity of the Holy Ghost—upon the Articles of the Christian Faith, as comprehended in the Apostles' and Nicene Creeds.

"Also I direct, that thirty copies of the eight Divinity Lecture Sermons shall be always printed, within two months after they are preached, and one copy shall be given to the Chancellor of the University, and one copy to the Head of every College, and one copy to the Mayor of the city of Oxford, and one copy to be put into the Bodleian Library; and the expense of printing them shall be paid out of the revenue of the Land or Estates given for establishing the Divinity Lecture Sermons; and the Preacher shall not be paid, nor be entitled to the revenue, before they are printed.

"Also I direct and appoint, that no person shall be qualified to preach the Divinity Lecture Sermons, unless he hath taken the degree of Master of Arts at least, in one of the two Universities of Oxford or Cambridge; and that the same person shall never preach the Divinity Lecture Sermons twice."

SERMON I.

TITUS i. 9.

Holding fast the faithful word as he hath been taught, that he may be able by sound doctrine both to exhort and to convince the gainsayers.

To a person well grounded in the principles of Revealed Religion, and whose faith has never yet been shaken by any attempts to subvert it, matter of astonishment and perplexity is continually presented, in contemplating the prodigious diversity of religious opinions which agitate the Christian world. That Christianity itself should be opposed by any who have had sufficient opportunities of examining its pretensions, is a phenomenon not easily explained upon the ordinary principles of human conduct. But still more inexplicable does it appear, that, among those who professedly agree as to the *general* truth of the Gospel, there should be found any irreconcilable difference respecting its *particular* doctrines; and that such a difference should exist even on points acknowledged, on all sides, to be of fundamental importance. It also increases this perplexity, that the Sacred Writers strenuously urge unanimity, as well as sincerity, in the profession of the Faith. They exhort that all dissensions and divisions should be avoided, although they allow not of any compromise of truth for the sake of peace and amity. Whence we are naturally led to infer, that truth is certainly attainable by a right application of the rule of faith which these inspired Teachers have left us; and that a disagreement in the application of it indicates, on the part of some of its interpreters, a deviation from the rule itself. Nevertheless, it is a fact beyond dispute, that these apostolical injunctions have not hitherto produced their full effect; since, from the earliest ages of the Church to the present day, heresies and schisms have arisen in rapid succession, baffling every attempt at their entire extirpation.

This would be a circumstance very discouraging to the sincere believer in God's word, had not that same word forewarned him of the event; giving also directions for conducting this warfare betwixt truth and falsehood, and clearly predicting its successful issue.

SERMON I.

Among many other instructions to the same effect, St. Paul, in the words of the text, warns the Christian minister to be prepared for the work of controversy. " To exhort and " to convince the gainsayers," he represents as an indispensable part of the pastoral office. He represents it also as a duty, for which he is to qualify himself by " sound doctrine;" by doctrine obtained from the fountain-head of Scripture truth, " the faithful word ;" the word delivered by holy men, inspired of God, who exhibited incontrovertible credentials of their Divine commission to instruct mankind.

No great research is requisite, to shew the necessity of this admonition, or to prove how large a portion of good has, under Divine Providence, resulted from the apparent evil which renders it necessary. Every day's experience testifies, that the truth is more and more illustrated by that investigation which the perverseness of its opponents continually calls forth. This benefit the Christian Church has abundant reason to acknowledge. What article of the Faith has not received some additional confirmation; nay, what support has not the Faith itself, in general, received; from the profound and elaborate disquisitions which its adversaries have provoked? So ample, indeed, have been the contributions thus made to the stores of theological knowledge, that, on many of its weightiest subjects, more information perhaps is now to be obtained from polemical than from merely didactic treatises. Of this description were the greater part of the writings of the early Fathers of the Church; occasioned by the efforts, either of Infidels, to subvert the whole fabric of Christianity, or of Heretics, to despoil it of its essential doctrines. Nay, the writings of the Apostles themselves (excepting their historical narratives) appear to have been, for the most part, controversial; written, not so much for the purpose of elementary instruction, as for the refutation of errors which had already crept into the Church. And who does not know, that, in these latter times, the most successful promoters of religious truth are to be found among those who have been challenged to its defence, by bold oppugners of the Faith, or by abettors of specious heresy?

But while we gratefully acknowledge this good to have been eventually derived from the labours thus called forth, let us not overlook the positive evils that attend it, nor forget the awful denunciation of our blessed Master, "Woe unto the world because of offences[a]!"

[a] Matth. xviii. 7.

The offences hereby occasioned are, indeed, neither light nor few. The faith of multitudes is shaken; of some, entirely overthrown. Many are confirmed in unbelief. The corrupt passions of men are fostered; their prejudices strengthened; and unchristian acrimony and bitterness too often engendered. Therefore, "although it must needs be that "offences come," and although the providence of God renders them instrumental to good more than proportionate to the evil, yet for that portion of evil, whatever it may be, is the assailant of the truth responsible:— "Woe unto that man by whom the offence "cometh!"

Religious controversy, then, is not to be considered as in itself indicative of an unchristian spirit. It is good or evil, according to the principles which it upholds, the purpose in which it originates, the object to which it is applied, and the temper with which it is conducted. If it spring from a mere spirit of contention; from desire of victory, not love of truth; or from stubbornness that will not be brought into captivity to the obedience of Christ; Christianity will not acknowledge it for her own. If it be employed on questions unbefitting human disputation; questions, inaccessible to our finite understandings, unnecessary or unimportant in their issue, and only tending to perpetuate strife, or to unsettle the opinions and disquiet the minds of men; then is it also unworthy of the Christian character. Nor is it void of offence, when, however sound its principle, however important its subject, however irrefragable its argument, it is made the vehicle of personal malignity; when it is carried on with a spirit that rends asunder the social ties, and exasperates, instead of endeavouring to soften, the irritable feelings which, even in its mildest aspect, it is but too apt to excite.

But these evil consequences, which flow from the abuse of controversy and from causes by no means necessarily connected with religious discussion, ought not to deter us from its proper use, when truth requires its aid. Controversy is worse than useless, if it have no better end in view than a display of mental superiority, or the self-gratification which, to minds of a certain cast, it appears to afford. For as, in secular disputes, it is the legitimate end of warfare to produce peace; so, in polemical discussion, the attainment of unanimity ought to be the main object. War is waged, because peace cannot be obtained without it. Religious controversy is maintained, because agreement in the truth is not otherwise to be effected. When this necessity is laid upon us, we do but acquit ourselves of an indispensable duty, in defending the charge committed to our care, by the use of those weapons with which the armoury of the Divine Word supplies us.

Nevertheless, there prevails, in the present day, a spurious kind of liberality, which would teach us to regard with equal complacency almost every diversity of religious opinion, however irreconcilable with the tenets which we ourselves believe to be the unsophisticated doctrine of God's word. Hence, though that word is made by many the instrument of spreading religious error, yet, because it is appealed to for the sanction of error as well as of truth, we are often called upon to give the right hand of fellowship even to those by whom it is thus perverted. As if the time were already come when " the " wolf should dwell with the lamb, and the " leopard lie down with the kid[b]," and nothing should " hurt or destroy in all God's " holy mountain[c]," many are lulled into security under a persuasion that error and falsehood are harmless in their nature, and

[b] Isa. xi. 6.   [c] Isa. xi. 9.

will cease to molest us, if we admit them into our fold. According to this persuasion, Christian charity seems to have lost one of its distinctive characters, that of " rejoicing in the " truth[d]," and to rejoice rather in sacrificing the truth for the semblance of concord. " The " bond of peace" is no longer to be found in " unity of spirit[e];" but diversity and disunion are to work the happy effect. A boundless latitudinarianism is to supply the place of fixed principles: and to every religionist who professes to derive his tenets from the Scriptures, the plea is to be allowed of an equal adherence to Divine truth; as if the word of God were responsible for whatever of confusion or contrariety may be engrafted upon it by human devices!

Were these sentiments generally admitted, and practically carried to their full extent, there would indeed be no longer occasion for the study of controversial Divinity. St. Paul's admonition to "hold fast the faithful word," for the purpose of " exhorting and convincing "gainsayers," might be regarded as an obsolete precept, superseded by later discoveries. Error and Truth might go hand in hand. Credulity and Incredulity might concur in erecting a motley fabric, of divers proportions and of

[d] 1 Cor. xiii. 6.   [e] Ephes. iv. 3.

fantastic forms, on the ruins of the solid and venerable edifice of Christian unanimity.

Every argument, however, that can be urged, to shew the necessity of " contending " for the faith," and endeavouring to " con-" vince the gainsayers," proceeds on the supposition that there is some acknowledged foundation on which the matter in discussion rests. It also presupposes some acknowledged rules or maxims, by which the discussion is to be regulated. Otherwise, instead of being able to adapt to our case the Apostle's expressions, " So run I, not as uncertainly; so " fight I, not as one that beateth the air[f];" we may at last be found among the number of those whom the same Apostle describes as " ever learning, but never able to come to " the knowledge of the truth[g]."

Controversy, therefore, as it respects professed Christian believers, is but another term for maintaining what, on either side, is supposed to be the true intent and meaning of the Sacred Word. The right Interpretation of Scripture is the direct object of its research. The authenticity, authority, and truth, of that Word, are assumed as axioms or postulates, on which the whole inquiry is founded. It is presumed also, that truth, and truth

[f] 1 Cor. ix. 26.   [g] 2 Tim. iii. 7.

only, can issue from this Divine source of knowledge; for, as contrary positions in human science cannot be received as true, so is it impossible that contrary doctrines in theology should have any real foundation in Holy Writ. With infidels, indeed, these postulates are not to be assumed, without proof or evidence deduced from some other principles admitted both by the unbeliever and the Christian. But among professed believers a mutual agreement on these points is necessarily implied, and any departure from them in the course of argument may justly be deemed inadmissible:—a rule, however, not unfrequently violated in the wantonness of polemical disputation.

It is evident, then, that, for the preservation of Christian truth and Christian unity, there must be a general recognition of some fixed principles of Scripture-Interpretation; without which, it is impossible that we should "all speak the same thing[h]," that our Jerusalem should be "as a city that is at unity "in itself[i]," or that, however widely the Scriptures be diffused, any security can be had against their perversion. Men may be conversant with the Word of life, but read it neither

[h] 1 Cor. i. 10. [i] Psalm cxxii. 3.

with the spirit nor with the understanding requisite to a right apprehension of its contents.

Nor does this view of the subject derogate, in any respect, from the sufficiency of the Sacred Writings for the purpose they were intended to effect. For though it be most true, that they "are able to make us wise unto sal-"vation[k]," yet that implies not that the effect will be produced without due care and diligence on the part of those who receive them. The Scriptures themselves intimate the contrary, in their admonitions that we beware of "corrupting the word of God[l]," of being led away by "false teachers[m]," of "handling the "word of God deceitfully[n]," and of being "wise in our own conceits[o]." To prevent these evils, the providence of God hath ordained, that in this, as in other concerns, the strong should assist the weak, and they who have abundance should minister to such as are in need. Perhaps no man was ever entirely self-instructed in his knowledge of the Bible: nor do we read of any instances of conversion to Christianity (except in cases purely miraculous) without the instrument-

---

[k] 2 Tim. iii. 15. [l] 2 Cor. ii. 17. [m] 2 Peter ii. 1.
[n] 2 Cor. iv. 2. [o] Rom. xii. 16.

ality of human teaching The Word has never been, either under the Jewish or the Christian dispensation, unaccompanied with the ordinance of a ministry to promulgate its truth. Nevertheless, the Word itself contains all that is necessary to salvation. Provision only is to be made, that neither the ignorant nor the unstable should "wrest it to their "destruction." For we may affirm, on the authority of an Apostle, that to such a purpose, not only "some things hard to be un-"derstood[p]" in St. Paul's writings, but also "the other Scriptures" are liable to be perverted.

The proficient in ecclesiastical history will require no detail of evidence to convince him that the Scriptures have thus oftentimes been forced from their direct and proper channel, to yield supplies to error. To a perverse endeavour thus to obtain a colour of sacred authority for its opinions, religious error may indeed be chiefly ascribed. For, does not every sect or denomination of Christians maintain, that it has the sanction of Scripture for its own Creed? And how could this be, if, among so many contending parties, some, at least, did not ground their interpretation of it upon erroneous principles? The fact

[p] 2 Pet. iii. 17.

SERMON I.

speaks for itself, and shews that whatever some may dream of the facility of extracting from the Scriptures a correct and coherent system of Divine truth, this is hardly to be effected without such qualifications and attainments as we shall in vain look for among a very considerable portion of mankind.

It is a duty, then, which we owe to that God who caused these Scriptures to be "writ-"ten for our learning[q]," that we use our best faculties, and resort to the best helps that can be obtained, for security against their misinterpretation. More especially is this incumbent upon them who are called to the Ministerial Office. An awful responsibility lies upon them, to "hold fast the faithful "word as they have been taught, that they "may be able, by sound doctrine, both to ex-"hort and to convince the gainsayers." And since the effectual discharge of this duty demands a competent acquaintance, not only with the ordinary rules of criticism, the original languages of the Sacred Writings, and the proofs of their divine authority, but also with the leading errors which have from time to time prevailed, and the sources from which they have sprung; it will immediately be perceived how wide a field of inquiry pre-

[q] Rom. xv. 4.

sents itself to the sincere and diligent investigator of Scripture truth.

It may, therefore, be neither unseasonable with respect to the present state of religious opinions, nor unsuitable to the design of the institution which calls forth these annual labours in the cause of truth, if an attempt be made to establish some general rules and principles of Scripture-Interpretation, and to shew the necessity of adhering to them for the preservation of truth, and the refutation of error. " To confirm and establish the " Christian Faith, and to confute heretics and " schismatics," are among the declared purposes which the pious Founder of this Lecture had in view; purposes, to which the proposed investigation cannot be deemed irrelevant. And if any one period more than another may render a discussion of this kind necessary, does it not seem to be when there prevails, as in the present moment, an extraordinary zeal for the dissemination of the Scriptures; a zeal, which, however pure and laudable in itself, seems to call for a correspondent care to guard against the perversion to which even that best gift of God is liable?

There would, however, be much difficulty to encounter in the course of such an inquiry, were it necessary to exhibit in detail the vast mass of matter which the subject offers to our contemplation. The field of controversy is of wide extent, and is so crowded with an intermixture of objects not readily distinguishable from each other, that a full developement of what it comprises would hardly be attainable, within the compass prescribed to the present undertaking. But to attempt this, is neither necessary nor expedient. For, though Error is multiform, Truth is, for the most part, simple and undivided: and the straight line being once ascertained, every deviation from it will be readily discerned. Clear and distinct conceptions of the main points which constitute the system of our Faith, are, however, indispensable; because, these being accurately formed, every subordinate or collateral topic will the more easily be arranged in its proper place; and the difficulty will be much diminished, of shewing its agreement or disagreement with those essential parts of the system to which it appears to belong.

That truths thus essential to the system are to be collected from the Sacred Writings; and that, when established, they form the proper test of all religious opinions of minor consideration; are positions virtually recognized in every Creed or Confession of Faith introduced into the Christian Church. To regard such formularies as unwarrantable impositions on Christian liberty, is to overlook their obvious utility, if not necessity, towards the preservation of sound doctrine, or of any real unanimity in articles of Faith. And though a liberty must be allowed of examining whether any such Creed, compiled by human authority, declares the genuine truths of Holy Writ; yet if, upon a fair examination, it be found to preserve the essentials of the Faith entire and uncorrupted, no difference of opinion on lesser matters will warrant the violation of Christian unity. Were this duly regarded, it might tend to diminish considerably the number of controversial points: many of which would probably be dismissed as unworthy of serious contention; while others, of greater magnitude and importance, would become more prominent to observation, and, being disencumbered of extraneous matter, would be more easily defended against their assailants.

It is important then to ascertain in what these essentials consist. But this cannot be done, without deciding upon certain preliminary questions which affect the whole inquiry. To agree in the interpretation of

Scripture, there must be a concurrence in the general principles of interpretation. Some variety of opinion may indeed be expected, notwithstanding such a general concurrence: but a variation so circumstanced can hardly involve an error, on either side, dangerous or incapable of adjustment. On the other hand, a radical disagreement concerning these first principles of the subject to be discussed, precludes the hope of bringing men to be " per-" fectly joined together in the same mind " and in the same judgment [r]."

The method, by which it is intended to pursue the present inquiry, will be adapted to this view of the subject. There can be no necessity for a minute consideration of rules of criticism common to every species of writing, and on which scarcely any difference of opinion may be supposed to exist. These appertain to the interpreter of Scripture as a general scholar, rather than as a theologian: and though it be most true, that the theologian would be justly exposed to contempt, who, in his endeavour to expound the Sacred Word, should violate any established canon of ordinary criticism; yet if the Scriptures themselves have a peculiar and extraordinary character impressed upon them, which

[r] 1 Cor. i. 10.

takes them out of the class of ordinary writings, that character, whatever it be, ought unquestionably to form the basis of his judgment respecting the matters which they contain.

The knowledge of Divine truth is indeed perfectly distinct from human science, in that it emanates immediately from the Fountain of infinite wisdom. Yet has it this in common with human science, that it is made by its heavenly Author to flow through the channel of human instruction. While therefore we "receive it not as the word of men, "but, as it is in truth, the word of God[s];" we must nevertheless examine it as it is delivered to us, clothed in the language of men, and subject to the general rules of human composition. The deference due to it as a Divine production does not interfere with this province of human learning; it only exacts submission with respect to the subject-matter of the revelation, to which the critical investigation is entirely subordinate.

For the fuller developement of these general principles, it is purposed to consider, in the first place, the moral qualifications requisite for a right apprehension of the Sacred Word[t]. An inquiry will then be instituted

[s] 1 Thess. ii. 13.   [t] Lect. II.

SERMON I.

into the paramount authority of that Word as the rule of faith, and its own interpreter [u]: and, in connection with this, will follow a consideration of the subsidiary means by which, subject to that authority, its interpretation must be sought [x]. The ground being thus cleared of preliminary difficulties, and a secure basis laid for a solid fabric of Scripture truth; the question, how the superstructure is to be raised, will then remain to be considered. This will lead to some observations upon the proper mode of analyzing [y] the contents of Scripture, and of combining [z] them again into a coherent and harmonious system. As supplementary also to this part of the inquiry, some remarks will be necessary upon the distinction between the literal and figurative sense of Scripture [a]; a distinction, affecting in its result many important controversies in the Christian Church.

Under these several heads may be introduced all that is necessary for a compendious view of the subject; and occasion will be given for as much detail of its particulars, as may suffice for the mere purpose of illustration. It will also incidentally be seen, how

[u] Lect. III.   [x] Lect. IV.   [y] Lect. V.   [z] Lect. VI.
[a] Lect. VII.

far an agreement on points essential to salvation has hitherto prevailed in the Church Catholic, and whence have sprung the leading errors and corruptions, which have from time to time made inroads on the Faith. The inquiry may then be closed with a brief consideration of the sacred charge committed to the Church[b], of preserving the Truth inviolate; accompanied with some not unseasonable observations on the conduct of our own Church in particular, in this respect; on its purity in doctrine and in discipline, its safety as a guide to Scripture truth, and its adherence to those sound principles of interpretation, which afford the best security against the "perverse disputings of men of "corrupt minds[c]," and can alone prevent us from being "carried about with every wind "of doctrine[d]."

Of the difficulty, as well as the importance of these subjects, none ought to be more sensible than he who attempts to discuss them. It is only a just sense of that difficulty, which can induce such a dispassionate and soberminded consideration of them, as may be expected to lead to successful results. They indeed who have been most conversant with such disquisitions, will be the most cautious

[b] Lect. VIII.   [c] 1 Tim. vi. 5.   [d] Ephes. iv. 14.

and the most candid in forming their decisions. "Masters in Israel" will hardly expect, from a work necessarily so circumscribed in its extent, any considerable accessions of knowledge on topics already familiar to their minds. But to less experienced students, nothing is unimportant which may open a way for pursuing a safe and satisfactory course of inquiry into religious truth. Knowing by what principles the Christian scholar is to conduct that inquiry, and what helps are necessary to ensure its success, they will be better able to judge of the various matters of controversy presented to their view, and better armed against the errors of an age, unstable and unwary, prone to follow every phantom that flits before it, and lightly to regard the attainments of former times. The labour will not be lost, if, through the Divine blessing on the endeavour, faith be, in any instance, strengthened by hearing, and hearing lead to a right understanding of the word of God.

SERMON II.

JOHN vii. 17.

If any man will do his will, he shall know of the doctrine, whether it be of God.

MANY difficulties present themselves in attempting the solution of that important question, Whence comes religious error? For, not only are the several species of error so various and discordant, as to make it scarcely possible to trace them all to similar causes; but no less different are the dispositions, the habits, and the attainments, of those by whom they are upholden. On the one hand, we see the thoughtless and the considerate, the vain and the modest, the sober and the licentious, the illiterate and the scholar, linked together by some common bond of opinions respecting what they deem to be the truth: on the other hand, we see persons for the most part similar in their moral and intellectual qualities, who, on these subjects, appear to be irreconcilably at variance. This anomaly in the human character it may not be easy to explain. But of one thing we are certain, that whatever is repugnant to truth, is repugnant to the Divine will. That the merciful God and Father of all would " have all men to be " saved and to come to the knowledge of the " truth[a]," is a maxim entirely consonant with every notion we can form of the Divine perfections, as well as with the declarations of Holy Writ. No error can be supposed to issue from Divine wisdom, or to be the object of Divine approbation. Its source must be sought elsewhere; since the very term error denotes a deviation from some line of rectitude: and what but rectitude can proceed from Him who is the acknowledged Fountain of perfection?

Searching the Scriptures for an elucidation of this subject, we there find not only unbelief, but heresy and schism also, ascribed partly to human perverseness, and partly to the influence of a spiritual adversary operating upon fallen man's predisposition to evil. This indeed is the solution there offered to us of moral evil in general, as well as of that particular species of it which leads men to " make shipwreck of their faith." The parables of the sower and of the tares place

[a] 1 Tim. ii. 4.

the subject in this point of view: and various apostolical admonitions concur in representing that the will of man, whether yielding to its own inward propensities, or to some evil suggestions from without, is deeply concerned in every departure from the truth.

Conformably with this representation, our Lord frequently charges the Jews with wilfulness and obstinacy in rejecting his doctrine. He addresses them as persons possessing the means of reasonable conviction, but not disposed to use them aright. He says of them, that they had " no cloke for their sin[b]" in this respect; that they " would not come to " him that they might have life[c];" and that they " loved darkness rather than light, be-" cause their deeds were evil[d]." In the words of the text he virtually conveys a similar reproof; intimating that their ignorance of the justness of his pretensions (if ignorance it might be called) proceeded from an indisposition to do the will of God.

The Jewish Scribes and Pharisees despised our Lord for the want of those attainments in religious learning, which they arrogated to themselves; and they alleged this supposed deficiency on his part as the ground of their unbelief: " How knoweth this man letters,

[b] John xv. 22.   [c] John v. 40.   [d] John iii. 19.

" having never learned^e ?" An objection, the same in substance with that, of which we read in another part of the Evangelical history, " Is not this the carpenter's son ? is not his " mother called Mary ? and his brethren, " James, and Joses, and Simon, and Judas ? " and his sisters, are not they all with us ? " Whence then hath this man all these " things^f ?" With such contempt did they regard that lowly station which seemed to have precluded him from the advantages of a superior education!

To these cavils our Lord replies, that his pretensions were not founded on any such advantages, but depended on testimonies of a very different description; on proofs of a much higher nature, and such as they were well able to appreciate, if disposed to receive them. " My doctrine," says he, " is not mine, " but his that sent me^g." " His word was " with power^h." It was accompanied with incontrovertible evidences of its Divine original: and so clear were those evidences, that he adds, without reserve, " If any man will do " His will," that is, the will of God, " he shall " know of the doctrine, whether it be of God, " or whether I speak of myself." He then

^e John vii. 15.   ^f Matth. xiii. 55, 56.
^g John vii. 16.   ^h Luke iv. 32.

proceeds to shew their perverseness in submitting to the Law, and to the authority of Moses, and yet rejecting His claims, founded upon similar and even stronger grounds of acceptance : and he closes the conference with declaring, that, notwithstanding their pretended doubts, they "both knew him, and " knew from whence he came[j]."

The words of the text, then, were addressed immediately to the Jews, and had especial reference to their peculiar case. The Jews had advantages above other persons, for trying the validity of our Lord's pretensions and the truth of his doctrine. To them had been committed the ancient oracles of God, "the " law and the testimony[k]," which were to form the criterion of every subsequent revelation. Our Lord declared, that "not one " tittle of that law should pass away till all " had been fulfilled[l]." His appeal therefore was made to their own Scriptures: and had they been sincerely desirous of conforming to the will of God, as set forth in those Scriptures, they would have found no difficulty in acknowledging his claims. But having perversely corrupted their own Law, and being obstinately prejudiced against every thing interfering with their secular views, the light

[j] John vii. 28.   [k] Isaiah viii. 20.   [l] Matth. v. 18.

of preceding revelations shone upon them in vain, and their understandings were darkened, that they could not discern the truth.

But though this censure was specially applied to the Jews, it is not to be restricted to them alone. It is couched in general terms, and expressed as if intended to be taken in a more enlarged signification. It is not said, If *ye* will do his will, *ye* shall know of the doctrine; but, If *any* man will do it;—any one who investigates the subject with a disposition to attain to such knowledge. Whence an inference appears to be deducible, that every error respecting the Christian Faith proceeds, more or less, from some perverseness in the mind; or, at least, that an earnest desire to know and to do the will of God, is so far a necessary preparative for a right understanding of its doctrines, that without it no proficiency in that respect is reasonably to be expected. Caution, however, is necessary, that while we maintain the general importance of this maxim, we do not strain it beyond its probable intent; lest, in regarding every deviation from the standard of perfect truth as chargeable upon the will, rather than upon the understanding of man, and ascribing it to an *intentional* disregard of the will of God, we should seem unmindful of that Christian charity, which "beareth all things, believeth "all things, hopeth all things, endureth all "things^m."

Endeavouring then to divest ourselves of any undue bias in this discussion, let us proceed to a more particular examination of the text, with reference both to its precise signification, and to the application of which it is capable to our general subject.

The *disposition* to do the will of God appears to be the point on which the great stress of our Lord's observation is laid :—$\epsilon\alpha\nu$ $\tau\iota\varsigma$ $\theta\epsilon\lambda\eta$, if any man *be willing* to do the will of God, "he shall know of the doctrine whe-"ther it be of God." This willingness relates simply to the Divine authority of the doctrine propounded. It implies a readiness to abide by such a knowledge of God's will as may be obtained from any well-authenticated revelation. It is not therefore the general disposition of a person habitually practising moral and religious duties, which is here intended, (though this is unquestionably of great importance in all inquiries after Sacred truth) but it is the specific character of a person free from prejudices unfavourable to the object of inquiry, and prepared, nay desirous, to profit

---

m 1 Cor. xiii. 7.

by its researches. To him whose mind is thus open to conviction, our Lord holds out the assurance of success; prejudice and indisposition to the object of research being as films and mists to the sight, which render the objects of vision obscure and indistinct; whereas, these being removed, whatever is within reach of the faculty itself is readily discerned.

The question indeed, how far the understanding is dependent upon the will, though, abstractedly and metaphysically considered, it appears to be of a subtle and difficult kind, is practically easy to be apprehended. For, although we are conscious that the will cannot absolutely control the understanding, so as to make it believe or disbelieve, contrary to its own convictions, yet are we equally conscious that it can indispose it to the reception, or even to the consideration, of particular truths; thus diminishing the force of that intellectual application which may be requisite for the purpose. And whatever be the motive by which the will is thus prompted to blind or to mislead the understanding, the effect may be the same. Whether the bondage be that of ignorance, of prejudice, or of moral corruption, the mind may be equally debarred of the free exercise of its powers, and in the midst of light remain in darkness.

It does not, therefore, necessarily follow, that because religious error has gained possession of the mind, there must be totally vitiated affections or an incurable depravity of heart. Neither does it follow, on the other hand, that uprightness and sincerity, accompanied with well-disciplined and pure intentions, afford entire security against the admission of error. As the understanding is in some measure dependent upon the will, so the will may be influenced by special motives and impulses, greatly altering the complexion of the case with respect to its moral aspect, although the result be substantially the same. Hence there may not unfrequently be found a propensity to imbibe false opinions in religion, and a disinclination to the truth, where it would be difficult to fix the stain of immorality or vice.

Nevertheless, our Lord's aphorism is both just and of universal application. If there be, from whatever cause, an indisposition to do the will of God, there will ever be a proportionate difficulty in coming to the knowledge of the truth: and if the mind be free from adverse prepossessions, obstacles will be so much the more easily removed. This we may conceive to be the full scope and meaning of the text. Let us now consider how it may be applied to our proposed subject of Scripture-interpretation.

At first sight, it may appear that the position, "If any man will do his will, he shall "know of the doctrine whether it be of God," applies rather to the belief or disbelief of God's word in general, than to the interpretation of its particular doctrines. We may easily perceive the influence of a predisposition to conform to the Divine will, in prevailing upon men to embrace what is proposed to them as a Divine revelation; but we may not so clearly discern how a right exposition of what is contained in that revelation depends on such a frame of mind. The connection between virtue and faith on the one hand, or vice and infidelity on the other, is undoubtedly much more obvious to common apprehension, than the connection of a right or wrong interpretation of the Scriptures with a good or evil disposition.

For the elucidation then of this point, let it be observed, that, in the pursuit of every kind of knowledge, an earnest desire to obtain correct views of it greatly facilitates the labour, and is necessary to ensure its success. And if this be true of other studies, still more evidently is it so in that of Revealed Religion. It is a circumstance which distinguishes this from every other study, that the knowledge it obtains is derived from the authority of an Instructor whose wisdom is infallible, and whose will is above control. It is essential to the sincere inquirer, that he should enter upon the research with this consideration deeply engraven upon his mind. Such moral dispositions as are requisite in other pursuits, and especially that love of truth which is the powerful stimulus to improvement of every kind, are doubtless indispensable also in the character of the Sacred interpreter. But to complete that character, something more is also required. The Bible has pretensions exclusively its own. In his interpretation of it, the critic must ever bear in mind, that it is the work of Sacred Penmen, not of unassisted human powers. Therefore, not only an ordinary solicitude to avoid error, but also a readiness to submit, where the subject requires it, the understanding and the affections to what is propounded on such authority, becomes the duty of the theological student; a duty, never to be unconditionally exacted, where the composition is merely human; never to be on any pretence dispensed with, where it is confessedly Divine.

This frame of mind is evidently included in that faith which the Scriptures represent as the proper inlet to spiritual knowledge. This is the main spring by which the work of religion operates both upon the heart and upon the intellect of man. It opens the eye to see the wonders of the Divine law: it opens the ear to hear the voice of heavenly wisdom: it removes mountains in the way to knowledge: it invigorates every faculty for the labour it has to accomplish.

The Scriptures abound in declarations to this effect. Yet none of these may be understood to affirm, that faith, however lively or sincere, shall enable the inquirer to comprehend all mysteries and all knowledge, by giving him powers of discernment beyond the reach of man; or that he shall hence be qualified, without the aid of human learning, to interpret the Sacred Word aright. On the contrary, a willingness to know and to do the will of God, implies a willingness to resort to all necessary helps for advancement in the truth, and for security against error. The meaning therefore of any such passages can only be, that without faith, without the disposition to conform to the Divine will, none will be adequately qualified for the purpose, however otherwise gifted with the best natural or acquired endowments. Hence St. Paul says, " If any man think himself wise, let him

SERMON II.   35

" become a fool that he may be wise[n];" that is, let him renounce any pretensions to a wisdom superior to that which the word of God imparts to him. Hence also our Lord warned his disciples, that " except they became as lit-" tle children[o]," they could not enter into his kingdom; and gave thanks to his heavenly Father, that he had " hidden those things " from the wise and prudent, and revealed " them unto babes[p]." In the same sense we may also interpret the promise, that " to him " that hath shall be given, and he shall have " more abundance[q];" implying, that where that which has been already communicated is carefully improved, there will be the greatest proficiency in religious knowledge. The interpretation of the Sacred Word will, doubtless, be most easily ascertained by those whose dispositions are most congenial with its character: and the tendency of all these Scriptural illustrations is, to shew that the first requisite in the study of Divine truth (whether with reference to the general credibility of Revealed Religion, or to the interpretation of its particular doctrines) is a genuine singleness of heart, which has one main object

[n] 1 Cor. iii. 18.   [o] Matth. xviii. 3.
[p] Matth. xi. 25.   [q] Matth. xiii. 12.

in all its researches, that of knowing and obeying the will of God.

To the case of avowed unbelievers there cannot be much difficulty in applying this criterion. For, though there may be many whose generally virtuous conduct seems to give them a claim of exemption from the charge of intentional disregard of truth; yet strong presumptive evidence will almost always appear of a radical indisposition in the will to a careful investigation of the subject. Few, if any, manifest a serious inclination to " receive with meekness the engrafted word," as an authority to which they owe submission. On the contrary, some principle repugnant to it, some root of bitterness that admits not of its cordial reception, usually betrays itself, where infidelity has taken fast hold upon the mind. This it is, which magnifies every difficulty, generates suspicion and distrust, and misleads the judgment by presenting the object of contemplation to the understanding through a fallacious medium.

Nor is it much more difficult to adapt this same criterion to those who, professing a general belief of Christianity, maintain opinions at variance with its essential doctrines. Want of *faith* is more or less discoverable in almost all who depart from the standard of Scripture truth. Not that this is rashly to be assumed, in cases where only slight shades of difference prevail, or respecting the exposition of doctrines transcending the comprehension of the human intellect and revealed to us only in general terms. But where a doctrine inseparable from Christianity itself is either rejected or misinterpreted, from evident prepossessions of the mind against it, (for this it is which properly constitutes heretical pravity,) there we can hardly avoid imputing that perversity of the will which our Lord teaches us to regard as the proximate cause of all religious error.

The fact appears to be, that a very great proportion of the heresies, which have from time to time sprung up in the Christian Church, may be traced to some lurking principle of infidelity operating upon the mind. A favourite maxim of false philosophy, or a vain conceit of the imagination, takes possession of the understanding; and, fully persuaded of the unanswerable truth of the opinions thus adopted, yet unwilling entirely to relinquish the Faith, the slave of prejudices adverse to Revealed Religion commences the work of new interpretation, and exercises his ingenuity in endeavouring to adapt Scripture to his preconceptions. Do we ask, then, how it happens that errors, even of the worst kind, are the fruit of his labours? The answer is readily given. He is regardless of the Divine admonition in the text. Instead of being willing to abide by the revealed will of God, he is predisposed to abide by his own will: and it being found impracticable to reconcile these to each other, without wresting the Scriptures from their obvious meaning, some more recondite sense is sought for, and the simplicity of truth is sacrificed at the shrine of vanity.

The rule, then, that "if any man will do " his will, he shall know of the doctrine, " whether it be of God," admits, we may perceive, of a more special and circumstantial application than might at first be apprehended: and although it may behove us to exercise the greatest charity and discretion in judging others by this rule, it will, in scrutinizing our own opinions, be necessary to apply it with unsparing freedom. A suspicion of some wrong bent in the mind ought indeed always to be entertained, when we are conscious of a secret wish to set aside any doctrine, apparently forming a part of that system which, in its general character, we acknowledge to proceed from God.

If, however, it should still be asked, how

the concurrence of the will of man with the will of God can thus facilitate either the belief or the right interpretation of the Sacred Word?—this further answer may be given.

The mere disposition to concur with the Divine will we may conceive to be productive of these results, both by its own natural efficacy, and by the powerful co-operation of that Divine aid which gives a blessing to human endeavours.

Its natural and immediate tendency is, to ensure earnest attention to the subject, diligent inquiry into proofs and evidences, perseverance in surmounting difficulties, deliberation in framing decisions, modesty in proposing doubts, readiness to retract error, firmness in adhering to well-grounded conviction. The effect of these excellent qualities, in removing obstacles to the truth, in disencumbering the judgment of what may impede its progress, and increasing the thirst for those acquirements which enlarge and strengthen the mental powers, may readily be conceived. Not to ascribe to them their due share in the acquisition of truth, would be to derogate from the wisdom of that Providence, who, in bestowing upon man the gifts of understanding and of free-will, evidently designed that the honest application of these talents should largely contribute to produce the desired effect.

Nor is it less evident, that the inquirer after religious truth, cultivating this genuine disposition to know and to do the will of God, may well confide in that communication of heavenly aid, which, if duly sought for, will not fail to be bestowed, as a blessing upon his endeavours, by him who "giveth to " all men liberally, and upbraideth not [r]." For, if the Almighty hath actually imparted his will to mankind, is it not with the intent that they should thankfully receive it, and diligently search its meaning? And can we doubt that every indication of such a disposition will be regarded with special favour by the great Author and Finisher of our Faith? Can we doubt that the grace of God will assist in perfecting what the humble aspirant after truth is already striving to accomplish, by the use of those means which the providence of God has placed within his reach? What further satisfaction on this point can be requisite, than that assurance of our blessed Lord and Master, " Ask, and it shall " be given you; seek, and ye shall find; " knock, and it shall be opened unto you [s]?"

In whatever point of view, then, we con-

[r] James i. 5.   [s] Matth. vii. 7.

sider the subject, we shall find this position incontrovertibly established, that the willing and ingenuous mind, the free and unrestrained surrender of every thought and purpose, of every imagination and affection, to the all-perfect will of God, is the first principle of religious duty, the germ of every thing which is afterwards to expand and ripen into action. It is that, which can alone produce the fruit of sound Christian knowledge; and to which, when duly planted and watered by human industry, the Divine Benefactor will assuredly give the increase.

Thus we have advanced one step in our inquiry, by shewing what disposition of mind is previously requisite in those who enter upon the interpretation of Holy Writ. The main source of all contentions respecting the sense of Scripture, on points of fundamental importance, may be traced to a reluctance, on one side or the other, to renounce prepossessions militating against an entire reception of the truth. Men are led by partiality to their own opinions, or undue deference to those of others, not only to irreconcilable dissensions among themselves, but eventually to a departure from the plain and obvious meaning of the Word of God. It was the error of the ancient Jews, that they "set up "idols in their heart," and "put a stumbling-block before their face [t]," so that God would not be inquired of by them. And so it is with multitudes in the present day. They are in their hearts devoted to some favourite object of pursuit, to some theory or opinion which they cannot relinquish; and they consequently enter upon the research with almost a certainty of failure.

But, perhaps, the force of our Lord's maxim in the text will be still more sensibly felt, by considering it in its negative as well as its affirmative sense; as if it were said, (which indeed is implied in the terms of the proposition,) "if any man will *not* do his will, he "shall *not* know of the doctrine, whether it "be of God."

The moral qualities comprised in the character of a sound and faithful interpreter of the Word, have been already enumerated. The dispositions repugnant to that character, are carelessness, indifference to truth, indolence, rashness, a spirit of scepticism and self-conceit, pertinacity in retaining opinions hastily taken up, love of novelty, and a proneness to abandon what is sanctioned by long established authority and well tried experience. It is easy to perceive how these dis-

[t] Ezek. xiv. 4.

positions must operate on the intellectual powers, in preventing the full and free exercise of the faculties most necessary to be called forth in such disquisitions, and in diminishing the desire of such attainments as can give any reasonable hope of success.

In a word, that which we understand by the term, docility, or an aptitude to receive instruction, is the first requisite towards the acquisition of Scriptural knowledge. The mind ought to be unbiassed by any thing that would lead it astray from the simple truth, and disposed to " lay aside every " weight [u]," which may retard its progress. In this consists the willingness, to which is held out the promise of such a knowledge of the Divine word as cannot otherwise be obtained.

We are not to wonder, then, if instances oftentimes occur, where splendid talents and rare acquirements are employed in the service of Error, and even in endeavouring to subvert the fundamental truths of Revealed Religion. These are, in themselves, no security against error. On the contrary, when not controlled by a powerful sense of duty, they rather incite to bold and hazardous speculations, by the vanity and self-confi-

[u] Heb. xii. 1.

dence they are wont to create. Caution therefore is necessary, lest we be dazzled and led astray by genius and learning thus mischievously employed. For to this subject is our Lord's saying especially applicable, "He "that exalteth himself shall be abased, and "he that humbleth himself shall be exalt-"ed [x]." That profound submission, that prostration of heart and mind, which desires instantly to receive and obey whatever comes from God, is the sentiment which best befits the inquirer after sacred truth. Hence, both in the general defence of Christianity, and in the successful interpretation of its essential doctrines, none have more signally distinguished themselves, than they who to a grasp of intellect above their fellows have united the profoundest reverence and humility, in exploring the depths of heavenly wisdom.

Caution however is necessary, on the other hand, that we do not hastily impute either moral or intellectual defects, in every ordinary case of erroneous persuasion. To lay these to the charge of the multitudes who are merely followers of specious heresies, and who, from early habits of education, or other untoward circumstances scarcely under their control, have pertinaciously adhered to them;

[x] Luke xiv. 11.

would be a precipitate, if not uncharitable, censure. Perhaps too it may not unreasonably be questioned, whether, in some instances, Heresiarchs themselves have not been rather misled by weak and erroneous judgment, than by deliberate and intentional opposition to the Divine will. The errors of such persons might, perhaps, have been rectified, under more auspicious circumstances. The question, therefore, whether, in any particular cases, heresy be wilful, or ignorance invincible, should be regarded as of too momentous a nature to be lightly treated, and not always capable of being peremptorily decided by human authority.

But the more necessary these cautions may be, respecting particular points of controversy, or the personal characters of the parties engaged in them; the greater necessity will exist, for vigilance in guarding ourselves against any disposition that tends to darken the understanding and betray it into error. Here our Lord's admonition in the text demands the most profound consideration, as a fundamental maxim on which all consistency and correct knowledge of religion must depend. With Solomon's exhortation to the same effect, the subject may, therefore, now be closed. " My son, if thou wilt re-

"ceive my words, and hide my command-
"ments with thee, so that thou incline thine
"ear to wisdom, and apply thine heart to
"understanding; yea, if thou criest after
"knowledge, and liftest up thy voice for
"understanding; if thou seekest her as sil-
"ver, and searchest for her as for hid trea-
"sures; then shalt thou understand the fear
"of the Lord, and find the knowledge of
"God [y]."

[y] Prov. ii. 1—5.

SERMON III.

1 PETER iv. 11.

If any man speak, let him speak as the oracles of God.

THE necessity of a constant recurrence to first principles, as a preventive of any deviation from truth, is in no case more apparent than in the study of Holy Writ. For, since the great foundation on which Revealed Religion is established is an absolutely DIVINE authority, every thing which tends to displace that fundamental basis will endanger the whole system: and the consequences must be infinitely more injurious to the best interests of mankind, than any similar violation of principles in matters of human science; according to the acknowledged maxims, that the worst of abuses is the abuse of that which is best in itself, and that no truth can be made more certain than by sufficient evidence that it proceeds from God.

The apostolical injunction in the text evidently rests upon the supposition of this supreme authority of Holy Scripture, as the rule of faith and the interpreter of its own doctrine. " If any man speak, let him speak " as the oracles of God :" let him, both as to the doctrine and the interpretation, be careful to advance nothing contrary to those Sacred Oracles, nothing that may bring into competition with them authority of a different kind.

But however indisputable the principle may appear on which this injunction is founded, it is not only continually violated through ignorance or inadvertency, but a very great portion of the errors and corruptions prevalent in the Christian world evidently spring from systems, virtually, if not formally, opposed to it; from maintaining the necessity of some ulterior tribunal of appeal, for the decision of controversies and for framing unerring standards of interpretation.

Besides the moral dispositions, therefore, already shewn to be requisite in the search after spiritual knowledge, it is necessary to determine this great preliminary question, Whether there be any authority paramount or even equivalent to the Sacred Word, which, either as jointly connected with it or as its judicial superior, may claim our unreserved obedience ? If there be any such, the sincere inquirer after truth must submit to its pretensions. If there be not, to admit such pretensions is not only superfluous but dangerous; as derogating from the authority which possesses the rightful claim.

Upon this head St. Peter's admonition might be deemed decisive: and there are other texts of Scripture which ought to place it beyond dispute. Nevertheless, they who argue on the contrary side would fain allege the sanction of Scripture for their views of the subject: a circumstance, which renders it so much the more necessary to examine their pretensions, lest we stumble at the very threshold of our inquiries.

And here it will be found that we have three distinct parties to contend with; all widely differing from each other, yet all asserting principles injurious to the just preeminence of Scriptural authority.

The first of these, the Papist, insists on the necessity of an infallible Judge or Interpreter of doctrine, in the person of some visible Head of the Church, from whom there shall be no appeal. The second, comprising various Sects, contends that every doctrine of Holy Writ must bend to the decision of human Reason as the supreme judge in matters of faith. The third, a multifarious order of Interpreters, gives supreme sway to a supposed inward Light, or immediate communication from the Holy Spirit, supplementary to Scripture, and infallible as well as irresistible in its operations. An examination of the respective pretensions of these different claimants to assume authority above the Scriptures, will fully occupy us for the present. The regard due to them in a subsidiary and subordinate capacity must be made the subject of another Discourse.

I. The great points in controversy between Papists and Protestants, as far as relates to the present question, are the infallibility of the Church and the authority of unwritten Traditions; Traditions, supposed to have been originally of Apostolical origin, but not recorded in Holy Writ.

In arguing these points, it is presumed, on both sides, that the Scriptures are the Word of God, and therefore must be true. The Romanist, however unguardedly he may sometimes speak of the written Word, does not venture openly to contravene this position. Consequently, no arguments are admissible in the present discussion, which oppose what the Scripture itself affirms: and the debate might be reduced to a simple inquiry, what the Sacred Writings declare upon the subject.

The *infallibility* of the Scriptures is taken for granted: their *sufficiency* is the controverted point. If then it should appear that the Scriptures, which the Romanist confesses to be infallible, assert, either expressly or virtually, their own sufficiency as the rule of faith, the matter at issue would be thus far decided; and even on his own principles, the opponent would stand defeated.

The proof, however, of this point is not so clearly deducible from any particular texts of Scripture declaratory upon the subject, as from the general scope and design of these Sacred Records, and the extraordinary endowments of the writers themselves. It rests upon the plenary inspiration of those writers; upon their exclusive authority to declare the Divine will; and upon the want of satisfactory evidence, on the other hand, to prove any doctrine to be really theirs, which is not contained in the written Word. These positions being established, the sufficiency of Scripture for its intended purpose will be fully made out, and all competition with its authority effectually precluded.

There are indeed texts both in the Old and New Testament, which, if understood as relating to the whole Sacred Canon, might seem to put the question beyond dispute. Thus

David, speaking of the Word as it existed under the Jewish dispensation, declares it to be "a lamp unto the feet and a light unto "the paths[a];" a "perfect law, converting the "soul; and a testimony that is sure, making "wise the simple[b]." St. Paul likewise speaks of the Scriptures in general, as "able to make "us wise unto salvation," and "making the "man of God perfect, thoroughly furnished "unto all good works[c]." These expressions may be understood not only as ascribing to the Sacred Writings a character and authority above those of merely human compositions, but also as intimating that nothing more was necessary for our instruction than what the Almighty had thus been pleased to reveal.

But since every declaration of this kind (unless we conceive it to have been *proleptically* delivered) can in strictness have reference only to the writings extant at the time when it was used; something more may be thought requisite for our present argument. And this may be obtained from the tenor of our Lord's promises to his Apostles. He declares, that the Comforter, the Holy Spirit, should " guide them into ALL truth and shew

---

[a] Ps. cxix. 105.   [b] Ps. xix. 7.   [c] 2 Tim. iii. 15, 17.

SERMON III.

"them things to come[d]," should "teach them "ALL things," "bring ALL things to their re-"membrance whatsoever he had said unto "them[e]," and "give them a mouth and wis-"dom which all their adversaries should not "be able to gainsay, nor resist[f]." These promises were strikingly fulfilled in that preeminent degree of inspiration of which the Apostles exhibited most convincing proofs. Nor did they ever intimate that any other persons (not even those upon whom, through their ministration, many excellent and extraordinary gifts were bestowed) were to succeed them in the special office of making further revelations of the Divine will. On the contrary, they affirm of themselves only, that they spake by that Spirit which "searcheth "all things, yea, even the deep things of "God[g];" that the mystery "of Christ, which "in other ages was not made known unto the "sons of men, was revealed unto them by the "Spirit[h]." They denounce that if "even an "Angel from Heaven should preach another "Gospel than that which they had preached, "he should be accursed[i]." They make adherence to "the Faith once delivered to the

[d] John xvi. 13. [e] John xiv. 26. [f] Luke xxi. 15.
[g] 1 Cor. ii. 10. [h] Eph. iii. 4, 5. [i] Gal. i. 8.

"Saints[k]," to be the test of sound doctrine:—"We," says St. John, "are of God: he that knoweth God, heareth us; he that is not of God, heareth not us: hereby know we the Spirit of truth, and the Spirit of error[l]."

These declarations, with the facts accompanying them, afford most convincing proof of the plenary inspiration of the Apostles. They serve also to establish their exclusive commission to reveal the will of God, and to complete the Sacred Canon. And upon this ground we may be warranted in extending to the whole of that Canon the threatening which St. John applies to his own Revelations in particular: "If any man shall add unto these things, God shall add unto him the plagues that are written in this book; and if any man shall take away from the words of the book of this prophecy, God shall take away his part out of the book of life[m]."

Against all subsequent pretences to infallibility, for the purpose either of making further revelations of the Divine will, or of interpreting what is already revealed, these considerations may be deemed decisive. Infallibility implies an immediately Divine guidance. It is no human attribute, nor can, without flagrant impiety, be assumed by any

[k] Jude 3. [l] 1 John iv. 6. [m] Rev. xxii. 18, 19.

uninspired being. Were the plea once to be admitted without preternatural evidence of the fact, it would be difficult to preclude any claim that might be grounded upon it to introduce new doctrines and new revelations. For, who should deny to acknowledged infallibility, that which would be conceded without hesitation to any other miraculous gift? Or what gift could in itself be more miraculous, or give surer testimony of Divine inspiration? From infallibility, therefore, in interpreting God's Word, it is but a short step to infallibility in proposing new articles of Faith, and new modes of Worship. And how readily the one pretence may succeed to the other, the practice of the Romish Church has but too evidently proved.

But the Romanist is not thus to be driven out of the field. Whatever respect or deference he may acknowledge to be due to Holy Writ, he will have recourse to a species of reasoning well adapted to perplex the subject. He will contend that the Scriptures cannot be deemed an infallible rule to the unlearned, who read them in translations only, and who must, in that case, depend on the infallibility of translators; whereas translators not unfrequently disagree in rendering the sense of the original; and there is, besides, so much inherent obscurity in the original itself, as to require some authoritative and infallible interpreter to render it an unerring standard of truth.

To this train of reasoning it might be sufficient to reply, that the proposed expedient by no means obviates the alleged difficulty; inasmuch as the very same impediments to a right apprehension of the rule of faith would still remain. For, how shall he, whose want of learning precludes him from distinguishing an infallible translator, be qualified to distinguish an infallible interpreter? The necessity of such an infallibility would create a necessity for some infallible criterion, to ascertain where it is to be found: and it would be impossible, without the continual intervention of miracles, to determine which, out of many authorities that might advance such pretensions, had substantiated the claim to an implicit faith in its decisions.

But to disentangle the subject from this sophistry, let us consider the question as we are wont to do in the case of a work of merely human authority. Were the purpose simply to ascertain the sense of such a work, that sense (whatever helps might be found useful for its illustration) would be sought for in the work itself, and the book be interpreted, as far as possible, in conformity with its own declared principles. Whether those principles be true or not, is a matter of distinct inquiry. But if we admit them to be true, what more is necessary for the satisfaction of the interpreter, than to make it evident that he has elicited the author's meaning? And how is that to be made evident, but by an ultimate appeal to the writing he undertakes to expound, or, if that be possible, to the author himself? The mere interpreter and the author can never stand upon one and the same footing of authority: nor can it be otherwise than that the work of interpretation must always lie open to the censure and revision of other interpreters competently qualified for the undertaking. But in this case, an appeal to the Author from the writing itself is no less than an assumption of Divine inspiration; and this assumption, whether on the part of the Church or of any of its individual members, calls for the same substantial proofs of the fact assumed as those which the Sacred Writers themselves produced, and without which no such pretensions are admissible. It is therefore a mere fallacy, to put the Church, as the interpreter of Scripture, on an equality, in point of authority, with the Scripture itself. Nay, it savours of hazardous presumption. For, here God is the Author, and man the interpreter: and unless the interpreter can produce evidence of Divine inspiration equal to that produced by them whose writings we receive as the Word of God; to allow in both the same stamp of authority, is, so far, exalting the creature to a level with the Creator.

There is moreover a want of faith and trust in God, as well as of due reverence towards Him, in contending for the necessity of such an expedient to carry on the work of Divine instruction. What ground is there for suspecting that the Apostles failed to commit to writing, for the benefit of succeeding ages, all that was necessary to salvation? Being "guided into all truth," is it to be supposed that they preached any thing essential to the Christian faith, which is not, in substance at least, left upon record in their writings? If so, might we not reasonably have expected some intimation from them, that the Scriptures they had drawn up were not intended as complete instructions for after-ages; but that their omissions were to be supplied by the authority, with which the ruling powers in the Church would afterwards be invested, to add to the Sacred Word as occasion should require? As our blessed Saviour said to the

Apostles before his resurrection, " I have " many things to say unto you, but ye cannot " bear them now [m]," would not the Apostles also in such a case have said to their appointed successors, " What we now write for " your instruction, is but a part of those sav-" ing truths which ye are hereafter to pro-" mulgate to the world; when the converts " to the Faith shall be better able to receive " them, than they are to whom we are com-" missioned to make known the will of God?" —But where are any such intimations to be found?

In truth, no reason can be assigned to justify the expectation of a continued infallibility in the Church, for the purpose of interpreting the Word of God, or adding new articles of faith to those therein contained, which does not virtually arraign the perfection or the authority of the Word itself. Nor can the Scriptures be properly called the Rule of Faith, if such additional security be necessary. Whatever be the authority that assumes a power to determine, *suo jure*, the sense of Scripture, or to impose articles of belief derived from any other source; that authority itself, if its right be admitted, be-

---

[m] John xvi. 12.

comes the Rule of Faith, and virtually supersedes the other.

Here however some further inquiry is called for, respecting the authority of unwritten traditions, which the Romanist holds to be equal to that of the written Word.

Traditions, in the sense in which the observance of them is enjoined by the Apostles, are received by Protestants with as much reverence as by the Romish Church. For, according to the apostolical usage of the word, the traditions enjoined to be observed, are the doctrines and precepts delivered, whether orally or in writing, by the Apostles themselves. " Stand fast," says St. Paul to the Thessalonians, "and hold the traditions which " ye have been taught, whether by word or " our epistle[n]:" that is, whatever has been personally delivered to you by me, either in preaching or in writing. Protestants do not question the truth of the position, that the word of an inspired Apostle, whether written or unwritten, is to be regarded with entire deference; since, in whatever way the Word of God be communicated to us, it has the same claim to our submission, provided we know that it proceeds from Him. But here is the question from which the Romanist has

[n] 2 Thess. iii. 15.

no escape:—can after-ages have the same kind of assurance respecting the authenticity of the written and of the unwritten Word? We contend, that there cannot now be sufficient evidence of the authenticity of any such unwritten traditions; and that, therefore, on the written Word only we can with safety rely. On this ground, the Scripture is maintained to be now the only Rule of Faith: and whatever benefit may be derived from other writings, reporting to us, as apostolical traditions, additional matters illustrative of our faith and worship; to them is to be assigned no more than a secondary rank, as being subsidiary, not essential, to our Creed.

In thus denying to unwritten traditions the same authority as to the Scriptures, no just prerogative of the Church is invaded, nor is any injurious reflection cast on the primitive Fathers, who, on this point, above all others, are entitled to our especial regard. For it is evident that the governors of the Church never intended such authority to be assigned to them; since they record no intimation given by the Sacred Writers themselves, that their oral communications were to be transmitted to succeeding generations, or promulgated by the Church as authentic documents. On this is founded the distinction between Scripture and unwritten tradition. The former is a structure, compact, and resting on an immoveable basis; the latter is composed of uncemented materials, and unsupported by any solid foundation.

But here the subject is sometimes perplexed by another sophistical kind of argument. The Romanist will contend that the authority of the Church is above that of Scripture, because Scripture itself is received through the medium of the Church, from whose declaratory judgment it derives that stamp of validity by which it is recognized as the word of God. The fallacy of which reasoning consists in not rightly distinguishing between the weight of testimony to the authenticity of a writing, and that of judicial decision upon its authority. " There is," says an incomparable writer on this subject °, " no " judge of faith, but God : if the Church " were judge of faith, it would set her above " God." The Canon of Scripture was determined by the Church, upon evidence of its genuineness and authenticity; and to this the Church bears witness. The Truth of Scripture rests on other grounds; on the " witness of God," as well as " the witness of " men." So is it with respect to Interpreta-

° Leslie.

tion. The Church directs her members to the right sense and meaning of Scripture: but that sense does not depend on her judgment, nor is it imposed arbitrarily as her own; but she refers to Scripture itself, for proof that *there* it is to be found. Were she to take upon her to be a judge of faith in a higher sense than this, she would assume the attributes of the Author of Holy Writ, rather than the character of its Interpreter.

Respecting traditions, therefore, as well as infallibility, Scripture must be resorted to, as the original fountain of authority, from which the pretensions either of the Church at large, or of General Councils as its representative body, or of the Pope as its supposed visible and universal head, ought to be derived. And this will follow from the concessions of the adversary himself; who, in acknowledging the Scriptures to be Divine, virtually admits that there can be no higher jurisdiction to which submission is due.

II. We are next to consider the controversy with those who set up human Reason as the supreme arbiter in matters of faith.

Here (since we are contending not with declared unbelievers, but with those who profess to receive the Christian Religion as a Divine revelation) the question seems to lie between what Reason can make known to us on religious subjects without Revelation, and what Revelation has actually taught us:—whether the former be so clear and perfect in its conceptions, as justly to claim an ascendancy over the latter; or whether it ought to acknowledge its inferiority with respect to its means and sources of information?

Without intending any depreciation of Reason itself, considered as the gift of God originally bestowed on man for his guidance to truth and rectitude, it is necessary to examine, not only its abstract pretensions, but its comparative claims when brought into competition with a Divine revelation. That human reason, as well as Revealed Religion, partakes of a Divine authority, is a position, which, though true in a limited sense, does not reach the present question. The gifts, though bestowed originally by the same hand, may differ in value and in kind, being adapted to different purposes, and suited to different exigencies: so that the superiority of the one to the other will depend upon the evidence to be produced of the degree of deference required to be paid to them respectively, by their all-wise and benevolent Giver. If reason, whatever were its original powers, were sufficient when enlightened by nature only, why was the light of revelation superadded? and if the light of revelation has actually been superadded, how can the superior authority of reason be maintained, without depreciating the utility of the subsequent gift?

But it is also to be kept in mind, that man's reason, however originally perfect it might have been, is now, we are assured, in a deteriorated state, and, consequently, no longer sufficient, by itself, to secure us against error. Revelation, therefore, being given to supply its defects, and to impart to it knowledge otherwise unattainable, it must be the province of reason, with respect to the subject-matter of what is thus revealed, to submit, not to dictate; to receive the commandment, not to prescribe the law. The disproportion also between the subjects on which unenlightened reason exercises its judgment, and those which Revelation presents to it, affords another argument to the same effect. Scripture reveals such things as "eye hath "not seen, nor ear heard, neither have en- "tered into the heart of man to conceive°." If it were otherwise, reason might, with less evident impropriety, advance pretensions to a co-ordinate, if not to a supreme authority.

° 1 Cor. ii. 9.

But if reason be a finite power, (and surely none will deny this of human reason,) it cannot be a competent judge of infinites. Now, the Scriptures (those parts of them, especially, which relate to its more mysterious doctrines, and which are among the very essentials of its system) affirm many things of this description; many truths concerning the nature, and attributes, and counsels of the Godhead, so entirely beyond the limits of any natural faculty of our reason, that they can only be received upon the credit of the Sacred Oracles; being, to our apprehensions, incapable of any thing resembling scientific demonstration. If, therefore, in matters even of this description, our reason might be allowed to overrule the written word, where could we cast anchor in the depths of moral and metaphysical speculation? Where would be our security against errors, however pernicious, which the devices of human imagination might suggest, and of which the capricious standard of every man's corrupt or fallible judgment would be made the criterion?

The dangerous position, (dangerous, that is, when taken in its broad and unqualified acceptation,) that the authority of Scripture must bend to that of reason, has been the source of numberless errors and corruptions among persons professing the Christian Faith. In the earliest periods of its history, we find the Gnostics distinguishing themselves (as their assumed title implied) by pretensions to profounder attainments than those of their fellow Christians, and boasting of the improvements they were enabled to engraft upon the Christian religion, by the aid of human philosophy. Of some who drew their notions of the Gospel from these interpreters, it is remarked by Mosheim, that " they looked " upon it as a noble and glorious task, to " bring the doctrines of celestial wisdom into " a certain subjection to the precepts of their " philosophy, and to make deep and pro-" found researches into the intimate and " hidden nature of those truths which the " Divine Saviour had delivered to his dis-" ciples." This vain affectation of a wisdom superior to that which dictated the revelation they professed to receive, prepared the way for many a wild and incoherent system of imaginary truths, for daring innovations on the Faith, and, in not a few instances, for an almost entire desecration of the Sacred Oracles. Many of the early Heretics rejected large portions of Holy Writ, and even the whole of the Old Testament, not upon any alleged ground of their want of authenticity, but solely because they found them irreconcilable with the philosophical tenets they had espoused, and from the mere wantonness of speculation on matters above the reach of human conception. Tertullian, Origen, Augustin, Jerome, and other Fathers of the Church, continually charge them with the rejection, or the mutilation, of various parts of Scripture, for the unwarrantable purpose of adapting them to their own extravagant persuasions.

To the same source may also be traced most of the errors among philosophizing Christians in after-times; especially the many strange and fantastic theories which gained acceptance, respecting the doctrine of the Trinity, and that of the twofold nature of our blessed Saviour. Vain attempts to explicate points which, to our present apprehensions, must ever remain enveloped in a certain degree of mystery, and to make them conformable to opinions wholly incapable of proof or evidence, led multitudes to "make " shipwreck of their Faith."

This evil is perhaps inseparable from the propensity to make Revealed Religion subservient to philosophical theories, and from regarding the Scriptures as secondary to human science. It arises from not rightly distinguishing between the objects with which each is exclusively conversant, and thus assigning to neither its proper rank and office. As the Scriptures were not intended to instruct men in human philosophy, so neither can human philosophy instruct them in the matters which the Scriptures reveal. This, however, is to be understood of that only which is properly the subject-matter of Revelation; of facts and doctrines which it was its express purpose to make known to mankind; not of matters incidentally connected with it which may be capable of physical demonstration. And surely there are truths of Revealed Religion sufficiently attested to us by its general evidences, which it is not in the power of the human understanding to refute by arguments grounded on any antecedent principles. Can, for instance, the doctrines respecting the essential nature of the Godhead be brought to any test of human science? Can the Miraculous Conception, the Incarnation, the Resurrection, the Ascension of our Lord, or any thing properly miraculous in the Christian dispensation, be proved or disproved otherwise than by competent evidence, on one side or the other, respecting the alleged facts? Or can the doctrines of Atonement and Grace be established or invalidated by any abstract reasoning on their necessity or expediency? The utmost that our limited reasoning faculty may in such cases attempt is, in the first place, to satisfy itself of the genuineness of the text and its Divine authority, and so to interpret the doctrine that Scripture shall not be made to contradict itself; and, in the next place, to make it harmonize, as far as may be, with those moral and physical truths, of which we have, from other sources, clear and indisputable evidence, and which are even recognized as true by the general tenor of Holy Writ.

Nevertheless, in these latter as well as in former times, Socinians and other sects professing more liberal and enlarged modes of thinking, are wont to contend, if not overtly yet by implication, for the supremacy of the human understanding in all matters of Faith; regarding it as its undoubted prerogative, to decide, by its own natural faculties, upon the truth of every doctrine of Revealed Religion and the wisdom and expediency of the Divine dispensations, as well as upon the testimony by which they are supported. It is manifestly upon this principle, rather than upon the ground of any known law of evidence or legitimate canons of criticism, that considerable and very important portions, extending not only to single words or paragraphs, but even to entire chapters of the Sacred Writings, are regarded by persons of this description as spurious and interpolated; or are made to undergo such forced and unnatural expositions, as would hardly occur to the thoughts of persons whose judgments were not warped by some strong prepossessions against their plain and obvious signification.

In opposition to these or any similar endeavours to elevate the uninspired Critic above the divinely-inspired Authors of the Sacred Oracles, it behoves us to maintain our ground. Not that it is hereby intended (as will in the sequel more fully appear) to countenance the notions of those who would treat man as altogether incapable of understanding religious truths without the immediate act of Divine inspiration; much less, to depreciate the value of those attainments in human science and literature, which exalt and dignify our nature, and, together with that moral culture which is still more indispensable, prepare the soil for the reception of heavenly wisdom. The design is, merely to shew that the Word of God, as such, is not to be submitted to the human understanding as to a superior power or an authoritative judge, in matters which are, from the very nature of the subjects, removed out of its reach, and placed beyond the limits of its proper jurisdiction.

III. It remains now to consider, in the last place, the pretensions of a very different class of interpreters; those who hold the necessity of a supposed inward Light, or immediate communication from the Holy Spirit, as supplementary to Scripture, and, when obtained, infallible and irresistible in its operations.

Here, as in the other cases, the question may be brought to a ready issue, by adhering to the proofs already adduced of the sufficiency and perfection of the Holy Scriptures. If these Scriptures are "able to make us wise " unto salvation;" if every man who speaks of Divine things, is to speak only as those Oracles direct him; if our Lord declared that the Holy Spirit should guide his chosen Apostles " into ALL truth;" if one Apostle issues an anathema against those who preach any other Gospel than that he preached, and another Apostle denounces obliteration out of the book of life on such as should add to or take from his inspired volume;—what further proof can we desire, that, in the estimation of these Sacred Writers themselves, no claim of special illumination might be brought into competition with what was thus attested to be in truth the work of God? But if, on the ground of any such claim, a new sense may be imposed upon the Sacred Word; or if inspired interpreters, as well as inspired writers, be deemed necessary for Christian edification; what security have we against the setting up of a criterion amenable itself to no superior authority; or against the admission of imposture and fanaticism, acting under no other guidance or control than their pretended or imaginary obedience to a heavenly mandate?

It is easy indeed to perceive, that, by the admission of such a plea, no less danger would ensue to the purity and just pre-eminence of Scripture truth, than by allowing to the Church itself the claim of infallibility. For this is, in effect, transferring from the Church to individuals a privilege of a similar kind. The teacher who sets up a private spirit of his own for the introduction either of new doctrines or new interpretations of doctrine, and who founds his pretensions to do so on being specially gifted for the purpose;—what does he but assume to himself a Divine commission, and so far virtually lay claim to infallibility? A bold pretence to such spiritual communications with God, like that of Papal infallibility, throws the authority of Scripture into the shade, obtruding upon our notice a new and more attractive claim. And, when it is believed that God hath spoken to the individual who takes upon him to instruct others, it is hardly to be expected that deliberate inquiry will be made into the conformity of his doctrine with preceding revelations. Whether he come in the character of a preacher of new doctrines, or an interpreter of old ones, implicit deference will be required to his authority; and the credulous will fear to oppose it, " lest haply " they should be found to fight against God[p]."

The assurances therefore which we have of the absolute sufficiency of the Holy Scriptures, and of the exclusive authority with which their authors were invested for the revelation of the truths they contain, are strenuously to be pleaded in bar of any subsequent pretensions of a similar kind; it being manifestly derogatory to those writings and their authors, to deem any further communications from above to be requisite for the instruction of those who have access themselves to the Sacred Records, and who have, together with the aid of appointed

[p] Acts v. 39.

guides and pastors, such other means as Divine Providence affords them of applying these invaluable treasures to their spiritual improvement.

This hypothesis, indeed, as well as that of an infallible Interpreter at the head of the Church, appears to rest on an assumption, that the knowledge of Divine truth cannot be perpetuated without a continuation of the extraordinary and supernatural means by which it was at first communicated to mankind. But by what evidence or argument is this assumption supported? Is it not repugnant to the ordinary dealings of the Almighty; who is never found to encumber the work of his hands with unnecessary machinery, or to exert superfluous powers for the accomplishment of his purposes? Various indeed in their specific characters, and wonderfully adapted to the exigencies of mankind under their respective circumstances, were the several Divine dispensations antecedent to our Lord's coming into the world. But God having " in these last days spoken " unto us by his Son[q]," whose doctrine and instruction we receive through his Apostles and Evangelists, no ulterior revelation is to be expected; nothing more is to be looked

[q] Heb. i. 2.

for in the way of immediate communication from above. The Sacred Volume is closed: and with it terminated the age of special and extraordinary illuminations. Such pretensions therefore are now to be regarded not only with suspicion, but with dread, from their tendency to weaken that which is already stamped with the seal of Divine authority. Nor do they present themselves under a less formidable aspect, when advanced for the purpose of giving weight to particular interpretations of God's Word. "The Faith once " delivered to the Saints" was committed to writing by the Sacred Penmen, that we might believe " through their word[r]." Nothing therefore is now necessary, but to bring to their elucidation the best human attainments, moral and intellectual; together with those ordinary aids of the Holy Spirit, which the great Author and Finisher of our Faith has promised to them who sincerely seek the truth.

Claims, however, of extraordinary illumination, for the purpose of more fully revealing the Divine will, have been productive of some of the most baleful heresies in the Christian Church. As, in its earliest ages, the various sects who corrupted the Faith by false

[r] John xvii. 20.

philosophy were afterwards blended into one mass under the general denomination of Gnostics; so a variety of Enthusiasts, pretending to special revelations from God, lost, in process of time, their specific distinctions, and were known by the general title of Pneumatics, or persons affecting to act under the immediate influence of the Holy Spirit. The former arrogated to themselves extraordinary intellectual powers, in the discernment of heavenly truths: the latter laid claim to spiritual communications, enabling them to see farther than others could do into Divine mysteries. Thus a door was opened for the reveries of intellectual pride on the one hand, and spiritual pride on the other; and the followers of each having once imbibed a persuasion that more was necessary to be known or believed than the Scriptures had revealed, were disposed to listen to any presumptuous teachers, and to receive with avidity doctrines which could hardly have obtained an hearing, had not the supreme authority of the Sacred Oracles been first virtually done away.

The abettors however of this fanatical principle are not inexpert in their endeavours to uphold it by Scriptural authority. Many texts have been pressed into their service, which to examine in detail would lead to a prolix discussion. But the obvious distinction between the ordinary and extraordinary gifts of the Spirit will, for the most part, afford an easy solution of the difficulties with which the subject is usually embarrassed. And if we bear in mind, that whatever was once immediately communicated to the Sacred writers by Divine inspiration, has been, in effect, mediately communicated through them to the rest of mankind, so that they having been " taught of God," we also have, by their instrumentality, been taught of Him; we shall perceive that nothing more is wanting to the entire fulfilment of His promises, than that we should faithfully abide by the written Word as the exclusive Rule of Faith.

Thus far then may suffice to shew the radical unsoundness of the chief anti-scriptural principles which have contributed to the dissemination of religious error. Different as they appear to be in their specific characters, there are some striking points of resemblance between them. They all pervert that which is good and useful as a secondary object, by treating it as one that is primary in importance. They all give unbounded scope to human invention, to the disparagement of that which has the stamp of Divine authority. They all proceed likewise on a supposition that there is some imperfection or insufficiency in the Scriptures, which is to be supplied by one or other of these infallible remedies. In these false conceptions of the subject, each is equally reprehensible. Each confounds, what ought to be carefully distinguished, the obscurity of the doctrines revealed in Scripture with the obscurity of Scripture itself; as if a doctrine might not be laid down in a clear and distinct manner, although it be in itself above the full comprehension of the human faculties. Each is also equally defective in the remedy it proposes. For it is not oral tradition, nor human infallibility, (if such were to be found,) nor the utmost perfection of human reason, nor such illuminations as Enthusiasts rely upon, that can throw more light upon the doctrines than the Scriptures have already shed upon them. The same insurmountable barriers betwixt Divine and human knowledge will still remain, and by faith alone will the doctrines be received.

Still let us not suppose that Church-authority, or reason, or the cooperation of the Holy Spirit, may be lightly esteemed in the work of Scripture-interpretation. These are all evidently intended by their Divine Author to be instrumental to this great purpose.

But a fuller discussion of their just and proper limits, as helps to the knowledge of God's will, must be reserved for our further continuation of the subject in the next Discourse. In the mean while, with reference to the errors we have now been considering, let us remember that there are lights which dazzle and mislead; which blind the judgment instead of shewing objects in their true shades and colours. "Take heed, therefore;"—it is the emphatical warning of the Redeemer himself;—"Take heed, that the light which is in "thee be not darkness[s]!"

[s] Luke xi. 35.

SERMON IV.

1 PETER iv. 11.

If any man speak, let him speak as the oracles of God.

THE general proneness of mankind to adopt extremes in matters of Religion renders it especially necessary, on the part of a sincere inquirer after truth, to beware that in refuting one error he give no encouragement to another.

To a neglect of this maxim may be attributed many prevailing mistakes on points of great importance. When men, eager to combat some false and dangerous persuasion, conceive that the only effectual means of doing so is to establish the doctrine most diametrically opposite to it, they not unfrequently involve themselves in perplexities scarcely less mischievous than those they are solicitous to avoid. Hence disputes are carried on, wherein both parties confidently ground the truth of their own opinions on the overthrow of those of their adversaries; when probably a moderator in the controversy might easily shew, that, although each was successful in convicting his opponent of error, each was unsuccessful in establishing the truth of his own positions.

To the subjects entered upon in the last Discourse, this observation will be found particularly applicable. "If any man speak," says the Apostle, "let him speak as the ora-"cles of God:"—let him found his doctrine on the Word of God; let him search there for what he intends to deliver as sacred truth; let his first inquiry and his last appeal be directed to that Fountain of heavenly Wisdom. In opposition to this principle, different maxims have been inculcated by different parties. "If any man speak," says the Papist, "let "him speak as the oracles of the CHURCH;" —according to primitive Traditions, to General Councils, or to the Pope's Decretals; whose decisions are infallible, nay, on whose authority the verity of Scripture itself depends. "If any man speak," says the self-called Rationalist, "let him speak as the ora-"cles of REASON;"—according to the measure of his own understanding, or the agreement of what is proposed to him with the notions he has formed of that which is most befitting the Divine Wisdom and Goodness.

"If any man speak," says the Fanatic, "let " him speak as the oracles of the INWARD " LIGHT;"—trusting to a special illumination of the understanding by the immediate agency of the Holy Spirit, bestowed upon the chosen few, the faithful, the Elect of God, for their infallible guidance and direction.

With these several parties the sound Scriptural Christian has to contend, in maintaining the supreme authority of the oracles of God. Upon the genuine principles of the Protestant Reformation, undebased by any impure admixture infused into it by mistaken zeal or sceptical indifference, he has to establish this main foundation of Revealed Religion. He is bound to shew that no dictates of Church-authority, or of unenlightened Reason, or of Spiritual Illumination, can supersede the claims of these Sacred Writings to the highest rank in our estimation. Their sufficiency, their perfection, their preeminence above all pretensions of human wisdom or authority, and above all imaginations of preternatural gifts, are points never to be yielded, by those who have resolved to keep the Faith committed to them whole and undefiled.

This then is the first duty of the Christian

expositor. But if, in resisting the claims of these opponents, he hastily conclude that all the oracles which they reverence are to be despised as nothing worth; he will soon find himself on untenable ground. To deny to them that secondary rank to which they are entitled, and to reject them even as auxiliaries in the interpretation of Scripture, must be injurious to the truth itself. On this head, a species of enthusiasm occasionally prevails, which it is highly necessary to counteract; many being inclined to suppose, that the sufficiency and perfection of the Scriptures cannot effectually be maintained, without disallowing any coadjutors in its interpretation; that it needs no authorized ministry, no helps of human learning, no Divine blessing upon the study of it, to enable the reader to deduce from it an entire and consistent body of truth. The affirmative of which opinion will by no means follow from the negative of those which it is intended to refute. For, though we reject all pretensions of public or of private judgment, to supersede the authority of God's Word; yet we may, and must, (unless we yield ourselves to a blind and superstitious use of it,) call in these helps to its elucidation. Nay, it is evident from Scripture itself, that these are to be regarded as subsidiary to the work of spiritual instruction.

There are, indeed, texts of Scripture, which seem to speak in such absolute and unqualified terms of a certain internal power and efficacy in the Sacred Writings, that an undiscerning reader may possibly be led to suppose, that none of these helps are necessary for general edification. But when the same Scriptures admonish us of the duty of "obeying " them that have the rule over us[a]" in spiritual concerns;—when they declare, that God gave not only " Apostles," and " Prophets," and " Evangelists," but also " Pastors and " Teachers, for the perfecting of the saints, " for the work of the ministry, for the edify-" ing of the body of Christ[b];"—when they exhort us to be " men in understanding[c]," to " be ready always to give a reason of the hope " that is in us[d]," and to " prove all things, " and hold fast that which is good[e];"—and when they further teach us, that by " the " Spirit of wisdom the eyes of our under-" standing are enlightened[f];"—these suggestions are undoubtedly to be regarded as modifications of those texts which otherwise might appear capable of a more general and

[a] Heb. xiii. 17.   [b] Eph. iv. 11, 12.   [c] 1 Cor. xiv. 20.
[d] 1 Pet. iii. 15.   [e] 1 Thess. v. 21.   [f] Eph. i. 17, 18.

indefinite construction. Nor is it difficult to render these different representations of the subject perfectly consistent with each other; the necessity of such aids in the study of Holy Writ being in no wise incompatible with the most unreserved acknowledgment of its absolute perfection.

To regard the Sacred Word as an insulated production, entirely unconnected with human knowledge, is indeed a species of extravagance, scarcely less prejudicial to Divine truth, than those anti-scriptural theories, to which apparently it stands opposed. Ecclesiastical History bears witness to the many pernicious errors which have arisen from this mistaken principle. In the middle ages especially, there were men, who, with a zeal very laudable in itself, opposed the mischievous subtleties of scholastic Divines; many of whom they justly regarded as mere dialecticians in theology, intent only upon a display of their talents for disputation, and wholly negligent of the reverence due to sacred subjects. These opponents, however, unhappily fell into the other extreme; and disclaiming altogether the use of human learning in the investigation of the truth, began to speculate on the oracles of God with uninformed minds and ill-regulated piety. Of some of them it is recorded, that assuming to themselves a denomination expressive of their being purely Scriptural Divines, they discarded all other studies but that of the Sacred Writings. And what was the consequence?—Their crude conceptions, their abortive labours, produced strange and ill-formed theories, betraying in every feature the want of sound learning and well-disciplined understandings. From these sprung a new race of Mystics, far different from those who cultivated the philosophy of Plato and of Aristotle, but equally, if not more, injurious to the cause they professed to uphold. Hence arose interminable disputes between the advocates of Faith on the one side, and of Reason on the other; as if these were necessarily contrary to each other, and incapable of being brought to an agreement in the truth. These again give birth, in succeeding times, to various enthusiastic sects, entering upon the study of the Scriptures with a predetermination to neglect all mental culture, and to submit to no discipline which might restrain their unruly imaginations. Nor was even the Protestant Reformation, though in itself largely indebted to the revival of pure and genuine learning for its success, wholly unsullied by fanaticism of this kind: against which however its most distinguished leaders, Luther, Melancthon, and others, did not fail most strenuously to caution their disciples. And can we say, that our own times (boasting, nevertheless, of progressive improvement in every branch of knowledge) are entirely free from the same reproach? Are there not yet among us those who foster delusions of the grossest kind, by encouraging the pernicious notion, that human acquirements are altogether superseded by the Divine Word, and that unlettered ignorance is no disqualification for the office of the Sacred Interpreter?

To guard then against such mistaken views of the subject, and against any misconstruction of what has already been advanced in the foregoing Discourse, I proceed now to consider what deference is justly due to Church-authority, to human Reason, and to the ordinary assistance of the Holy Spirit; and what advantages may be derived from these, in subordination to the authority of Scripture itself.

I. On the first of these points, Papists and Protestants (with the exception of those among the latter who entirely separate from the Church as a visible community) are thus far agreed, that they mutually acknowledge the Divine ordinance of a Ministry, by whom the Sacred Word is to be promulgated and expounded. But with respect to the nature and extent of its authority, there exists between them this manifest difference. The Papist looks to one visible Head of the whole Christian Church, the universal Arbiter of religious controversies, infallible in his decisions, and from whom there is no appeal. The Protestant acknowledges no such universal Head, nor deems the Church itself, acting even by its legitimate rulers, to be either gifted with infallibility, or vested with such authority as may annul the right of its individual members to appeal to Scripture itself. The Church, he contends, has no lawful power to enjoin any doctrine or observance militating against the written Word. And the reason is this:—that the authority of the Church being derived from Scripture, as the charter by virtue of which it governs, it cannot with impunity violate the charter itself. Subject however to this restriction, the Church may be said to have a certain judicial power in matters of Faith. It is the constituted Guardian of the truth; and may do whatever the Scripture enjoins or permits, for the government and edification of the body at large; though it cannot originate, as of its own right, doctrines or duties really necessary to salvation.

The difference then between the parties (it has been well observed) is simply this:— "one demands absolute assent and unlimited "obedience; the other, only conditional as- "sent and cautionary obedience." The Protestant steers a middle course between superstitious veneration and lawless contempt of authority. Of the injury done to truth by departing from this golden mean, the history of the Church supplies abundant proof. Heresies at first sprang up, from want of due respect and subordination to ecclesiastical powers. After a while, on the depression of the turbulent spirits who introduced them, the Romish Church began to arrogate to herself an authority above the Sacred Word. And when this assumption of power received a sudden check from the counteracting force of the Protestant Reformation, then again there arose, among them who renounced her communion, some who were disposed to exercise unwarrantable liberties, and whose disorganizing principles gave occasion to the revival of many an exploded error, not without the addition of novelties equally detrimental to the purity of the Faith. The people were taught to spurn at every attempt to secure the sound exposition of Scripture by Liturgies, and Creeds, and Articles; as derogating from its sacred character. Hence new lights were continually sought for, and many an *ignis fatuus* was pursued by the inconsiderate and admiring multitude.

Such evils are only to be avoided by duly considering, that, though the Word of God is in itself a perfect rule of Faith, yet to the far greater portion of mankind it can only become so through some medium of human instruction. That medium the Scripture itself has pointed out to be the Christian ministry. Though the private Christian therefore, however uneducated, is not bound to rely upon any man, or upon any body of men, as infallible; yet is he bound, in prudence and in conscience, to look to such authorized teachers for necessary information. If he wantonly or perversely disregard their authority, it is at his peril that he does so; and should the result be that he fall into error, the fault can hardly be altogether venial. Nay, even from persons whose talents and acquirements give them much higher pretensions, some deference may reasonably be expected, to those who claim, upon the ground of institutions, not only long-established and long-venerated, but even of Divine appointment, the character of spiritual Guides;— claims, which ought at least to be thoroughly and dispassionately examined, before they are set at nought.

The modesty, however, which scruples to dissent from the highest human authorities, may be carried to a culpable excess. It is carried to that excess in the Romish Church; tending to preclude a general advancement in Scriptural knowledge, and leading to a blindfold acquiescence in the dictates of spiritual rulers. Christian modesty does not bind us to such servility. It warns us, not rashly to gainsay doctrines declared by the Church to be deduced from Holy Writ: but it does not require us to renounce our understandings, or to admit, as necessary articles of faith, positions which cannot be proved from the Word of God.

To yield altogether the right of private judgment, is indeed scarcely practicable: and if it were practicable, the surrender of conscience to human authority of any kind, would be a manifest violation of the first of all religious principles, that we are to "obey God rather than men [g]." But, on the other hand, the same principle obliges every man to obey the Divine will, rather than follow his own: and if in the Scriptures conditional obedience be enjoined to spiritual

[g] Acts v. 29.

rulers, it must be hazardous to disobey the injunction. In this respect, private judgment stands upon a similar footing with Church-authority. Both must submit to the Word of God; and neither may assume a right over the other, contrary to that Word. The individual may not conform to the Church in opposition to Scripture: the Church may not allow the departure of her members from what Scripture declares to be necessary to salvation. As the obedience required on the one hand is conditional, so is the right conferred on the other. Both are limited by the obedience due to the Supreme Power; both are equally subject to HIM who " ruleth over all." The responsibility therefore, on either side, is great: and nothing but a careful adjustment upon this principle, of the respective claims of private conscience and public authority, can ensure the practical exercise of that great rule of Christian conduct, " endeavouring to keep the unity of the " Spirit in the bond of peace [h]."

But the question immediately before us relates not so much to the authority of the Church over the private individual, as to the grounds on which it may presume to frame Articles of Faith. It is an inquiry, how far,

[h] Ephes. iv. 3.

on either side, recourse may be had to human authority, in the work of Scripture-interpretation.

On this head, much discussion has from time to time arisen, respecting the deference due to the writings of the primitive Fathers of the Church, and the use and value of ecclesiastical antiquity;—points of considerable moment, and deserving of attentive examination.

It seems to be indisputable, that the primitive Fathers are not to be regarded as Divinely-inspired; since otherwise their writings would necessarily have formed a part of the Sacred Canon. The question therefore is, whether, admitting them to have no more than human authority, they have any special claim to our reverential regard, which places them on higher ground than that of their ecclesiastical successors. And this question is to be determined by a fair consideration of any peculiar advantages they might possess, and of their ability and disposition to turn them to good account.

Against any such deference being paid to these our spiritual forefathers, it has been sometimes contended, that their writings now extant are few in number; that several of them, if not spurious, are adulterated, through the pious frauds, the sinister designs, or the ignorance of after-ages; that their style and reasoning are obscure; that, in their zeal to defeat opponents, they occasionally suppress or disguise the truth; that they are on certain points inconsistent with each other, and with themselves; and that it is often difficult to ascertain, whether the opinions they advance are meant to be declaratory of the judgment of the Church, or delivered only as their own private interpretations. For these and similar reasons, it has been alleged, that their testimony as genuine witnesses of the Faith may deservedly be impeached; and that neither Protestants nor Papists have hesitated occasionally to depart from their authority.

But of these charges it has repeatedly been shewn, that many are greatly exaggerated; some wholly unfounded; whilst others affect not their writings, more than the writings of almost all controversial authors of ancient date, adverting (as they must necessarily do) to times, and persons, and local circumstances, now but imperfectly known, and which cast a shade of obscurity over some of their narratives and their reasonings. These afford no good argument for laying their productions under a general interdict. Against an implicit submission to their authority, they are, doubtless, important considerations: but against the use and application of them as documents of more than ordinary value, they merit but little attention.

In answer therefore to such objections, it may suffice to observe, that supposing the primitive Fathers to have been men of only common discernment and integrity, their testimony respecting the doctrines then actually received by the Church, and maintained against the heresies then prevailing, must have peculiar weight. Those among them who had been personally conversant with the Apostles, and who derived their knowledge of the Christian Faith from what they continually heard of their preaching and discourse, as well as from their writings, seem to have claim to a regard only short of that which was due to their inspired Preceptors. To place such men as Clement, Ignatius, and Polycarp, no higher in the scale of authority, with respect to the value of their testimony on these points, than Bishops and Pastors in later times, betrays an error of judgment, which on any other subject of investigation analogous to this, would be deemed preposterous. On the part of their immediate successors, somewhat of the same extraordinary claim to acceptance still presents itself, though

with a certain diminution of its force. Descending still lower in the scale of history, this authority rapidly diminishes; and our judgment in their favour will be chiefly, if not solely, influenced, by the internal evidence their writings afford of some superior qualifications in the authors themselves. Yet, until the great schism between the Eastern and Western Churches, and the full establishment of the Papal Usurpation, the Fathers of the Church appear to have been deeply sensible of the obligation laid upon them to "contend for the Faith once de-
"livered to the saints[i]," and to guard the sacred deposit committed to their charge against every vain imagination which the Heretic or Schismatic might labour to introduce.

Disclaiming, therefore, any superstitious reverence towards these venerable men, it may reasonably be urged, that their peculiarly advantageous circumstances demand especial consideration; and that unless their characters, both moral and intellectual, could be so successfully impeached as to prove them wholly unworthy of credit, their testimony is of the very first importance in ascertaining the primitive Faith. In matters requisite to the formation of the Church; in framing

[i] Jude 3.

Confessions of Faith more or less explicit according to the errors it was necessary to discountenance; and in adopting means for the perpetuation of these benefits to the latest ages; they appear as having been at first deputed by the Apostles for purposes the most important, and as acting under impressions of a most awful responsibility. To them were also confided those Sacred Oracles, on which our Faith now most essentially depends. Through their ministry we have received these invaluable treasures: to their zeal and fidelity, under Providence, we owe the transmission of the pure Word of God to these present times: and the charge thus consigned to our care, we are bound to deliver unimpaired to succeeding generations.

If, in addition to these special grounds of confidence in the early Fathers, we admit, what has been contended for by learned and judicious Divines, that the extraordinary gifts of the Spirit, (especially that of " discerning " of spirits [k],") were not entirely withdrawn from the Church till long after the time of the Apostles; this would give still stronger confirmation to their claims. For, though we should not be warranted in a supposition that even these extraordinary gifts conferred

[k] 1 Cor. xii. 10.

authority for promulgating new articles of Faith, or infringing on any exclusive prerogative of the Sacred Writers; yet it would go far towards establishing interpretations of Christian doctrine thus received and sanctioned, on a firmer basis than any on which their less gifted successors can ground their pretensions.

But, not to insist on any disputable points, the use and value of ecclesiastical antiquity in general, and of its earliest productions in particular, is sufficiently evident, upon the ordinary principles of criticism and evidence. As works so nearly contemporary with those of the Sacred Canon, they illustrate the diction and phraseology of the inspired Penmen; they give an insight into the history of the age in which the writings of the New Testament were composed; they explain allusions to rites and customs, which otherwise might be involved in much obscurity; and, what is of still more importance, they assist in fixing the sense of controverted texts of Scripture, by the substantial evidence they afford of their generally received interpretation in the primitive ages of the Church. These advantages are derived to us from the public acts of the Church recorded in the most ancient ecclesiastical histories; from the prescribed formularies of Faith then in general use; and from the censures authoritatively passed upon such as departed from these standards of reputed orthodoxy. Hence we are assured of the care and solicitude manifested from the beginning by spiritual rulers, to preserve the truth from corruption: and when the importance of the doctrines themselves, as well as the opportunities they enjoyed of tracing them to the fountain-head, are duly considered; it can hardly be conceived, that they who had the guidance and government of the primitive Church should either be universally uninformed as to any fundamental truth, or universally embrace any fundamental error.

It is, therefore, with no common reverence that these authorities are to be regarded: nor can we detract from their just pretensions without hazard to some of the main foundations of our Faith. "No man," says Bishop Bull, " can oppose Catholic consent, but he " will at last be found to oppose both the Di- " vine Oracles and sound Reason." Nevertheless, we do not claim for them any infallibility, any commission to make further revelations of the Divine will, or any absolute authority as Scripture-interpreters. The appeal still lies from them, as from all other religious instructors, to that Word itself, which was no less their rule of Faith than it is ours: and the highest degree of deference that can be due to them, may be paid without any infringement of that inviolable maxim, " If any " man speak, let him speak as the oracles of " God."

II. We are now to consider, secondly, what degree of deference is due to the authority of human Reason in the investigation of Sacred Truth; and what advantages may be derived from calling in the aids of human science.

Whatever may be the inherent weakness or corruption of human Reason, we are not warranted in ascribing to it such total darkness or depravation, as would render it incapable of assisting us in these researches. At a very early period of life, the human mind discovers an ability to discern between good and evil, truth and falsehood, which, when duly cultivated, becomes a powerful auxiliary in the attainment of spiritual knowledge. And the accuracy of that knowledge which is obtained from the investigation of Scripture itself, may be expected to bear some proportion to the degree of cultivation bestowed upon this natural faculty. But it is necessary to ascertain what is the proper sphere of Reason in these inquiries; since upon its being occupied within or without that sphere, will depend the measure of its actual utility.

In searching the Scriptures for spiritual instruction, ample scope is afforded to the exercise of every faculty of the human intellect. Its powers of simple apprehension, of judgment, of argumentation, and of arrangement and combination of the several parts of the subject are continually called forth, in proving the genuineness of the text, or the authenticity of the Canon of Scripture, and in digesting the matter diffused through the Sacred Volume into a compact and coherent body of truth. The well cultivated mind cannot be more profitably occupied than in the labours connected with this research; in solving doubts, in removing difficulties, in clearing up ambiguities, in reconciling what seems to be at variance, and in illustrating by human science what it nevertheless receives as grounded upon Divine testimony. This is the legitimate province of man's Reason, when engaged in the service of Revealed Religion. But if it overstep this boundary; if, instead of the interpreter, it assume the character of an arbiter and judge; it may become injurious to the party in whose service it is employed; it may darken the subject, instead of throwing light upon it; and by introducing into the discussion authorities or principles irrelevant to the matter in hand, it may confound what ought to be kept distinct, and perplex what would otherwise be rendered clear and intelligible.

Here, then, care must be taken to distinguish between what can be discerned or apprehended through faith only, and what the natural intellect has power to discover or excogitate from its own external or internal resources. Truths of the latter description, however clear and irrefragable, are seldom proper criteria of truths of the former class. They have reference to different kinds of objects, and depend upon different kinds of evidence. Yet it is chiefly by confounding these, and arguing from one to the other by mistaken analogies, that bold adventurers in theology are led virtually to assert such a supremacy of human Reason, as would place it even above Divine control. It is also from similar confusion or misapprehension, that men of stronger piety than judgment are wont to shrink from any exercise of their mental powers in discussing Scriptural truth, lest they should seem to derogate from the Divine authority of Revealed Religion.

But to preserve the medium betwixt these extremes, and to assign their proper boundary to human reason and human science, is not surely a work of insuperable difficulty. The Scriptures comprehend a vast extent of knowledge, human as well as divine; and, in the illustration of them, scarcely any acquisitions of human learning are useless or unimportant. The adept in ancient languages, in philology, rhetoric, logic, ethics, metaphysics, geography, chronology, history ancient and modern, will have a conspicuous advantage in the study of the Sacred Writings, over him who is deficient in these attainments. Where these are capable of application to the subject, no competent student need be fearful of pursuing his inquiries to their utmost extent. The only just grounds of apprehension would lie in a slight and superficial knowledge, enough to discover difficulties, but not enough to remove them; or in attempting to stretch even the best attainments to points beyond their reach. But the value of solid acquirements of this kind, soberly and discreetly applied, is fully proved by the signal benefits which the Christian Faith has actually derived from the various improvements and discoveries of modern times in literature and science, tending to corroborate many important truths in the Sacred Records, and enabling us to retort upon the sceptic and the scoffer many a formidable blow, aimed at it in the vain confidence of irresistible strength.

There are indeed, in every branch of human knowledge, certain principles, and certain facts, so clearly and indubitably established, as to make it incredible that any system of Divine truth, rightly understood, should be found to contradict them; and by such a test, many a false interpretation of Scripture has been detected and exposed. But to apply this test successfully, is not the work of a rash or unskilful hand. Every principle and every fact resting upon human authority only, must be placed beyond the reach of controversy, before it can here be admitted as evidence: nor may even such evidence be admitted, if it be not strictly applicable to the subject under discussion. And since, in this respect, considerable doubts and difficulties may occasionally arise, it will well become the man of science, rather to mistrust his own judgment in the case, than hastily to infer that reason and revelation are irreconcilably at variance.

Subject to these restrictions, we need not hesitate to give to human reason and science their full share in the interpretation of the Sacred Oracles. To apply to this purpose every intellectual endowment which God has bestowed upon us, is so far effectually to fulfil his will; remembering, however, the infinite disparity between ourselves and HIM. The energies of the human mind may thus be brought successfully to lend their aid in the acquisition of spiritual knowledge. Though incompetent in themselves to the discovery of that knowledge, yet, when discovered, they are competent to discern, to examine, to compare, to illustrate, and to confirm it, by means similar to those which, in every other pursuit, lead most certainly to improvement and perfection.

III. It now only remains, to add a few observations respecting the ordinary assistance of the Holy Spirit, promised to individuals for their advancement in religious knowledge; and the reliance which may be placed upon it, in subordination to the authority of Scripture.

No devout believer in the Scriptures will be regardless of St. Paul's declaration, that " our sufficiency is of God[1]." Nor need we hesitate to affirm, that the ablest as well as safest expositors of Holy Writ are generally to be found among those who have been most distinguished by the dispositions emphatically called in Scripture, " the fruit of the Spirit[m]."

[1] 2 Cor. iii. 5.   [m] Gal. v. 22, 23.

Among the opposite characteristics, "the "works of the flesh[n]," the Apostle enumerates "variance, strife, and heresies:" and they who wantonly separate from the Church are declared to be "sensual, having not the "Spirit[o]." We are, therefore, warranted in maintaining, that in the work of interpreting Scripture, as well as in other Christian duties, "every good and every perfect gift is from "above, and cometh down from the Father of "lights[p]."

But this truth is of a general nature only, applicable to this subject in common with whatever appertains to the character of a faithful disciple of Christ. Whether engaged in the study of the Scriptures, or in any other means of working out his salvation, the devout Christian acknowledges that "it is God "who worketh in him both to will and to do "of his good pleasure[q]," and that for every degree of light and information of which he is conscious, he is to give God the glory. This assurance, however, of Divine help to further his own exertions, he knows, is not to be expected as a special or extraordinary gift; much less as intended to supersede the use of any other helps or means, with which the

[n] Gal. v. 19, 20, 21.   [o] Jude 19.
[p] James i. 17.   [q] Phil. ii. 13.

providence of God has blessed him. In the infancy of the Church, there were "diver-"sities of gifts," proceeding from "the same "Spirit[r]," for the great work of spreading the Gospel far and wide, and for the immediate edification of those who could not have been brought, without such extraordinary means, to the knowledge and acceptance of the Gospel. These gifts appear to have been limited to persons holding official stations in the Church, and to have continued no longer than the exigencies of the Church required. In process of time, they were gradually withdrawn: and their place is now to be supplied by the use of the Holy Scriptures, accompanied with such attainments as the light of human learning, bearing some faint analogy to the light of inspiration, enables us to bring to the inquiry. Upon the diligent application of these, and the ordinary imperceptible aids of Divine grace to render them efficient, we are now to rely.

While therefore we entirely reject pretensions to special illumination of the understanding, as a warrant for obtruding unauthorized interpretations of Holy Writ;—while we acknowledge that the age of extraordinary inspiration, as well as that of mira-

[r] 1 Cor. xii. 4.

cles and prophecy, has long since passed away;—while we strenuously insist upon the danger of neglecting the ordinary means of improvement which the Providence of God affords us, from a vain expectation of more than ordinary gifts of Grace;—we, nevertheless, are far from depreciating the value of that spiritual aid, which is the assured privilege of every faithful member of Christ, and to which the Scriptures themselves invariably direct us to ascribe whatever proficiency we make in wisdom and in knowledge.

The dispositions, indeed, implied in a sober and well-regulated confidence in this aid, cannot but greatly facilitate the attainment of the object: and to the want of these we may ascribe much heterodox exposition of Holy Writ, as well as much of that infidelity, which is to be found in Christian countries. And, doubtless, (as has been already more fully noticed,) there is the promise of an especial blessing annexed to such dispositions. For, "God resisteth the proud, but giveth " grace to the humble[s]." What wonder then, if they who trust only to human sagacity, and to ingenuity rendered more conspicuous, perhaps, in distorting than in simplifying the truth, should exemplify what the Prophet af-

[s] James iv. 6.

firms of such as "made them crooked paths,"—" We wait for light, but behold obscurity; "for brightness, but we walk in darkness[t]?"—What wonder, if the *judicial* consequences of rash and unhallowed attempts at Scripture-interpretation, by those who are regardless of the ordinary and appointed means of attaining to it, should be that "strong delusion," which, the Apostle warns us, may be sent upon them who "receive not the love of the "truth[u]?"

The distinction, then, between the Fanatic and the sober-minded Christian in this respect is manifest. The former presumes upon the aid of the Spirit, to the neglect of human acquirements: the latter avails himself of both. The former despises the natural gifts of which he is in possession; expecting preternatural gifts, of which he has no reasonable assurance: the latter diligently cultivates every talent bestowed upon him; relying, at the same time, for help from above to perfect his endeavours. For this blessing on his labours, he confidently trusts in God; knowing that "whosoever thus believeth in HIM "shall not be ashamed[w]."

Thus we have brought to a termination the first general division of our subject, respecting

[t] Isa. lix. 8, 9.   [u] 2 Thess. ii. 10, 11.   [w] Rom. x. 11.

those great leading principles, by which all inquiries into the truths of Revealed Religion, and every specific rule of Scripture-interpretation, are to be regulated and adjusted. We have seen, on the one hand, the errors of those who would set up authorities of their own devising above that of the Oracles of God; and the errors of those, on the other hand, who would reject the means, which the Providence of God has placed in their hands, of guarding the Sacred Word against perversion and misinterpretation. It is to one or other of these extremes, that the Church may justly attribute some of the worst corruptions of the Christian Faith. By the undue elevation of ecclesiastical authority, of human philosophy, or of imaginary inspiration; sacerdotal, intellectual, and spiritual Pride, have, in their turns, domineered over the faith of mankind, and "taught for doc-"trines of God the commandments of men[x]." By vilifying all these; by spurning at restraint of every kind; and by closing up all the avenues to wholesome instruction and mental improvement; ignorance, licentiousness, and irreligious apathy, have rendered the Scriptures themselves instrumental to delusion. These prime sources of error being

[x] Matth. xv. 9.

removed, the inquirer will come to the investigation of Scripture truth, with a mind free from dangerous prepossessions, and better able to profit by the research.

" Other foundation can no man lay, than " that is laid, which is Jesus Christ[y]."—He is " Head over all things to the Church[z]."— His Word " giveth light and understanding " to the simple[a]."—His Grace " is sufficient " for us[b]." These are first principles, invariably to be adhered to, and to which every other rule is secondary and subordinate. But in the application of these principles to the purposes of spiritual instruction and improvement, our own cooperation is made requisite by Him who is " the Author and Finisher of " our Faith[c]." He hath taught us that whatever talents, natural or spiritual, are bestowed upon us, must be used in His service; and that with them we are to " occupy till He " come[d]." For, " of Him, and through Him, " and to Him, are all things; to whom be " glory for ever. Amen[e]."

[y] 1 Cor. iii. 11.   [z] Ephes. i. 22.   [a] Psal. cxix. 130.
[b] 2 Cor. xii. 9.   [c] Heb. xii. 2.   [d] Luke xix. 13.
[e] Rom. xi. 36.

SERMON V.

2 TIMOTHY ii. 15.
Rightly dividing the word of truth.

IN the course of the inquiry already instituted into the subject of Scripture-interpretation, those points have chiefly been discussed, which relate to certain primary principles necessarily affecting every subordinate rule, and indispensably requisite towards the attainment of a clear and consistent view of the Christian system. These principles being established, it remains to consider how we may most securely build on such foundations. And here we may select, in the first place, as a topic of main importance, the admonition in the text, given by St. Paul to Timothy, that he should "study to shew "himself approved of God, a workman that "needeth not to be ashamed, RIGHTLY DIVID-"ING THE WORD OF TRUTH."

The Apostle, in giving this direction to him whom he calls his "own son in the Faith," undoubtedly intended the edification, not of Timothy only, but also of all who, after him, should succeed to the Office of the Ministry; since upon a right division or distribution of the truth into its respective parts, by the Preacher of the Word, would depend the clear conception of it by the people committed to their charge, and their security against any counterfeit representations which false or ignorant teachers might attempt to impose upon them. And although it concerns not the plain unlettered Christian to be an adept in the arts of controversy, or to be able to unravel every perplexity in which minute inquirers may seek to entangle him; yet is it highly important, that he should not, either through his own misapprehension or that of his appointed instructors, be led to hold opinions subversive of " the hope that is in him;" —a hope, intended to be " an anchor of the " soul, both sure and stedfast[a]."

What then is the purport of the Apostle's injunction, " rightly to divide the word of " truth?"

On the critical meaning of the word ὀρθοτομοῦντα, here rendered " rightly dividing," it is unnecessary to dilate. Whatever metaphorical signification we assign to it, (for it is

[a] Heb. vi. 19.

capable of more than one,) its application in this passage will be nearly the same. It denotes a judicious distribution or arrangement of the subject-matter of Holy Writ; such an analysis of its component parts, as may enable the reader to judge of their respective purposes, and of their connection with the general design. This cannot but be requisite in a work so multifarious in its contents, composed by various authors, treating on various subjects, referring to various times, persons, and occurrences, and yet manifesting one uniform and consistent purpose, in which all mankind are equally concerned. It is also the more necessary, because, for obvious reasons, the Scriptures themselves are not presented to us in a systematic form. The several dispensations of Revealed Religion had reference to the special exigencies of mankind at certain periods, as well as to the general purpose of Divine Revelation. The Sacred Writings, therefore, were particularly adapted to the improvement of those to whom they were at first addressed, whilst they at the same time shed a light intended to be universally beneficial. Hence they admit a somewhat diversified mode in the arrangement or classification of their contents, although the truths they deliver are substantially the same. But, whatever be the method pursued, the same leading principles must be adhered to, and the same accuracy of discrimination will be requisite, in examining the constituent parts of so stupendous a work.

In discoursing then upon the injunction in the text, we may consider it as comprising, in general terms, whatever is necessary for the clear *analysis* of Scripture truth. "Rightly "to divide the truth," is rightly to separate what ought to be kept distinct. And how important this rule is, to a correct interpretation of Holy Writ, may be evidenced by a brief examination of the following points:—First, the general distinction between what is properly *fundamental* in Scripture truth, and what is not so;—Secondly, the specific distinctions to be observed in the several *dispensations* of Revealed Religion, by which, at different periods, the Almighty saw fit to communicate his will to mankind;—Thirdly, the variety of *subject-matter* contained in the Sacred Writings, and connected with these particular dispensations;—Fourthly, the immediate *occasions* and *purposes*, whether general or special, for which certain books or portions of Holy Writ appear to have been composed.

I. First then, we are to consider the general distinction, as far as it can be made, between what is properly *fundamental* in Scripture truth, and what is not so.

It is not every truth clearly deducible from Scripture, or manifestly necessary to be believed, that can with propriety be called fundamental. For though no man may safely deny any doctrine proved from Scripture; yet all truths, however certain and indisputable, are not to be placed on the same level, with respect to their essential importance. Some it is the direct purpose of Scripture to reveal to us: others it recognizes only as truths already received, or collaterally connected with its design: and greater stress is evidently laid upon some of these points than upon others. Hence we find reiterated injunctions respecting particular doctrines and duties, as if almost the whole of religion consisted in these; and many compendious rules of faith and practice, which, if taken in the abstract only, might seem to preclude the necessity of inquiring farther into what we are to believe or to do.

But though truths thus urged may justly claim especial consideration, yet the number of those which are to be regarded as fundamental will be too much circumscribed, if we attempt thus to reduce them to one or two comprehensive articles. It seems indeed impracticable to frame articles so comprehensive as some desire to have them, without giving latitude to a great diversity and even contrariety of opinions which may be engrafted upon them. If, for instance, from St. Paul's general maxim, " Other foundation can " no man lay, than that is laid, which is Je-" sus Christ [b]," it were inferred that the bare acknowledgment of this one truth, " Jesus is " the Christ," is sufficient in itself as a creed in which all may conscientiously unite ; what security could be had against a multitude of erroneous tenets respecting the various points virtually included in that general proposition ? or what difficulty would be found, even by men holding the most opposite opinions on those points, in acceding to so broad and indefinite a rule of Faith ? Yet, it is not evident, that the several specific truths inseparable from that proposition are no less essential to a right profession of the Faith, than the proposition itself? For, when the Apostle speaks of Jesus Christ as the foundation of our Faith, must we not infer, that whatever necessarily belongs to it becomes,

[b] 1 Cor. iii. 11.

in effect, a fundamental article of Belief? The question, therefore, what is fundamental, still remains open to inquiry; and the answer is to be sought for in the developement of the Apostle's aphorism. The aphorism itself may contain all that is necessary to be believed, and may afford a clue to the discovery of such contents:—but it does not itself give the definitive answer. It only cuts off every pretence for establishing any opposite principle of religion to that which rests on faith in Christ; by declaring the authority of the Christian Revelation to be that to which every other must bow and obey.

In like manner, wherever compendious texts occur in Scripture, which seem to comprise in one single proposition all that is necessary in faith or practice, they are to be considered either as combining several essential truths, or as intended to be taken in conjunction with others, no less essential, dispersed through the Sacred Writings. Scripture indeed no where sets before us a synopsis, or collective view, of such essentials. This is left to be done by those whose charge it is to feed the flock of Christ: and in this the skill of the judicious interpreter will be most profitably displayed.

The desire, however, of simplifying, as

much as possible, the truths of the Christian Faith, and of cutting off occasions of disputation, seems to have led many to attempts at *generalizing* its system, more than is consistent with a distinct delineation of its design. Thus it has been affirmed, that nothing is fundamentally necessary to be believed, but that Jesus is the Messiah; or that those articles alone are fundamental, on which all Christians are agreed; or, again, that what is essential to the Faith is to be determined solely by its practical tendency and effect:— all which are but ambiguous or defective criteria of a right belief; affording no direct evidence of the specific articles which constitute the Faith itself, much less of the sense in which they are to be received, so as not to be rendered inconsistent with each other. Such indefinite views of the subject tend indeed to create indifference to correct apprehensions of the truth, and to shelter dangerous errors under the cover of a latitudinarianism specious, but delusive.

Among the many directions, therefore, which have been given for our guidance in this respect, none, perhaps, is so entirely unexceptionable, as the rule laid down by an eminent Divine of our Church [a], that "what-

[a] Dr. Waterland.

"ever verities are found to be plainly and directly *essential* to the doctrine of the *Gos-pel-Covenant*, they are *fundamental verities;* and whatever errors are plainly and directly *subversive* of it, they are *fundamental errors.*"

That such fundamental truths are discernible in the Holy Scriptures, may be inferred from the purpose for which those Scriptures were written. Every thing in the Sacred Volume tends to one great central point, the Covenant of God with man for his final justification and acceptance. Whatever inseparably appertains to this, is fundamental in its kind, and indispensable to a saving faith. Whatever is repugnant to this, is an error that endangers salvation. Numberless other truths there may be, consequent upon these, or collaterally connected with them, or even entirely distinct from them, which, as Scripture-verities, we are also bound to believe. But those only are strictly *fundamental* in the system, which immediately affect that great charter of our salvation, the Christian Covenant. And what these are, the nature and the terms of the Covenant will sufficiently ascertain.

The Gospel presupposes, not only the existence of God, but the mode of his existence as Father, Son, and Holy Ghost, and those essential attributes by which he was moved to bestow this inestimable blessing upon mankind. It also presupposes the contraction of actual guilt on the part of man; whence arose the necessity of this merciful interposition of the Almighty, to save him from destruction. It further assumes, that man has freedom of will to accept or reject the proffered mercy, and that it is the indisputable right of his Divine Benefactor to prescribe the stipulations, or conditions, on which its benefits shall depend.

The points thus assumed are therefore to be regarded as forming the basis of the Christian system, and, consequently, as fundamental doctrines. They involve the truth and the validity of the whole scheme of religion deduced from revelation. Hence it is our first concern, to form correct opinions on these topics. To know God, and to know in what relation we stand to Him under this gracious dispensation, are essential to a right apprehension of the dispensation itself, as well as to the profitable application of it to ourselves. Contrariety of sentiment on such leading questions must not only preclude accommodation as to many lesser points, but will make each party appear to the other as virtually renouncing Christianity itself.

For similar reasons, the acknowledgment of our Lord Jesus Christ as the *Mediator* between God and man, combining in his person the twofold nature, human and Divine, must, if the doctrine be true, be essential to the Covenant; and, therefore, to err on this point, is to err fundamentally. Inseparably connected with this, is the doctrine also of *Atonement* through the Redeemer; according to our belief or disbelief of which, Christianity assumes a totally different character; different in kind and in substance, not merely in form and circumstance.

The same may be said respecting the *conditions* of salvation through Christ. A *Covenant* without condition seems to be a contradiction in terms. If the Gospel were simply a *Promise* of salvation, it might be absolute and unrestricted. But as a *Covenant*, it is necessarily conditional. Therefore, though it originated in God's free Grace, and is founded entirely on His Promises, which are "yea " and amen," and which he might have withholden or not, at his good pleasure; yet these Promises being delivered under the form, and substance, and denomination of a Covenant, they must be regarded in that light: and to represent the Almighty as making this offer irrespectively and unconditionally, is to undermine the very foundations of the Gospel. It cannot, therefore, but be matter of importance, to determine whether we will admit the necessity of Repentance and Obedience in conjunction with Faith; or, so rely on Faith only, as virtually to supersede that necessity:—whether we imagine Christ to have done all for us, and that nothing more is requisite than to lay hold on him by Faith; or admit, that there is, on our part, something to be done, as well as to be believed, that we may attain to eternal life.

Nor is the doctrine we hold concerning the nature and operations of the Holy Spirit, and its efficacy in the work of our *Sanctification*, less strongly marked as to its fundamental character. If we doubt "whether there "be any Holy Ghost," any Divine Person so denominated, the Spirit of God and of Christ, by whom "the whole body of the Church is "governed and sanctified;" it may well be asked, "Unto what then were we baptized [b]?" —And again, as to the mode of its operation;—whether we persuade ourselves that this Spirit works in us irresistibly, and by its perceptible operations gives us an inward as-

[b] Acts xix. 3.

surance of its saving effects; or believe that our own cooperation with it is indispensable, and that its presence with us is apprehended by faith, not by sensible perception;—these cannot be questions of secondary importance. In their results they affect the very vitals of Christianity. Truth concerning them must be radical truth: error concerning them must vitiate the whole mass of our Creed.

Perhaps, too, we shall be well warranted, in placing among these fundamental articles, a due estimation of the Christian Sacraments, and the Christian Priesthood. The question, whether these are essential, or not, to our actual reception of the benefits of the Covenant, involves, on the one hand, our safety in placing any reliance upon them; and, on the other, our danger in disregarding them, if necessary to ensure our acceptance with God. If the Sacraments be not only signs or emblems of spiritual benefits, but the instituted means of conveying those benefits;—and if the ministration of the Priesthood, as a Divine ordinance, be necessary to give the Sacraments their validity and effect;—then are these interwoven into the very substance of Christianity, and inseparable from its general design. So much, indeed, is said in Scripture of the Church of God, as a spiritual society, subsisting under a visible government, and administered by means of these ordinances; that to treat the consideration of these points as of little weight, appears to be depreciating, if not the system of Christianity itself, yet the mode which infinite Wisdom has ordained of carrying it into effect. Here, therefore, as in other fundamental points, errors, whether of excess or of defect, may be attended with most momentous consequences.

Thus it appears, that whatever relates generally to the Divine nature and attributes;—to the Father, Son, and Holy Spirit, by whom we are created, redeemed, and sanctified;—whatever specially appertains to the personal dignity and office of the Son as Mediator of the Covenant between God and man, or of the Holy Spirit as rendering us meet to become partakers of that Covenant;—whatever conditions are to be fulfilled on our part, to entitle us to the benefits of the Covenant;—and whatever means are ordained for carrying this gracious purpose of the Almighty into effect;—may be considered as Fundamentals of the Christian Faith. To these our attention is to be primarily directed: and in carefully discriminating between them and points not so distinctly revealed; or concerning which diversity of opinion may be entertained without affecting the hope of salvation; will be shewn, in the first place, our adherence to the Apostolical maxim, " rightly dividing the word of truth."

II. But, secondly, besides this *general* distinction, bearing reference to the one great purpose for which the whole system was revealed; there are also *specific* distinctions to be observed, respecting the several Dispensations of Revealed Religion, by which, at different periods, the Almighty saw fit to communicate His Will to mankind.

These Dispensations may be classed, either according to the order of time in which they took place, or according to some peculiar and essential characteristics in the Covenants with which they were accompanied.

Respecting the Covenants entered into by the Almighty with mankind, these also may be somewhat differently classed or subdivided, according as we view them in their general or specific characters. Some speak of two Covenants only;—the Covenant before the Fall, and the Covenant after it :—the former, bestowing the promise of Eternal Life on condition of man's continuing in a state of innocence and obedience; which, by the help of Divine Grace, he was rendered able to do ;—the latter, in which, after man had by transgression incurred the forfeiture of eternal life, new terms and conditions were offered for his restoration to it. According to this division of the subject, every intermediate Dispensation between the Fall of man and the end of the world, forms a part only of the second Covenant preparatory to its final completion.

Others adopt the same twofold division of the subject, under different denominations;—such as the Covenants of Nature and of Grace;—of Incorruptibility and the Resurrection;—of Works and of Faith;—all which distinctions, though not each expressed, perhaps, with equal accuracy, evidently relate to the general state of man before and after the Fall; without reference to any particular modifications of the latter Covenant, intervening between the first promise of a Redeemer, and the full accomplishment of the promise, in the person of the Messiah.

Now although these distinctions, rightly and clearly defined, may suffice for a general view of the design of Revealed Religion; yet, to prevent misconception in judging of the several parts of so vast a design, it is necessary that other distinctions, more specific, but equally important, should be constantly kept in view. For, with respect to the state of mankind since the Fall, it is manifest that the Almighty, in progressively carrying on the one great purpose of Divine Revelation, has, "at sundry times and in divers man-"ners c," adapted his proceedings to the various exigencies of those for whose benefit it was intended. With these circumstantial differences, therefore, the Scripture-critic ought to be well acquainted. Their occasions, their results, their separate purposes, and their instrumentality to the whole design, must be borne in mind, to enable him " rightly to divide the Word of Truth," and fully to apprehend the scope and intention of the Sacred Writers.

For the attainment of this object, however, it will suffice to mark the simple chronological order of the Divine transactions with mankind, as they occur in Holy Writ, under the Paradisiacal, the Patriarchal, the Mosaic, and the Christian dispensations;—an arrangement, the most obvious and convenient to the ordinary reader, while it combines every advantage of a more elaborate investigation. For, hence we shall readily perceive both the specific and the general characters of these Dispensations. We shall perceive

c Heb. i. 1.

that the Paradisiacal stands alone, comprehending the first general Covenant with man, and applicable only to that state of innocence and perfection in which he was at first created. We shall perceive also, that the Gospel, the second general Covenant made with man, did not commence at the time of our Lord's actual appearance upon earth, but was, in effect, coeval with the Fall; having its beginning in the promise made to our first parents, that "the seed of the woman "should bruise the serpent's head [d]." The Patriarchal Religion therefore was that of the Gospel, in promise or expectation. The Mosaic was that of the Gospel, in Type and Prophecy. The Christian was the completion of both. These are distinctions necessary to be well understood, that we may be enabled to enter into the true spirit and meaning of many of the Apostolical writings, where arguments are continually addressed to Jews, or Gentiles, or Christian Believers, grounded entirely upon these important considerations.

III. But, thirdly, the Scripture-interpreter will find it also expedient, to conduct his inquiries with reference to the great variety of

[d] Gen. iii. 15.

subject-matter contained in the Sacred Writings, and connected with these several Dispensations.

The order, in which the books of the Old and New Testaments are canonically arranged, affords one general clue to a classification of their contents. Another of a more comprehensive cast, is the division of the Old Testament into the Pentateuch, the Historical Books, the Hagiographa, and the Prophecies; and of the New Testament into the Gospels, the Acts of the Apostles, the Epistles, and the Apocalypse. But whatever distribution we adopt, it is to be observed, that no one book is unconnected with the rest. And hence, (as well as to characterize it, by way of eminence, the Book above all others to be received and reverenced,) probably, these Writings have collectively obtained their appropriate appellation, the BIBLE; denoting that they constitute one entire work, notwithstanding the diversity of authors whose names they bear, and the variety of subjects on which they treat; a work, singular in its kind, whether considered with respect to its authority, its design, or its known effects wherever it has been introduced.

Nevertheless, while we affix this character to the Bible in its collective form, regard must be had to the particular subject of each separate work it contains. And here the skill and attainments of the expositor will continually be brought to the test.

In the Historical books special attention is necessary to the immediate scope and purpose of the narrative; lest more should be expected from it than that purpose requires, or attempts be made to deduce from the history what it will not clearly warrant. Much in these records is left untold, which is either unnecessary to be known, or which, if necessary, must be supplied from other sources. Here the aids of geography, chronology, and profane history may be successfully employed, in the adjustment of questionable points, and in connecting events and circumstances which the Sacred Writers have but cursorily or incidentally noticed. The labours of our best Commentators shew how valuable in this respect are the acquirements of extensive information and diligent research; while the rash and ill-digested cavils of sceptical critics no less clearly prove the necessity of the greatest care and circumspection, in comparing sacred with profane history, and in employing the one for the elucidation of the other. That which has affectedly been called the Pyrrhonism of history, (at best but a low and groveling species of criticism,) is never so misplaced as when sitting in judgment on these Divine Oracles; whose credit nothing may be allowed to impeach, but irreconcilable contradiction to facts and authorities established upon testimony the most indubitable, nay, which it is impossible to set aside. To an investigation whether they really exhibit any such contradiction, we may confidently challenge inquiry. But while the general evidence of their authenticity and of their Divine inspiration stands unshaken, they are not to be made the sport of wanton surmise or irreverent suspicion, as if they rested on no firmer grounds than the effusions of poetic fiction and legendary credulity. From criticism however of this description, it were well if all who are classed among Christian Commentators could be entirely exculpated!

To the interpreter of the Prophetical books of Scripture, such cautions are of still higher moment. In the study of these, a greater reach of erudition and judgment will be requisite. A knowledge of the time, the country, and the condition of the Prophet himself; and an acquaintance not only with those circumstances with which the Holy Seer was personally conversant, but with those of other times and countries far remote from his; will oftentimes be necessary, for the elucidation of these obscurer portions of Sacred Writ. Nor will less regard be due to the characteristic style of their respective authors; to their highly figurative diction, their parabolical illustrations, and (still more difficult to decipher) their enigmatical actions and demeanour, in awakening attention to the awful purposes of their mission. And to this must be added the care necessary in fixing the accomplishment of Prophecy; whether it be sought for in the events which the Prophet himself lived to see; or in some subsequent though not distant period; or in that "fulness of time," when Messiah appeared; or in still later ages, when various events, preparatory to our Lord's final coming, have successively verified the pretensions of these faithful Messengers of the Most High. In the discussion of these points, more than an ordinary portion of discernment, as well as of sound learning, will be requisite, to avoid rash and mischievous interpretations, such as ignorance, fanaticism, and party spirit, are continually obtruding upon the Christian world.

Respecting those entire books, or portions, of Holy Writ, which are purely doctrinal or practical, although the labour of interpretation may seem to be, in some respects, less arduous, yet is it, in others, attended with its peculiar difficulties; and, in its results, it may be productive of consequences still more important. This indeed is a branch of Scripture-criticism, with which the points of distinction already noticed will be found to have a close connection. The distinction between points really fundamental, or not so, is here often necessary, to guide us in the exposition of particular articles of faith, and of particular rules of conduct. That between the respective Dispensations, or Covenants of the Almighty with his creatures, will frequently assist us in determining to what times, and persons, and circumstances, any of these related; and how far they concern mankind in general, or ourselves in particular. The professed subject also of any book of Scripture will afford some clue to the proper application of its instructions in matters of faith and practice, and to their necessary limitation or extension.

IV. These observations, however, as well as those which preceded them, may be still further strengthened, by considering, in the last place, the several other occasions and purposes, whether general or special, for which different books or portions of Holy Writ appear to have been composed.

Whatever be the subject of investigation, whether Prophecy, History, matters of Faith and Practice, or the nature of the different Dispensations of Revealed Religion; we shall be exposed to continual difficulty, if we labour under misapprehension respecting the immediate scope and intention which the writer had in view. Though the Bible therefore is capable, for the most part, and perhaps throughout, of an application both to general and special purposes; yet these must not be confounded with each other: and to the want of due discrimination in this respect, may be attributed many errors of considerable magnitude.

Perhaps indeed the far greater part of that obscurity in the Scriptural Writings, which has often been made the ground of unreasonable complaint, might be removed if this were more carefully considered. It is not however to be expected that the system of Revealed Religion should, in all its parts and circumstances, be equally clear and intelligible to persons living in different ages of the world, and under different dispensations of the Divine will. It appears to have been the purpose of the Almighty, that the disclosure of what related to this vast design should be gradual and progressive. Some of its particulars therefore would, of necessity, be better understood at one period than at another. The Patriarchs cannot be supposed to have had so distinct a view of the mystery of redemption, as that which is vouchsafed to the Christian world; nor could the Jewish prophecies be so intelligible to those who lived at the time of their delivery, as to them who have seen their completion. On the other hand, many circumstances respecting the types, and ceremonies, and sacrifices under the Jewish and Patriarchal dispensations, being specially adapted to the habits, and sentiments, and conditions of those periods, might then be better understood than in these latter ages, when their use and necessity are done away. Still the general utility of the Scriptures is the same. As much may be known by all, as it is necessary for all to know: and the fact, that special situations afford special advantages for the elucidation of certain obscurities in the Sacred Writings, cannot justly be alleged as detracting from their universally beneficial tendency. It only proves how necessary it is to investigate them with reference to this fact; and not to expect satisfactory and consistent interpretations of them, without regard to these local or occasional purposes, as well as to their general design.

In illustration of this, so far as it respects a right apprehension of doctrinal points, we may observe that the Gospel of St. John in particular, and almost all the Epistles in the New Testament, were evidently written to meet the particular exigencies of the faithful in those times, and with direct reference to the religious opinions then prevailing. There is abundant evidence to shew that St. John wrote his Gospel when the gross errors of Cerinthus and his followers were gaining ground; and that the introductory part of it, respecting the Divinity of the Logos, was composed with an especial view to their refutation. Other heresies had also sprung up during the Apostolic age: and to these the Sacred Writers found it needful to supply an antidote. The full force, therefore, and the characteristic excellence of some of the most important portions of the New Testament, will be in a great measure lost upon the reader who is unapprised or regardless of these circumstances. The respective prejudices and prepossessions of the Jewish and the Gentile converts were also fruitful sources of difficulty to the first Preachers of the Gospel, and called for the utmost discretion and judgment in their endeavours to counteract them. Accordingly, it was an acknowledged principle with St. Paul, and we have no reason to doubt its being so with the rest of the Apostles, to " become all things unto all men[f];" that is, to adapt their mode of reasoning, as well as their personal conduct, to the attainments, characters, conditions, and opinions of those to whom their instructions were addressed. In discoursing, at one time, with Jews; at another, with Greeks; at another, with Infidels or Heretics; at another, with those who received the word with sincerity and singleness of heart; it is not to be conceived that one uniform method of instruction would equally avail. The strain of the argument would sometimes be simply didactic; at other times, profoundly argumentative and polemical; the persons concerned in the discussion, as well as the subject-matter of the discussion, necessarily requiring such discrimination. And although it be unquestionable, that, even on such special occasions, nothing would come from the pen of an inspired Apostle, which might not, in the exposition of Scripture-doctrine, be made generally and universally instructive; yet is it no less obvious, that to render such portions of

[f] 1 Cor. ix. 22.

Scripture thus edifying, it is necessary to regard them in connection with these occasional purposes. Continual misapplication may otherwise be made of positions and arguments separated from the concomitant circumstances which give the clue to their proper interpretation, and applied to topics irrelevant to the design of the authors themselves.

To matters of practical concern also, as well as to doctrinal points, this rule must be extended. In consulting the records of the Old Testament, unless regard be had to the state of manners, civilization, customs, and local peculiarities of the times to which they relate; we shall be perpetually liable to dangerous errors of judgment, both with respect to the characters set before us, and the lessons they afford for the regulation of our own conduct. Nor is this caution less necessary in the interpretation even of the moral precepts of the New Testament. Many of our Lord's injunctions and prohibitions, as well as those of his Apostles, had reference to the existing circumstances of his personal followers. Some concerned only the Pastors and Ministers of the Church; others, the Apostles in particular; others, the persecuted flock of Christ, hourly exposed to perils and temptations not of ordinary occurrences; others, to the special exigencies of an infant Church, struggling with poverty and reproach. To apply these to every succeeding age, or to a state of society altogether different from that of the primitive Christians, may lead, and indeed often has led, to mischievous consequences. It has induced men of eccentric minds to attempt strange fantastic modes of life, generally impracticable, or, if practicable, entirely subversive of the social character.

Still, again it must be urged, there are no actual precepts or doctrines of Revealed Religion, which may not, when regarded under their necessary modifications, afford universal as well as particular instruction: nor may we venture to affirm, of any single portion of Holy Writ, that to believers in any age or country it is of no concern. But there are doubtless many portions, of which the proper application to other persons and to other times, must depend on a right understanding of their intended application to those persons and times for which they were immediately written. It is thus that directions the most special and personal may afford general information to the rest of mankind. They teach them how to act when similarly circumstanced. They serve, either as specifications of general rules, or as limitations of those which are elsewhere more indefinitely expressed, or as enlargements of such as appear to be of a more limited and restricted nature. In all cases, they suggest what, *cæteris paribus*, or *mutatis mutandis*, is the proper test of obedience to the Divine Will. And thus the Christian becomes more thoroughly acquainted with his duty in special cases and under particular trials, as well as with its general principles. Where these however are confounded together, or substituted the one for the other, inconsistency and error will be the natural result. And, but for such perversion as this, the world had probably never heard of the follies of Christian Devotees and Anchorites; of the refusal of certain sects, to cooperate with the civil magistrate by the use of oaths or by the sword; or of the atrocities which blind Fanatics have occasionally wrought, under a persuasion or a pretext of propagating the pure Religion of the Gospel.

Such a detail as would be necessary for the full developement of these subjects, the extent of the present undertaking does not allow. But enough may have been said, to shew the importance of "rightly" analysing, or " dividing the Word of truth;" and to trace some leading features of the system, most requisite to be distinctly borne in mind, if we would form clear conceptions of the whole as well as of its constituent parts; or would attain to accurate notions of it, either as a rule of faith or of conduct.

These points being carefully secured, (subject to that first and greatest principle, the supreme authority of the Word itself, investing it with a dignity to which no human composition may pretend,) the work of interpretation may then be prosecuted with the same ardour of inquiry, the same exercise of the mental faculties, and the same freedom of sound and legitimate criticism, which ordinarily ensure proficiency in other pursuits. These too will be the critic's best security against any vain and ostentatious display of learning, for the support of a fanciful theory, or for giving a colour to opinions which cannot be maintained without some perversion of the Sacred Word from its plain and genuine meaning. This indeed is an exercise of talents, here worse than misplaced; it is "hand-" ling the Word of God deceitfully[g]." Yet without some such disengenuous dealing, what erroneous system of Theology could maintain its ground?

[g] 2 Cor. iv. 2.

But cautions of this kind belong rather to the moral, than to the critical department: nor perhaps will any rules of criticism suffice to secure the interpreter of Holy Writ against errors, however palpable, unless his mind be first thoroughly imbued with those sentiments of profound veneration for the subject, which will " bring into captivity every " thought to the obedience of Christ[h]."

" Who," then, " is sufficient for these " things?"—Not the careless, not the indolent, not the superficial, not the unlettered mind. The sound Expositor will ever be distinguished from the vain, though learned, Sceptic, on the one hand; and from the ignorant, though not less conceited, Enthusiast, on the other; by uniting the attainments of sound learning and sober judgment, to those of the profoundest reverence for the Sacred Word. Without these qualifications of the heart and the understanding, neither the utmost zeal for the dissemination of the Scriptures, nor the most overweening confidence on the part of the Expositor himself, will make him " thoroughly furnished" unto the work he takes in hand. That which by Divine inspiration was " written aforetime for " our learning[i]," is now, by God's blessing

[h] 2 Cor. x. 5.   [i] Rom. xv. 4.

on human labour and diligence, to be made effective to that end. Like every other gift, it is bestowed for our cultivation and improvement; and in proportion to the labour, it is promised shall be the recompence. For, " unto every one that hath, shall be given, " and he shall have abundance: but from " him that hath not, shall be taken away " even that which he seemeth to have[k]."

[k] Matt. xiii. 12. xxv. 29. and Luke viii. 18.

SERMON VI.

2 CORINTHIANS ii. 13.

Comparing spiritual things with spiritual.

THE farther we advance in the investigation of Scripture truth, the more clearly shall we perceive that a right interpretation of it depends principally upon a due reverence for Scripture itself, as the work of Divine Inspiration. Whatever aids we may collect from other sources, they are subordinate, in point of authority, to the work on which they are employed. Hence arises, independently of other considerations, the importance of the rule given in the text, that of "comparing spiritual things with spiritual."

The design of the Apostle in laying down this maxim, is discoverable from the context. Throughout the chapter he labours to convince the Corinthians, that if they would rightly appreciate his doctrine, they must not judge of it by "the spirit of the world[a]," nor reduce it to the standard of "man's wis-

[a] 1 Cor. ii. 12.

" dom[b]:"—that is, they were not to suppose the extent of Divine Revelation to be limited by what the mind of man is naturally able to discern;—but were to regard what was preached, as proceeding from the Fountain of infinite Wisdom, and relating to truths, which could not " have entered into the " heart of man[c]," unless supernaturally imparted to him. Hence he infers, that whatever difficulties might present themselves respecting detached parts of this Divine system, they were to be obviated, not so much by reference to what is known independently of Revelation, as by what may be collected from the Sacred Word. " The natural man," says he, " receiveth not the things of the Spi-" rit of God; for they are foolishness unto " him: neither can he know them, because " they are spiritually discerned[d]." Not that the mind of man is physically incapable of apprehending such truths, when propounded to him; nor that it requires some special illumination of the understanding to enable him to discern the terms of the propositions laid before him in Holy Writ;—but that these truths are not naturally to be discovered, even by the greatest exertion of his intellec-

[b] 1 Cor. ii. 13.   [c] 1 Cor. ii. 9.   [d] 1 Cor. ii. 14.

tual faculties. They cannot be known until revealed by the Spirit of God: nor will they perhaps even then be fully and readily received, but by the effect of the same Spirit in subduing the pride and the corrupt affections of the human heart.

Upon the same grounds, we may also argue, that the full and clear Interpretation of these truths does not so much depend upon principles unconnected with the subjects of Revealed Religion, or not recognized in Sacred Writ, as upon reasoning from Scripture itself, the prime source of intelligence respecting the matters of which it treats. It is to be obtained, by faithfully comparing together whatever the Word of God has made known to us concerning " spiritual things;" things above the reach of our natural faculties, and of which we can otherwise obtain no certain or satisfactory information.

This principle of interpreting Scripture by Scripture, is what Theologians call the Analogy of Faith; an expression borrowed perhaps from a passage in St. Paul's Epistle to the Romans, where he exhorts those who " prophesy" in the Church, (that is, those who exercise the office of authoritatively expounding the Scriptures,) to " prophesy ac-
" cording to the *proportion*," or, as the word

is in the original, the *analogy* " of Faith[e]." To the same effect many Commentators interpret St. Peter's maxim, that " no Prophecy " of the Scripture is of any private interpreta-" tion[f];" implying that the sense of any Prophecy is not to be determined by an abstract consideration of the passage itself, but by taking it in conjunction with other portions of Scripture relating to the subject:—a rule, which though it be especially applicable to the Prophetical Writings, is also of general importance in the exposition of the Sacred Volume.

Having then already shewn the necessity of a careful *analysis* of Scripture, or, as the Apostle expresses it, of " rightly dividing the " Word of truth;"—it now remains to consider the counterpart of the subject, that of combining its respective portions, thus assorted or arranged, into a systematic form:—without which the work of Interpretation will be but imperfectly performed. Systems of Divinity, judiciously framed upon this principle, and constructed with the aids of sound learning and critical skill, are among the most useful labours of the Theologian. Nor is it a mean instance of the wisdom and goodness of the great " Author and Finisher of our faith," that

[e] Rom. xii. 6.   [f] 2 Pet. i. 20.

this exercise of the human understanding should be made instrumentally efficacious to the attainment of Divine truth. For, thus the best natural talents of man are called forth in the service of his Creator: and, by means similar to those which are found successful in the investigation of human science, he is taught to prosecute his researches into " the wisdom that is from above." So truly is learning the handmaid to Religion: and so admirably do the ways of Nature and of Grace, or rather the ways of God in both, correspond with each other! And thus are we taught, though we become children in simplicity, yet " in understanding to be men[g]."

But, in pursuing the subject immediately before us, three chief points may be considered as comprised in the Apostolical rule, "comparing spiritual things with spiritual:"—First, the Verbal Analogy of Scripture, or the collation of parallel texts illustrative of its characteristic diction and phraseology:—Secondly, the Historical Analogy, or collation of parallel events and circumstances for the elucidation of facts:—Thirdly, the Doctrinal Analogy, or collation of parallel instructions relative to matters of Faith and Practice.—Upon each of these, a few observations may

[g] 1 Cor. xiv. 20.

be requisite, followed by the illustration of them in some specific examples.

I. The first of these comprehends all that appertains to the department of Sacred Philology.

In the Holy Scriptures, as in other compositions, it may be presumed that the style of the several writers is distinguishable by some characteristic peculiarities. There is no reason to suppose, that the Holy Spirit, in suggesting to the Sacred Penmen the matter and substance of what they wrote, or even, occasionally, the very terms in which it should be expressed, should so entirely overrule their natural faculties as to bring them all to one standard in this respect. To suppose this, were to derogate from that Omniscience, which knows how to render every instrument subservient to its purpose, without destroying the character and properties of the instrument itself. Nay, it were contradictory to the internal evidence of Scripture; which sufficiently manifests, to the discerning critic, a considerable diversity of diction, and manner, and whatever constitutes peculiarity of style, in its several productions. To this point, therefore, especial attention will be necessary, where doubt and difficulties arise respecting the meaning of particular texts.

But, notwithstanding any specific diversities of style in the Sacred Canon, there is a general cast of character and expression in the entire Work, eminently distinguishing it from all other productions. This is to be ascribed, partly to the supernatural endowments of the writer, partly to the exalted nature of the subjects presented to his contemplation: either of which would give to his thoughts and expressions an elevation beyond their ordinary reach. Hence that peculiar energy, that sublimity and grandeur, which the best judges of excellence in composition have universally ascribed to the Sacred Writings; and to which might not unaptly be applied St. Paul's forcible expressions, that "the Word of God is quick, and "powerful, and sharper than any two-edged "sword, piercing even to the dividing asun-"der of soul and spirit[h]."

This its general character, therefore, as well as the appropriate style and manner of its various writers, must be taken into account by the Scripture Critic. Otherwise his philological inquiries, however marked by acuteness or ingenuity, will fail of a successful issue. Nor is this exacting any superstitious reverence for Holy Writ, or a greater

[h] Heb. iv. 12.

labour of investigation than every scholar knows to be requisite in other branches of literature. The sense of all writers, indeed, inspired or uninspired, must necessarily be determined by regard to special circumstances, as well as by general rules. A general knowledge of the principles of grammar and criticism, and an acquaintance with the idioms of the language in which any work is written, are, in every instance, indispensable. But the correct interpretation of any particular author will depend also upon an historical, as well as critical, knowledge of the language. It must be deduced from the work of the writer himself, from the nature of his subject, and from the common acceptation of the terms he uses among his contemporaries. For, what author has not something appropriate in his manner of expression? What work does not receive a certain tincture of character, from the age, or country, or condition and circumstances of the writer? And what, for the most part, are the labours of commentators upon all compositions of ancient date, but inquiries into these particulars, on which their elucidation so much depends?

Conformably with these principles, it is chiefly by attention to the Verbal Analogy of

Scripture, that the Biblical is to be distinguished from the merely Classical Critic. Here his labours must begin: and the aid must be sought of a competent apparatus for the purpose; of Concordances, Scripture Lexicons, and other helps of a similar kind, which the industry and skill of the learned who have gone before have abundantly supplied, to facilitate such researches.

II. But, secondly, the Historical Analogy of Scripture, or collation of its circumstances and events, is further necessary for its accurate interpretation.

Some occurrences are but incidentally noticed in the Sacred Writings; others are more fully detailed; others are related by different writers, varying, in particular circumstances, according to their respective views of the subject.—Here the work of the faithful Interpreter is to bring together such passages of Scripture as have any connection with the event or fact to be examined; and so to expound each separate portion of the history, that no seeming incongruity in its parts may deface the whole. Incalculable is the value of labours of this description, in supplying materials for the vindication of Revealed Religion against the cavils of Sceptics and Unbelievers. By the help of these, the general evidences of Christianity have often been admirably illustrated and defended; and the Scoffer has been defeated with his own weapons: while the research necessary for this purpose has had the effect, not only of discomfiting the adversary, but also of disclosing many admirable proofs of the Divine Wisdom and Goodness in the moral government of the world, which might otherwise have passed unheeded or unknown.

Superior knowledge and discernment, however, may sometimes be requisite, successfully to execute this branch of the Interpreter's office. But here again the storehouse of Theology is amply furnished with supplies for the diligent and inquisitive. As Verbal Analogy is aided by the use of Concordances and Lexicons; so is Historical, by Harmonies of the Sacred Writings, exhibiting in a connected series the matters which lie scattered in their different narratives; and presenting the readiest means of collating Scripture facts. Thus Scripture becomes its own interpreter. Farther help, where necessary, must be obtained from studying the connections of Sacred with Profane History; from the testimonies of Jewish and Heathen writers to the records of the Old and New Testament; and from such information as the more recent discoveries of the learned have afforded, respecting the times and countries to which the narratives of the Sacred Historians relate.

III. But, thirdly, still more important, with respect to its immediate subject, is the Doctrinal Analogy of Scripture, or collation of its parallel instructions relative to matters of Faith or Practice. To this indeed both the others must be considered as chiefly instrumental; since in all questions respecting matters of verbal or historical discussion, such a solution is to be sought for as shall not violate any certain article of Christian Doctrine.

Here also we shall find it necessary to proceed on principles to a certain degree recognized in the exposition of other writings. When in any ordinary composition a passage occurs of doubtful meaning, with respect to the sentiment or doctrine it conveys, the obvious course of proceeding is, to examine what the author himself has in other parts of his work delivered upon the same subject; to weigh well the force of any particular expressions he is accustomed to use; and to inquire what there might be in the occasion or circumstances under which he wrote, tending to throw further light upon the immediate object he had in view. This is only to render common justice to the writer; it is necessary, both for the discovery of his real meaning, and to secure him against any wanton charge of error or inconsistency. Now, if this may justly be required in any ordinary work of uninspired composition; how much more indispensable must it be, when we sit in judgment upon the Sacred Volume; in which (if we acknowledge its Divine original) it is impossible even to imagine a failure, either in judgment or in integrity. How exact and scrupulous a care in these respects may reasonably be expected from the Scripture Critic; lest, through any inadvertency on his part, " the way of truth " should be evil spoken of [i] !"

A reputed saying of Rabbinical writers, that " there is no difficulty in their Law, of " which the Law itself does not afford a so- " lution," is applicable to the Scriptures in general, both of the Old and New Testament:—and the maxim of human jurisprudence, that " no particular Law is to be " judged of, without taking the whole Law " into consideration," is still more indispensable where the Law proceeds from a Divine Legislator. Difficulties, therefore, are to be

[i] 2 Pet. ii. 2.

removed, in the first place, by the help of Scripture itself. Detached texts may be rendered clearer by a collation with those analogous to them, either in verbal expression or in general sentiment. What in one is wrapped up in obscurer terms, may in another be more explicitly developed. Even slight variations will oftentimes serve for the purpose of reciprocal illustration. This will be more or less perceptible, according to the subject of investigation: but in almost every instance it will amply remunerate the labour. Where the subjects of the passages compared are correlative;—as in the case of Type and Antitype, or Prophecy and the Fulfilment of Prophecy;—its advantages will be instantly perceived. In certain cases, the benefit may arise from the effect of contrast only: in others, from the connection of subordinate points with those which are of higher moment. But, whatever mode of comparison be instituted, additional light cannot fail to be thrown on the point to be examined.

Respecting these rules for the Collation of Scripture, or "comparing spiritual things with " spiritual," it will readily be perceived, that they presuppose a due attention to those already suggested for its Analysis, or " rightly " dividing the Word of truth." The great leading distinction between points of doctrine fundamental or non-fundamental; and the subordinate distinctions, between the several Dispensations, or Covenants, of Revealed Religion, the various subjects of the Sacred Writings, and the general or special purposes for which they were composed;—these must lay the foundation for every systematic arrangement of Scripture truth. As, in the investigation of any subject of human science, we first endeavour by Analysis to resolve it into its elementary principles or constituent parts; and then, by a synthetic process, proceed from these simple truths to a comprehensive view of the whole;—so, in the study of Revealed Religion, a clear apprehension of its primary and essential truths prepares the way for combining into a coherent and well digested system the entire doctrine of Holy Writ. Regarding these as connected in unity of purpose and in effect, though distinct in character and in operation; every portion of Scripture derives additional interest from being thus made to accord with the rest: and the work of Interpretation proceeds with the best assurance that human fallibility may pretend to, of a successful result.

These several Analogies, then, are intended

to cooperate in explaining obscure passages by those which are clearer, in confirming those of a doubtful character by such as are beyond all question, and in regulating those of minor consideration by the great leading principles of the Christian Covenant. Their joint effect will be, to exhibit in a compendious view the entire Analogy of the Faith, such as we meet with in well-digested Bodies of Divinity; or such as in earlier times was comprised in those shorter summaries of Christian Doctrine to which we may conceive St. Paul to refer, when he says to Timothy, " Hold fast the form of sound " words, which thou hast heard of me, in " faith and love that is in Christ Jesus. " That good thing which was committed " unto thee, keep by the Holy Ghost, which " dwelleth in you[k]."

II. I proceed now to illustrate these observations by some specific examples.

And first, the doctrine of Regeneration presents itself, as a subject of radical importance in the Christian system, and on which a due regard to all these Analogies appears to be indispensable for the prevention of error.

The determinate sense of the word Regeneration depends upon the subject to which

[k] 2 Tim. i. 13, 14.

it relates. Abstractedly, it denotes an entrance upon any new state of being; a state, essentially different from that in which existence had already taken place. Thence it is taken to denote any thing new in the mode or condition of being. But what that newly modified state or condition may be, can only be ascertained by reference to the subject and the purpose, to which the term is applied. Here the aid of Verbal Analogy is called for. In the Scriptures, terms of similar import with Regeneration, such as *new Birth, a new Creature, born again*, and *created anew*, are frequently used. These are to be compared with each other, and with the several contexts of the passages where they occur; in order to discover the signification ordinarily attached to them by the Author. And when we find, that they are almost invariably employed to distinguish the state of a person admitted into the Christian Covenant, from that of one who is not so admitted; we shall beware of adopting any interpretation irrelevant to that view of the subject. We shall perceive, that the word Regeneration, in the Scriptural usage of it, means only our initiation, or entrance, by Baptism, into that Covenant, which gives us new privileges, new hopes, and a new principle of spiritual life; placing us in a totally different state from that, to which by nature only we could ever attain. The expression therefore cannot, without a direct violation of the verbal analogy of Scripture, be applied to any operation that takes place subsequent to that Baptismal change, with which alone it perfectly corresponds.

In like manner, Historical Analogy may be applied to this particular point. Had the Sacred Writers used the term Regeneration, and the expressions synonymous with it, in a sense, not only peculiar to themselves, but dissimilar to any in which they had before been used; still, having expressed themselves so clearly upon the subject to which the terms are applied, there could be little difficulty in determining the acceptation in which those terms ought to be taken. But we have further evidence than this. Our Lord, in discoursing with Nicodemus on the necessity of being " born again," reproves this " master of Israel" for not already " know-" ing these things[1]:" that is, for not readily perceiving the force and propriety of a figure of speech, which ought to have been familiar to a Jewish teacher. And that this

[1] John iii. 10.

reproof was justly merited, we collect from the best writers on Jewish antiquities; from whom it appears, that terms of similar import were in frequent use among the Jews, to describe those Gentiles who had been converted from Heathenism, and admitted into the Jewish Church. Here then is historical evidence, strongly confirming that which is adduced from verbal analogy. This directs us to the sense in which such expressions would naturally be interpreted by those who heard them; and, consequently, to that in which it is most probable that the Sacred Writers intended them to be understood.

But if any doubt should yet remain upon this point, a still stronger confirmation is obtained from Doctrinal Analogy, or what is more largely called the Analogy of Faith. Regeneration is represented, by a certain class of interpreters, as an instantaneous, perceptible, and irresistible operation of the Holy Spirit upon the heart and mind; which, whether the person have been baptized or not, affords the only certain evidence of his conversion to a saving and justifying Faith. By others, it is regarded as a continued and progressive work of the Spirit; or as a state, commencing in Baptism, but not completed until, by perseverance to the end, the individual has "finished his course[m]," and is about to enter upon his final reward. Others, again, separating what the Scriptures state to be joined together in the work of the new birth, maintain a distinction between Baptismal and Spiritual Regeneration;—the former taking place in the Sacrament of Baptism;— the latter subsequent to it, and, whether progressive or instantaneous in its operation, equally necessary with Baptism to a state of salvation.

But here the Analogy of Faith seems to be violated throughout. For, how can any of these views of Regeneration consist with the plain and simple notion of it as an entrance upon a new state, or a sacramental initiation into the Christian Covenant? Nay, how can they consist with the terms and conditions of the Covenant itself?—If the Gospel be a Covenant, admission into which, on the terms of Faith and Repentance, gives an immediate title to its present privileges, with an assurance of the Spiritual helps necessary for the attainment of salvation;— and if Baptism be the divinely-appointed means of admission into that Covenant, and of a participation in those privileges;—is not the person so admitted actually brought into

[m] 2 Tim. iv. 7.

a new state? Has he not obtained " that " thing which by nature he cannot have[n]?" And being thus " regenerate and born anew " of water and of the Holy Ghost[o]," to what subsequent part of his Christian life can a term so peculiarly expressive of his first entrance upon it be with propriety applied? Moreover, must he not, after this, fulfil the conditions of the Covenant he has entered into, in order to obtain its final rewards? Must he not continue in that state unto his life's end; endeavouring, by further supplies of God's grace, to perfect, or to renew, his Repentances, his Faith, and his Obedience? But if Regeneration, or the new Birth, imply the completion as well as the commencement of his spiritual life; how is he ever to be assured of its having actually taken place, so long as his Christian course remains unfinished?

On the other hand, see how the sense, as deduced from Verbal and Historical Analogy, harmonizes with the general rule of Faith. By identifying Regeneration with the initiatory sacrament of Baptism, its full importance is assigned to it, as the instrument of Grace and Salvation, indispensable for admission to the privileges of the Cove-

[n] Office of Baptism. [o] Ibid.

SERMON VI. 167

nant, and conferring spiritual aid to perform its conditions. It is by entitling him to these benefits, that it makes the partaker "a new creature," "born of God," and "an heir of Eternal Life." Thenceforth he continues to be in a state of salvation, or salvable state, notwithstanding the errors and defections to which he is liable. He "may "depart from grace given, and fall into sin; "and by the grace of God may rise again, "and amend his life[p]." He may entirely forfeit his hopes and privileges by impenitency or unbelief: or he may recover them by repentance and renewal of faith. His spiritual birth, his Regeneration, is the beginning of his Christian life: his growth in grace, and his perseverance to the end, will be the result of a right use of those further supplies from above, which minister to his spiritual support and nourishment, and to which this first admission into the Covenant gives him a title and a claim. Here every thing is found to accord with the general design and purpose of the Christian Dispensation: and, having thus secured the concurrent evidence of sound verbal criticism, of historical testimony, and of doctrinal analogy, we need not doubt that the interpretation is that which

[p] Article XVI.

conveys the genuine and unsophisticated meaning of the word of God.

It is necessary, however, that in adjusting this Analogy of Faith, special attention be paid to the comparative importance of the doctrines under consideration and to the comparative clearness with which they are revealed. Primary and fundamental truths afford the proper standard of exposition, for such as are only secondary and subordinate; and doctrines obscurely or incidentally revealed, must be rendered conformable with those which admit of no misconstruction, and which it is the express purpose of Revelation to make known. Thus the questions of Predestination and the Divine Decrees, and of the Salvability of those who have never been admitted into the Christian Covenant, are dark and mysterious points; respecting which it does not appear to have been the purpose of Holy Writ to give direct and explicit information: they are among "the secret " things belonging unto the Lord our God[q]." But the Universality of man's Redemption, and the conditions of the Covenant through which it is to be obtained, are traced as with a sunbeam throughout the Sacred Volume. They are the foundations on which the

[q] Deut. xxix. 29.

SERMON VI. 169

whole Evangelical Dispensation rests. Whatever relates, therefore, to the former subjects, must be so explained, as to preserve the latter inviolate: these being among the things distinctly " revealed," which " belong unto " us and unto our children for ever^r."

Upon the same principle, where several doctrines of equal importance are proposed, and revealed with equal clearness; we must be careful to give to each its full and equal weight. Thus, that we are saved by the free Grace of God, and through Faith in Christ, is a doctrine too plainly affirmed by the Sacred Writers, to be set aside by any contravening position: for it is said, " By Grace ye " are saved through Faith; and that not of " yourselves: it is the gift of God^s." But so, on the other hand, are the doctrines of Repentance unto life, and of Obedience unto salvation: for, again, it is said, " Repent and " be converted, that your sins may be blotted " out^t," and, " If ye will enter into life, keep " the Commandments^u." To set either of these truths at variance with the others, would be to frustrate the declared purpose of the Gospel, and to make it of none effect. Points thus clearly established, and, from

^r Deut. xxix. 29.   ^s Ephes. ii. 8.
^t Acts iii. 19.   ^u Matth. xix. 17.

their very nature, indispensable, must be made to correspond with each other: and the exposition which best preserves them unimpaired and undiminished, will, in any case, be a safe interpretation, and, most probably, the true one. The Analogy of Faith will thus be kept entire, and will approve itself, in every respect, as becoming its Divine Author, and "worthy of all accepta-"tion."

Instances, however, of dangerous errors, originating in a disregard of these obvious maxims, have occurred in almost every age of the Christian Church.

On the first preaching of the Gospel, the Jewish converts were slow of belief, and prone to misinterpret its truths, from prejudices which indisposed them to perceive the connection between the several Covenants or Dispensations which God had entered into with mankind, from the Creation and Fall of Adam to the coming of Christ. They imagined, that the whole purpose of Revealed Religion centred in the Mosaic Dispensation: and, for the most part, they neither expected nor desired any thing beyond its extension and advancement. The analogy of their own Scriptures with the doctrines preached by our blessed Saviour and by St. Paul, and the

SERMON VI.

real correspondence which subsisted between the Jewish and Christian Dispensations, they obstinately refused to acknowledge; notwithstanding the distinct and luminous reasoning in which these were set before them. Their own method of interpreting the Law and the Prophets had, indeed, a directly contrary object in view. It aimed at proving the Religion of Moses and of Christ to be irreconcilable with each other. " Even unto this " day," says St. Paul, " when Moses is read, " the vail is upon their heart[w]." The great question, " Wherefore then serveth the " Law[x]?"—(that Law to which they nevertheless so pertinaciously adhered,) they were themselves unable to solve: nor would they receive its true solution, though coming from one of its most zealous advocates, brought up at the feet of Gamaliel, when, inspired with more than human wisdom, he shewed them its completion in the person of Christ, and the great purpose it had served in the œconomy of man's Redemption.

It is notorious also, that many early Heretics, of different denominations, derived a portion of their unscriptural tenets from errors similar to those of the unbelieving Jews and the Judaizing Christians of the

[w] 2 Cor. iii. 15.   [x] Gal. iii. 19.

Apostolic age. Nor is it less remarkable, that, in several instances, the same species of misapprehension led to heresies the most opposite to each other. While some were desirous of engrafting upon the Gospel Jewish laws and ordinances, altogether done away by the Christian dispensation; others cherished such an antipathy against every part of the Mosaic Institute, as entirely to reject the Scriptures of the Old Testament, and to ascribe them to the inspiration of an evil spirit. Monstrous as these opinions appear to us, they afford a striking illustration of the mischief arising from disconnected views of the Sacred Writings; from not carefully " comparing spiritual things with spiritual," so as to evince their mutual dependance upon each other.

Nor are modern times wholly free from the leaven of these pernicious principles. Too many are still wont to depreciate Judaism, as a system unimportant to us, both in its moral and religious purpose; and even as inculcating a spirit diametrically opposite to that of the Christian Religion. Because the Gospel superseded the use of the Jewish Ritual, they are led to regard all external ordinances as mere beggarly elements of Religion, unworthy of the evangelical and spiritualized believer. To this partial and erroneous view of the two Dispensations may perhaps be attributed the contempt which some Sects entertain for the Christian Sacraments and Priesthood, and their hostility even to any constitution of an external visible Church. Similar misapprehensions appear to have given rise to the narrow and circumscribed notions which others entertain of the Redemption through Christ. To the general privileges of the Gospel, and to the terms on which it holds out the offer of salvation, are applied arguments or expressions, relating solely to the Jewish Œconomy as contrasted with that of the Gospel. Interpreting what St. Paul says of the calling of the Gentiles and the rejection of the Jews, as if it related to the personal election and reprobation of individuals under the Christian Dispensation;—or, at other times, applying what is said of the special privileges of the Jews as a peculiar people, to the spiritual circumstances of a favoured few among Christian Believers, supposed to be exclusively ordained to eternal life;—these Expositors impute to the Almighty a system of arbitrary and absolute decrees respecting men's salvation, repugnant to the general tenor of the Gospel, and even directly at variance with the purpose of those Writings, from which their conclusions are so precipitately drawn.

These latter instances particularly shew the danger of disregarding Historical Analogy. Others may be adduced relating chiefly to the neglect of Analogies Verbal and Doctrinal. The violation of both these is strikingly exemplified in some of the contradictory errors which have prevailed respecting the doctrines of the Trinity and the Incarnation.

The Unity of the Godhead is a doctrine expressly and repeatedly declared in Holy Writ. The co-existence and co-equality of the Son and the Holy Spirit with the Father are also doctrines standing upon the same ground of irrefragable testimony. Again; the human nature of our Lord is indisputably proved from the history of his life. His Divine nature is declared and proved by the very same authority which records his actions as a human being. So firmly are these doctrines established, that the Infidel grounds his general disbelief of Christianity upon the incredibility of these particular articles; while the Sceptic, who dares not renounce the whole, is perplexed how to discard either of these doctrines without rejecting some portion of Scripture itself. To a plain, unprejudiced reader they are all indeed so evidently contained in Scripture, that, were they not accompanied with acknowledged difficulties in reconciling them with each other, they would, probably, be universally received. What then is the course which the Sacred Interpreter has to pursue?

The Analogy of Faith requires, as I have already stated, that all its articles should be received as equally true; and that in the interpretation of each, such a sense should be imposed as will not necessarily destroy or impair the rest. It has accordingly been the labour of the Christian Church, from its earliest to its latest periods, to guard these great and important truths, against the subtle attacks of their opponents, by affixing to each a meaning not contradictory to those with which it is connected. Whatever might be the difficulty of the task, the Church, as the faithful Expositor of Scripture, felt this to be its paramount duty. While the truth was strengthened on one side, it was not neglected on the other: and the balance was steadily held between contending parties. Hence, no Creeds or Articles of Faith, ancient or modern, appear to have been more elaborately or carefully drawn out, than those which relate to these particular doctrines.

But what is the course pursued by the impugners of these doctrines! The labours of Sabellians, Macedonians, Arians, and Socinians, to what purpose do they generally tend, but to set these truths in opposition to each other, and to establish one by the overthrow of another? The distinction of the several Persons in the Godhead is assumed to be irreconcilable with the Divine Unity. The union of the Divine and human nature in one person, is rejected upon a similar assumption. Thenceforth, Scripture is " di-"vided against itself ;" and every proof of one of its truths is brought to bear against the other. Thus we may account for the strange phenomenon of opposite heresies, deduced from the same premises; equally irreconcilable with Scripture truth and with each other. Some have " confounded the Persons" of the Godhead; others have " divided the " substance." Some have rejected the Godhead of Christ, because it was impossible to deny his Manhood; others, seeing his Divinity too plainly to doubt of it, have denied his human nature. In either case, the Analogy of Faith is violated; a part only of what is revealed in Scripture being received as truth, to the exclusion of the rest: and by thus offending against one essential article of Faith, the authority of all the others receives a dangerous blow. In the process also of such perverted criticism, liberties are sometimes taken, not to be reconciled with principles of strict integrity. Texts are examined, as if for the purpose of distorting them, by a certain dexterous ingenuity, from their accustomed signification, rather than of establishing their plain and obvious meaning. New Versions too of the Scriptures are brought forward, marked with a similar perverseness of character, when it is found that the renderings generally received will not admit of a ready accommodation to heretical views. And thus is the simplicity of truth discarded, to make way for the subtleties of a false and mischievous refinement.

The inquiry might easily be extended to much greater length, were we to enter upon an examination of the " divers and strange " doctrines[y]," which a disregard of true and legitimate principles of criticism has introduced into the Christian world. But even these, perhaps, are not so totally out of the reach of correction as those which proceed

[y] Heb. xiii. 9.

from a wild and disorderly Fanaticism, relying upon imaginary inspiration, and treating with contempt the sober application of reasoning and judgment to the Scriptures. By persons labouring under such a fatal delusion, the injunction to " compare spiritual things " with spiritual," seems to be regarded as implying nothing more than heaping together a multiplicity of texts, forcibly disjoined from their contexts, and unconnected by any proper Analogy. Hence the multitude are continually misled by teachers more conversant with the words than with the sense of Scripture; who conceive their point, whatever it may be, to have the sanction of Divine authority, when, by separating what ought to be united, or combining what ought to be kept distinct, they have made the word of God seem to bear testimony to their own crude conceptions.

Thus far we have carried on the inquiry into the internal helps which the Scriptures afford for their own interpretation. These at the same time point to the external aids necessary to give them their full effect. Commentators, Harmonists, Philologists, all must be called in to enable us thoroughly to analyse or to combine, rightly to divide or to compare, spiritual truths: and to neglect these, is virtually to neglect the means of profiting by the Bible itself.

But, since every aid that can be obtained, internal or external, is liable to misapplication; even these rules for " dividing the " word of truth" and " comparing spiritual " things with spiritual," must be accompanied with certain cautions. Care is to be taken, not to confound seeming with real analogies;—not to rely upon merely verbal resemblances, when the sense may require a different application;—not to interpret what is parallel only in one respect, as if it were so in all;—not to give to any parallel passages so absolute a sway in our decisions, as to overrule the clear and evident meaning of the text under consideration;—and, above all, not to suffer our eagerness in multiplying proofs of this kind, to betray us into a neglect of the immediate context of the passage in question, upon which its signification must principally depend.—The simplest mode of proceeding is, indeed, the safest. Every difficult or doubtful text is first to be considered by itself;—then, with its context;—then, with other passages of Scripture parallel to it in any respect;—and then, by the additional light of such extraneous illustrations as can be brought to it from the stores of human knowledge.

By due attention to these principles, accompanied with the great moral requisites already shewn to be indispensable, and with humble supplications to the throne of Grace for a blessing on his labours, the diligent inquirer after Scripture truth may confidently hope for success. The design of every portion of Holy Writ, its harmony with the rest, and the Divine perfection of the whole, will more and more fully be displayed. And thus will he be led, with increasing veneration and gratitude, to adore HIM, to whom every Sacred Book bears witness and every Divine Dispensation led the way;—even HIM, who is " Alpha and Omega, the First " and the Last[z]," " Jesus Christ, the same " yesterday, to day, and for ever[a]."

[z] Rev. i. 2.   [a] Heb. xiii. 8.

SERMON VII.

2 CORINTHIANS iii. 6.

Who also hath made us able ministers of the New Testament; not of the letter, but of the spirit: for the letter killeth, but the spirit giveth life.

IN suggesting rules to assist the ordinary reader of Scripture in the work of Interpretation, care is requisite, that we neither magnify nor diminish, beyond their just proportion, the difficulties to be encountered. From either extreme evil consequences may ensue: from the one, carelessness or presumption; from the other, blind submission to spiritual guides, or a morbid indisposition to rational inquiry. In either case also, encouragement will be given to the dissemination of error. Thus, in magnifying these difficulties, the Church of Rome finds an argument for withholding the Word of Life from the greater portion of her members. In diminishing them, the Fanatic discovers a pretence for assuming the office of a sacred Teacher, without any previous instruction, any preparatory acquirements.

That the truth lies betwixt these extremes, they who are most conversant with the Scriptures will be the most ready to allow. They will perceive that the Bible, though often profound and mysterious in its subject, does, for the most part, propose its truths in terms adapted to general apprehension; while, on the other hand, though it derives its authority purely from a Divine source, yet, in the exposition of it, it calls forth the exercise of the best faculties and attainments of the human mind. It is a mine of invaluable treasure; upon which the greater the labour and skill that are employed, the richer and more abundant will be the return. While, therefore, we give every encouragement to the humblest inquirer into spiritual truths; we are bound to admonish the adventurous and uninstructed, that no rash experiments may here be allowed. We are bound to warn him, that in this, beyond all other branches of knowledge, caution and sound judgment are requisite; that something may here be expected transcending the reach even of the most cultivated minds; and that, both as to the subject and the expression, many things may occasionally occur "hard to be understood[a]" by persons of inferior attainments.

The words of the text direct our attention to one important branch of Scripture-criticism, presenting difficulties of a peculiar kind; and which, though it may have been incidentally touched upon in the preceding inquiry, seems to call for distinct consideration.

St. Paul in this Epistle vindicates his authority as an inspired Teacher, against the cavils of those who endeavoured to sow dissension in the Church of Corinth. From the course of his argument it may be inferred, that the Judaizing converts were among his chief opponents. After reminding the Corinthians that the success of his ministry bore convincing testimony to the Divine blessing with which it was accompanied, he proceeds to state in what respects the New Testament, preached by him, was superior to the Old. He distinguishes the two Dispensations by the terms Letter and Spirit; intimating that the Law of Moses, in its literal acceptation, was fulfilled by the Gospel, in its spiritual sense; and that the former contained not in itself the power of delivering from sin and death, but pointed to the latter

[a] 2 Pet. iii. 16.

as bestowing life and immortality. By these remarkable expressions, the Apostle has been supposed to direct us to the contemplation of the Scriptures in a light which might not otherwise be sufficiently regarded; opening to the Interpreter a new field of research, into the mystical intent of many parts of the Sacred Writings. And since St. Paul himself occasionally has recourse to expositions of this kind, there is especial reason for investigating this as a distinct department of Theological inquiry.

Dismissing, therefore, any farther consideration of this particular text, I shall proceed to a more comprehensive view of the subject; endeavouring to shew, in the first place, the proper Use of this mode of interpretation, and the errors arising from its *neglect;* secondly, in what the Abuse of it consists, and the errors arising from carrying it to *excess*.

But here it may be expedient to premise some few observations upon the terms, *literal, figurative, spiritual*, and *mystical*.

Literal and *figurative* are terms which relate principally, if not exclusively, to modes of *verbal* expression. The literal sense is that which the words signify in their natural and proper acceptation. The figurative is that which they do not naturally denote, but which they nevertheless intend, under some figure or form of speech. These, therefore, thus explained, are terms purely of grammatical or rhetorical investigation; having no reference to any supposed occult or ulterior sense, in the writer's contemplation. They simply belong to the verbal signification; which, with respect to the sense, may be virtually the same, whether or not expressed by trope and figure. Thus, when *hardness* is applied to *iron* or *stone*, the expression is used *literally*, in its proper and natural signification:—when it is applied to the *heart*, it is used *figuratively*, or in an improper acceptation. Yet the sense, allowing for the change of subject, is virtually the same; its application being only transferred from a physical to a moral quality.

The terms *spiritual* and *mystical* stand in contradistinction to both these. They import that, besides the direct or immediate signification of the passage, whether literally or figuratively expressed, there is attached to it a more remote or recondite sense; a sense founded, not on a transfer of *words* from one signification to another, but on the entire application of the *matter* itself to a different subject. This is the foundation of all fictitious modes of instruction, such as fables, apologues, and allegories, used as vehicles of moral and religious instruction; where the hidden sense is a distinct subject of inquiry from that of the diction in which it is clothed. It is to be observed, however, that the term *figurative* is not unfrequently used, (especially when applied to Scripture,) in the same sense with the terms *spiritual* and *mystical*, though not perhaps with strict propriety.

Again; there are other terms relating to the subject which may require explanation. *Emblematical* and *symbolical* are terms relating to what is here meant by spiritual and mystical interpretation, not to merely verbal expression. They imply, as the words mystical and mysticism do, an occult or hidden sense intended by the writer, besides that which is open and manifest. The term *mysterious*, on the other hand, has no reference to this mode of interpretation. A doctrine may be mysterious, (that is, above our comprehension,) which is nevertheless expressed in the plainest language, and conveyed in the literal sense of the words. But *mystic* denotes another sense superadded to that which the words in their obvious signification convey.

SERMON VII. 187

The importance of these distinctions, with reference to the Interpretation of Scripture, may be illustrated by their application to some chief controversial points respecting the nature and design of the Holy Eucharist.

The words of our Lord, in the institution of this Sacrament, may be made to convey a very different meaning, according as they are literally or figuratively interpreted. The Romanist, taking them strictly in the literal sense, grounds upon them the monstrous doctrine of Transubstantiation; a doctrine, not only repugnant to the evidence of our senses and to every principle of reasoning founded upon such evidence, but also to Scripture itself; nay, even to the very words of the institution, when taken in connection with the circumstances under which they were delivered. For our Lord, in using these words, did not actually give his Body or his Blood to the Disciples; but gave them Bread and Wine as their Symbols. The plain inference is, that he did not intend his words to be understood in their literal sense. And this is further evident, from the conduct of the disciples themselves; who appear not to have testified any offence or surprise at so extraordinary a mode of expression, which they now rightly apprehended to be figuratively used; although on a former occasion they were shocked at the mention of our Lord's giving his flesh and blood to be meat and drink; conceiving him, at that time, to have spoken in the gross and literal sense of the terms. The figurative therefore must here be the true verbal sense: and the literal may, without hesitation, be rejected.

But the figurative interpretation thus established leads to a further inquiry, whether, beyond the mere signification of the words, there be not also a hidden or spiritual intent in the action itself. This relates to the *mystical* sense: and here there is room for further diversity of opinion. The Socinian, always solicitous to divest Christianity of every thing mysterious, regards the Eucharist as a bare commemorative act of devotion. He thus effectually removes the absurdity of the literal sense: but, at the same time, he reduces the figurative sense almost to a nullity, by setting aside the *sacramental* meaning of the institution, which consists in a right apprehension of what the symbols themselves were intended to represent. The Fanatic also equally admits the figurative and rejects the literal sense of the expressions; but by attributing all vital Religion to the *imme-*

diate agency of the Holy Spirit upon the soul of man, he betrays a similar misapprehension of the true force and meaning of these symbols, and alike depreciates their value; acknowledging no actual efficacy in the Eucharist, as the means of imparting to the communicant the benefits of our Lord's death and passion. By both these the spiritual or mystical application of our Lord's words is overlooked; the ordinance being reduced to a bare commemorative act, or a sign unaccompanied with the benefits of the thing signified. But since it is of the nature of every sacramental ordinance, to represent by an outward sign or token some inward benefit conveyed; the full sense of the words of the Institution is undoubtedly *mystical;* that is, it has reference to some deeper signification than the words abstractedly import. Interpreted, therefore, with due regard to its concomitant circumstances, to the known use of symbols among the Jews, and to the general analogy of Scripture language and doctrine, the passage may thus be paraphrased:
—" This Bread represents my Body, and this
" Wine represents my Blood: and this act
" of receiving Bread and Wine, according to
" my Institution and by virtue of its efficacy
" through Me, is, to the faithful communi-

" cant, the act of spiritually receiving my
" Body and Blood; that is, of receiving the
" benefits of the sacrifice which I am about
" to offer, in giving my Body, and shedding
" my Blood, for the remission of sins."

Thus far towards explaining the distinct meaning of the terms used in this inquiry. Let us now take a more general and comprehensive view of the proper Use of spiritual or mystical interpretation of Scripture, and of the errors arising from its *neglect*.

1. Great prejudices are frequently entertained against any tendency to this species of interpretation : but it is in vain to reason *à priori* for its total rejection, if the Scriptures themselves manifestly point to it as the clue to their full signification. The utility, indeed, if not necessity, of thus communicating spiritual truths appears, partly from the natural effect of imagery in arresting the attention and engaging the affections of mankind in general, partly from the nature of the truths themselves, which perhaps are not capable of being imparted to the human mind without the aid of figurative and symbolical expressions. Be that as it may, the frequent recurrence of such expressions in Holy Writ is unquestionable. And this being the case, an indiscriminate prejudice

against attempts to discover a spiritual sense beyond that which the letter conveys, may sometimes operate to prevent our discerning some of the most important matters it was intended to reveal to us.

There is moreover abundant evidence, that the Jews not only delighted, as other oriental nations did, in highly figurative modes of speech; but also, that, from the peculiar character of the Mosaic Ritual, they were habituated to mystical researches, and deemed them necessary to a right exposition of the Law and the Prophets. And although it be true that this species of interpretation was, on their part, often carried to a culpable excess, and in after-times degenerated into absurdities worse than frivolous and contemptible; yet it can hardly be denied, that much of the elucidation of the prophecies in the Old Testament respecting the Messiah, and of their accomplishment in the New, depends upon the judicious application of this kind of evidence;—a consideration in itself sufficient to warrant an attentive inquiry respecting this department of Scripture-criticism.

In determining the *extent* however of this species of interpretation, there is considerable difficulty. Some would confine it entirely to the expositions already given by our Lord and his Apostles. Others regard those expositions as ensamples only of what we are to apply universally to the Sacred Writings. The former, by too rigid a limitation of the rule, may possibly deprive us of many typical and prophetical adumbrations of the Gospel, not expressly interpreted as such by the writers of the New Testament. The latter, by giving too great latitude to the interpreter, seem to open a door to every extravagance of the human imagination. What middle course then presents itself to our acceptance?

The best writers on this subject seem to be agreed, that, before a figurative or a mystical interpretation be admitted, some urgent reason, even something like necessity, should be produced, either for receding from the literal meaning of the words, or for engrafting upon the words themselves, whether literally or figuratively understood, a higher sense than they naturally and immediately convey. If the literal meaning of the words be such as would derogate from the Divine perfections; as when bodily organs or human passions are attributed to the Almighty:—if, though their literal acceptation be not absolutely unworthy of the subject, yet the figurative be manifestly better adapted to its dignity and importance:—if, on the other hand, the expressions be of so elevated a cast, that to apply them literally would be altogether extravagant and absurd:—or if, with respect to the general intent and meaning of the whole passage, what is literally applicable to one event in Sacred History be so clearly applicable, in its figurative sense, to some other event of subsequent date, that the coincidence cannot be overlooked:—in all such cases, the internal evidence of Scripture itself, without giving undue scope to conjectural ingenuity, requires that the spiritual, or mystical interpretation be adopted. Again; if the inspired writers themselves, either expressly or by implication, direct us to such an interpretation, when otherwise we might not perceive its necessity; then we have an absolute *authority* for the exposition, which supersedes our own conjectures: and we are not only safe in abiding by that authority, but should be unwarranted in its rejection.

But though these rules may assist in determining whether, or not, the text require a mystical interpretation; it is another question, how that interpretation is to be regulated.

Here the general principles already laid

down must be taken into consideration. Every mystical portion of Scripture, and every figurative expression also, is to be explained consistently with other portions, or single expressions, whether figurative or not; and especially with those whose literal meaning is too plain to be misunderstood, or too important to be disregarded. The elucidation therefore of any mystical or figurative passage will depend upon an accurate examination of its subject, and upon a careful collation of its parallel passages. It will depend also upon care in applying either the metaphorical or emblematical sense so far, and so far only, as the case absolutely requires. For, it may be laid down as a maxim, that no fundamental article of faith, or necessary rule of practice, depends upon texts which are doubtful or obscure. Such texts may, when judiciously applied, be rendered serviceable in illustration of the most essential points. But whatever is generally necessary to salvation is, doubtless, somewhere propounded in Holy Writ, in terms sufficiently clear to preclude the necessity of searching for it in passages of abstruse and recondite meaning. Never therefore are we to interpret what is veiled in figure or imagery, in a sense irreconcilable with truths

SERMON VII. 195

more clearly expressed. And let the Commentator beware, that in exercising his ingenuity upon texts of such a description, he do not advance opinions unsupported by more substantial proofs.

But, perhaps, these observations will be better understood, by reference to the several kinds of mystical or emblematical writing which occur in the Holy Scriptures; and of which the chief may be considered under the distinct heads of Parable, Type, and Allegory.

Parables form a very important part of the Sacred Writings. Our Lord not only took frequent occasion to introduce them, but by his own exposition of some, taught us how to expound others. According to the Scriptural usage of the term, a Parable denotes a fictitious, but probable, narrative, illustrating certain matters of fact or doctrine, to which it bears resemblance. There is therefore in every Parable a twofold sense, the literal and the mystical, coinciding in signification. For example; the Parable of the Unforgiving Servant represents literally, that his Lord forgave him a debt of ten thousand talents: —mystically, that God remits to the penitent the punishment of innumerable offences. Literally it states, that this servant, on his refusal to exercise forbearance towards his fellow-servant, was delivered over to the tormentors :—mystically, that God will inflict the severest judgments on all who do not forgive to others their trespasses. The unity of sense in both interpretations is instantly perceptible. The literal is the external sense; the mystical, the internal. The literal must therefore be first explained; that the correspondence between it and the mystical may be more readily perceived. This correspondence, however, does not necessarily extend beyond the general purport of the similitude and its leading circumstances: nor is it always expedient to aim at tracing the parallel in every minute particular. Thus; in the Parable of the Ten Virgins, the main design is to shew the necessity of vigilance and circumspection in preparing for our entrance into eternal life. This the narrative very fully illustrates, by the different conduct of the wise and foolish in these respects. But the mystical signification of the lamps, and the oil, and other adventitious circumstances, as it is less evident, so is it comparatively unimportant; these being rather incidental to the narrative, than essential to its purpose. Generally, indeed, the more exactly the mystical exposition can be made to accord with the literal, the more perfect the Parable will appear to be: and therefore, though we ought carefully to distinguish between essential and merely circumstantial resemblances, yet where the latter admit of an easy and natural application, they are by no means to be overlooked: and it is observable, that in those Parables which our Lord himself interpreted to his Disciples, few, if any, of the circumstantial points are unapplied. But here great judgment is often necessary, neither to do too little, nor to attempt too much. Attention is principally requisite to the immediate design of the Parable; which, for the most part, is declared either at its beginning or its conclusion, or sufficiently appears from the occasion on which it was delivered. Some Parables, indeed, are evidently prophetical, and are to be explained by the same rules to which Prophecies in general are subject. Others serve to illustrate important points of doctrine. Others have the force of moral precepts. A competent knowledge, therefore, of this branch of mystical instruction is of very extensive importance.

Types form another conspicuous part of the Divine plan for the instruction of mankind. By pointing out some connection between persons, or events, remote from each other and apparently unconnected, they often become explanatory of the designs of the Almighty in the several Dispensations of Revealed Religion. A Type is a prefigurative action or occurrence, in which one event, person, or circumstance, is intended to represent another, similar to it in certain respects, but future and distant. It differs therefore from a Parable, in being grounded on a matter of fact, not on fictitious narrative. St. Peter speaks of the Ark in which Noah and his family were saved, as a Type of Baptism. St. Paul applies the passage of the Israelites through the Red Sea to the same purpose. The Rock, from which they were miraculously supplied with water, he also mentions as a Type of Christ: and our Lord refers to the Brazen Serpent and to Jonah, as Types of his Death and Resurrection. In these several instances the similitude arises out of an historical fact: and the coincidences we must suppose to have been preordained by Divine wisdom, and brought to pass by a special Providence. Sometimes, indeed, the Type differs no otherwise from a simple Prophecy, than in its being delivered by significant actions or gestures, instead of words; as in Jeremiah's yokes and bonds, Agabus's binding his own hands with Paul's girdle, and many similar instances recorded in the prophetical books. The Temple-service of the Jews and the whole Ceremonial Law of Moses, according to St. Paul's exposition of them in his Epistle to the Hebrews, may also be regarded as of a typical character, so far as respects their general design. But here, as in Parables and all figurative portions of Scripture, the parallel between the literal and mystical sense must not be too minutely extended; an error, into which fanciful Expositors are prone to fall, and by which the Sacred Writings have often been subjected to the ridicule of the undiscerning and the profane. Such Types, however, carry with them intrinsic evidence of their Divine original; and are not to be treated as mere casual coincidences, or ingenious accommodations of Scripture, where, though some resemblance may exist, yet no actual parallel was preordained. It is, indeed, essential to a Type, in the Scriptural acceptation of the term, that there should be competent evidence of the Divine *intention* in the correspondence between it and the Antitype; a matter, not left to the imagination of the Expositor to discover, but resting on some solid proof from Scripture itself, that this was really the case.

Similar observations are applicable to those other figurative portions of Holy Writ, which fall under the general denomination of Allegory. Parables and Types partake of the nature of allegorical representations; it being the character of every species of Allegory, that it represents one thing by the delineation of another. But though every Type or Parable is of an allegorical character; yet every Allegory is not a Type or Parable. Some historical facts of the Old Testament appear to be allegorized in the New, (that is, a spiritual application is given to them over and above their literal meaning,) although they cannot strictly be denominated Types. St. Paul, in applying the History of Sarah and Hagar to the Jewish and Christian Covenants, does not call it a Type; but only says, that in giving it such an application, he had allegorized the history. Such allegorical interpretations seem to form a distinct class. So, again, do Symbols. The symbolical language of the Prophets is almost a science in itself. None can fully comprehend the depth, sublimity, and force of their writings who are not thoroughly acquainted with the peculiar and appropriate imagery they were wont to use. This is the main key to many of the Prophecies: and without knowing how to apply it, the Interpreter will often in vain essay to discover their hidden treasures.

The importance, then, of figurative and mystical interpretation can hardly be called in question. The entire neglect of it must, in many cases, greatly vitiate expositions, however otherwise valuable for their erudition and judgment. In explaining the Prophetical Writings and the Mosaic Ordinances, this defect will be most striking; since, in consequence of it, not only the spirit and force of many passages will almost wholly evaporate, but erroneous conceptions may be formed of their real purport and intention.

II. But we are now to consider, on the other hand, the Misapplication or Abuse of this kind of Interpretation, and the errors which arise from carrying it to *excess*.

The most flagrant species of Abuse, is when it is made to militate against the plain and literal sense, or even to exclude it, although that sense involves no absurdity or falsehood, nor is contradictory to the rest of Scripture. Of this fault those Expositors are manifestly guilty, who, in their attempts to allegorize historical facts, virtually, if not expressly, reject the facts themselves. This is done by some, for the evident purpose of discrediting the Sacred History; by others, without any such sinister purpose, and purely from fondness for such interpretations, or from a persuasion that they afford the readiest means of repelling infidel objections. Hence many attempts have been made to substitute *allegorical* explanations of the Creation and Fall of man, and of several other narratives of the Old Testament, for the simple *historical* statements. That Unbelievers should have recourse to this, as the most plausible and specious mode of assailing the credibility of Holy Writ, is not surprising: and it is well known that two distinguished writers of this class, in the last century, adopted this allegorizing scheme; the one, to destroy the credit of Prophecy, the other, of Miracles. Others of like persuasion have, more or less systematically, attempted the same thing; well knowing that nothing could more effectually shake the whole fabric of Revealed Religion, than thus converting its history into fable and its realities into fiction. For if the narratives most usually selected for the purpose may thus be explained away; what part of the Sacred History will be secure against similar treatment? Nay, what doctrines, even those the most essential to Christianity, might not thus be undermined? For are not those doctrines dependent upon the *facts* recorded in Scripture, for the evidence of their truth? Does not, for instance, the whole system of our Redemption presuppose the reality of the Fall as an historical fact? And do not the proofs of the Divine authority of the whole, rest upon the verification of its Prophecies and Miracles, as events which have actually taken place? Allegory thus misapplied is, therefore, worse than frivolous or useless: it strikes a deadly blow at the very vitals of the Christian Faith.

It is natural however to the human mind to delight in Imagery: and the Sacred Writings so often administer occasions of gratifying this propensity, that men of ardent minds and luxuriant fancies may be led, without any suspicion of harm or danger, to extend Interpretations of this kind farther than a sound and sober judgment can approve. The supposed discovery of meanings deeply hidden and veiled from vulgar observation, gratifies the curiosity or flatters the vanity of the Interpreter; who will, in consequence, often satisfy himself with very slight evidence, or even with the mere semblance of correspondence between his own conceptions and those of the inspired writer. Hence the danger of great abuse and perversion of a talent of this kind, even where there is no intention to make way for the mystical sense by superseding the literal.

The practice of thus incautiously spiritualizing historical facts, and of indiscriminately applying to almost every part of Scripture some hidden and mysterious signification, appears to have owed its prevalence in the Christian Church, partly to Heathens, and partly to Jews.

When Christianity made such progress in the Roman empire as to threaten the total subversion of Paganism, and the absurdities of the Gentile superstition were in danger of falling into universal contempt, the advocates of the latter found it necessary to have recourse to allegorical expositions of its legendary fictions; that, by throwing over them the veil of mystic piety and wisdom, their deformities might be concealed. And surely they were " wise in their generation." For, what could render such gross and monstrous fictions palatable to a discerning mind but this mystic art? On the other hand, when these same ingenious advocates of a hopeless cause endeavoured to retaliate upon Revealed Religion by attacking the credibility of its historical records; Christian writers too readily fell into the practice of vindicating their own belief by this precarious mode of defence. When pressed with difficulties respecting the *literal* sense of certain Scripture narratives, they appear to have deemed it sufficient to shew that these, as well as Heathen legends, were capable of a satisfactory *allegorical* interpretation, to which the Heathen opponent could not consistently object. And in thus attempting to combat the adversary with his own weapons, they not unfrequently pushed the argument so far as to put to hazard the credit of the facts themselves.

The Jews also were instrumental to this evil. Their ancient Targums abounded with such interpretations. Philo delighted in them: and, in after-times, other Jewish writers engrafted upon them the innumerable absurdities of the Cabalistic Theology; affecting the discovery of profound mysteries in almost every word, syllable, or letter of the Sacred Oracles, and overlooking, in pursuit of these, the more solid and substantial matter.

From such corrupt sources some Christian Commentators appear to have unguardedly drawn their supplies. To these may be ascribed many strange reveries among the earliest heretics, and many mystic extravagancies which in later times have disgraced the annals of the Church; giving occasion of triumph to the scorner and the enthusiast, while the reverential believer has trembled for the cause of Truth confided to such injudicious hands.

This mode of interpretation may not, indeed, be safely intrusted even to the most learned or well-intentioned Expositor, unless he be content to circumscribe it within the limits of such necessary rules as those which have been here suggested. No faculty of the human mind requires to be kept under stricter discipline, than the Imagination; none being more difficult to control, none more eccentric or capricious when suffered to act without restraint. Nothing therefore may be deemed admissible in this branch of Scripture-criticism, which is not warranted either by the necessity of the case, or by clear Analogy from Scripture, or by the authority of some inspired Interpreter. *Spiritual improvements* (as they are sometimes called) of particular passages of Scripture;—

that is, deducing from them spiritual instructions for the practical edification of the reader;—whether or not they flow directly and naturally from the subject, may at least be harmless. But when brought forward for the purpose of Interpretation properly so called, they are to be viewed with caution and even with mistrust. For scarcely is there a favourite opinion which a fertile imagination may not thus extract from some portion of Scripture: and very different, nay, contrary interpretations of this kind have often been made of the very same texts, according to men's various fancies or inventions.

Nor is it a slight objection to the indiscriminate application of this species of exposition, that it renders the Scriptures in general too deep and mysterious for popular apprehension. Almost every mystical Expositor aims at novelty. His object is to make discoveries in spiritual knowledge. He sets out with a persuasion that a great portion of the Scriptures has hitherto been, as it were, a sealed Book, not fully understood, except by a chosen few, gifted with extraordinary powers to penetrate its interior, and to disclose its precious treasures. He adopts, moreover, a principle, which makes it scarcely possible to determine, when the *whole* truth is actually laid before us. For, if so excursive and volatile a faculty as the Imagination be permitted to range *ad libitum* in its airy regions, who shall say when it has arrived at the conclusion of its labours? What errors too in religious opinions may not receive a plausible appearance by the aid of a mode of interpretation so lax and flexible in itself, and affording such facilities for a perversion of the truth?

The advocates, however, for carrying this system to an unbounded extent, are wont to urge on its behalf St. Paul's distinction between " milk for babes who are unskilful in " the word of righteousness," and " strong " meat for them that are of full age[a];" as implying that the literal sense is fit only for novices in the Faith, and that the spiritual sense is the proper nourishment for more advanced Christians. But this appears to be a misapprehension of the Apostle's meaning. He reproaches those who, after having been taught " the first principles of the oracles of " God," faith, repentance, and the like, did not " go on unto perfection," but had " need to " be taught them again[b]," and who, in consequence, were both indisposed and unqualified to enter into his more profound disquisitions

[a] Heb v. 13, 14.   [b] Heb. v. 12. and vi. 1, 2.

respecting the connection between the Christian, the Mosaic, and the Patriarchal Dispensations. His censure falls upon those who, though they ought to have been themselves qualified to become teachers of the elementary doctrines of Christianity, had need to be instructed in what every ordinary disciple might be supposed to understand. But what is this to the question before us? Or, even if it did relate to it, how does it prove that greater importance is attached to deep and mystical subjects, than to the simple rudiments, or first principles, which constitute the very foundation of our Faith?

Whatever then may be said by the admirers of Allegory and Mysticism, respecting the transcendent excellence of such expositions, ought to be deemed of little weight, unless they can be shewn to have the sanction of Holy Writ. Without that sanction, the experiment is generally hazardous: and a due reverence for the Sacred Word will always incline us to hesitate in setting forth as the suggestions of Divine wisdom, what may eventually prove to be nothing more than human invention. Nor will it avail to argue, from some particular instances in Scripture of this mode of interpretation, to the application of it as an *universal* rule. No such universal rule is to be found in Scripture. It is no where laid down as a maxim, that there is in every part of the Sacred Writings, nor even in the greater part, a hidden spiritual sense, besides that which the literal expression conveys. The cases where it is exemplified are for the most part such as evidently require, or readily admit such an interpretation. And though we may find others also which appear to require or admit the same, yet great caution is to be used in its application; nor should it ever be regarded as of real necessity, where truth and sound doctrine can be obtained without it. To comprise all in a few short maxims:—figurative and mystical interpretations are never to be so applied as to destroy or supersede the literal sense, when that sense is sufficiently clear and intelligible;—they are never to be far-fetched, or pressed beyond the obvious meaning of the text;—they must be such as elucidate, not obscure or perplex the subject;—they are not to be made the foundation of articles of Faith, but adduced only for the illustration or confirmation of what is elsewhere more plainly revealed;—nor are they to be sought after in matters of little moment, or made the chief object of investigation.

To proceed farther into this vast and almost boundless field of inquiry would be productive of little benefit, unless the research were accompanied with such a detail of examples from Holy Writ as would form a very extensive commentary on the Bible. It is also the less necessary on the present occasion, because whatever has been now advanced must be considered as having reference to what has been already suggested respecting the Analysis and the Collation of Scripture truths. Nor has it been intended, in this or any other part of the discussion, to dogmatize on religious opinions, or to prejudge any particular interpretations of the Sacred Word. The sole object has been to shew on what general principles every disputed or disputable point in Revealed Religion ought to be argued; and thus to prevent that perplexity or indecision, which, in every science as well as in Theology, will arise from not having clear conceptions of the data or postulata on which the entire system depends. As want of knowledge in these respects makes Sciolists and Sophists in human learning; so does it give birth to strange and monstrous opinions in matters of Faith. And as well might the labourer attempt to make bricks without straw, or to erect a solid edifice on the sand, as the Theologian undertake to frame a substantial and consistent Creed without first laying his foundations deep in principles that will support his fabric, and acquainting himself with the necessary rules for raising a superstructure of just and congruous proportions.

In every department of Sacred Criticism, it is, indeed, of the first importance, that we " be not wise in our own conceits[d];" that we take heed neither to add to nor to diminish from the Word of God; and that we beware of confounding with His unerring wisdom the wanderings of our own wayward fancies. In no case are these cautions more necessary than with reference to the subject now before us. For here it is, that oftentimes the best disposed are in the greatest danger of being led astray. Eager to explore the depths of Divine knowledge, wrapped up in admiration of what he imagines he has discovered through some new channel of information, and relying implicitly on the Divine acceptance of his pious labours, the Mystic proceeds fearlessly, nor easily brooks restraint in the ardour of his pursuit. But let him take heed: if Reason may not usurp authority over the Written Word;—

[d] Rom. xii. 16.

if the Church, ordained by its heavenly Lord and Master for the preservation of the truth, must bow to that authority;—if neither public nor private Judgment may overstep its boundaries;—far less may such an unstable power as the human Imagination be allowed any absolute sway. Nevertheless, let not the dry and spiritless Critic conceive that he is shewing his superior wisdom, in fastidiously slighting any source of real information which that Word opens to him, whether conveyed in mystic terms or in those of plain and literal signification.

From the danger of either extreme due humility and reverence will be the Interpreter's best security. They will teach him, on the one hand, to " receive with meekness " the engrafted Word[e]," thankfully imbibing the Spirit as well as the Letter of its instructions. They will teach him, on the other hand, to beware of any attempts to become wise above that which is written, or of searching after new and unauthorized interpretations. They will admonish him not to " forsake the fountain of living waters," nor to " hew him out cisterns, broken cisterns, which " can hold no water[f];" but to " draw waters " out of the wells of Salvation[g]," unadulter-

[e] James i. 21.   [f] Jer. ii. 13.   [g] Isa. xii. 3.

ated by any admixture of human invention. And, " blessed are they who thus hunger " and thirst after righteousness; for they " shall be filled[h]."

[h] Matth. v. 6.

SERMON VIII.

1 TIMOTHY iii. 15.

Which is the Church of the living God, the pillar and ground of the Truth.

UPON a general review of the history of Revealed Religion, every intelligent observer may perceive, that it has not been left to *human* wisdom only to provide the means of communicating and perpetuating its blessings to mankind. Human instrumentality has been employed; but under the control of special laws and ordinances from above. Human learning has been made necessary for a right knowledge of its instructions; but in subserviency to the rule of Faith. Human authority has been ordained to administer its laws, and to dispense its privileges; but with no power to alter one tittle of its charter. The Wisdom which foresees and plans every thing from the beginning, and the Power which carries on and accomplishes whatever that Wisdom had devised, have clearly manifested a Divine superintendence of the whole: while the agency of man has been no less conspicuous in those various circumstances and events, which, without any *miraculous* interpositions of the Almighty, have contributed to its extension and completion.

In the words of the text the Apostle adverts to one special instance, in which this joint cooperation of divine and human powers is eminently conspicuous; the Institution of the CHURCH for the preservation of the Christian Faith:—" the Church of the living " God, the pillar and ground of the Truth."

Some difficulties have been raised respecting the precise meaning of these terms; difficulties created rather, perhaps, by the views of interpreters to their own particular systems, than by any ambiguity or obscurity in the text itself. Papists have endeavoured to ground upon this passage of Scripture an argument for the *infallibility* of the Church: to overthrow which, some would apply it, not to the *visible* Church known by its authorized governors and pastors, but to the *invisible*, known only to God, and consisting exclusively of those pure and faithful members of Christ who shall finally be made partakers of his everlasting kingdom. Others regard it as a personal exhortation to Timothy to shew himself " a pillar of the Truth" in the house or Church of God. Others, again, (not without some perplexity in the grammatical construction,) refer these expressions to " the " mystery of godliness" described by the Apostle in the subsequent verse.

But the more obvious application of the text to *the universal Church*, administered under an *external* and *visible* form of government, best accords with the context, and is liable to no solid objections. The words immediately follow a series of instructions to Timothy, how he in the office of a Bishop, and others in the inferior orders of the ministry, were to conduct themselves in the house of God; " which," adds the Apostle, " is the Church of the living God, the pillar " and ground of the Truth." His design is evidently to give additional weight to those preceding instructions, by suggesting the high and important purpose for which the Church was instituted; and thence to shew how necessary it was that they who were ordained to the Sacred Office of her ministers should "take heed unto themselves and unto " their doctrine[a]." In no other way can the passage be so easily and consistently explained.

[a] 1 Tim. iv. 16.

The Apostle, then, being understood to affirm of the Church Catholic, the Visible Church here on earth, that it was ordained by the Divine " Author and Finisher of our " Faith," to be the instrument of preserving that Faith in its genuine purity, and of upholding it for the general instruction of mankind; it becomes a matter of important inquiry, closely connected with those principles of Scripture-Interpretation which have formed the subject of the preceding Discourses, how far this great purpose appears to have been attained. And here these questions naturally occur:—First, What further insight do the Scriptures afford us into the Divine intentions in this respect? Secondly, What evidence have we, that the Church in general has been thus instrumental to the preservation of Truth, and to the prevention or removal of Error? Thirdly, What benefits of this kind are owing to our own Church in particular, that branch of the true Vine under the shelter of which the good Providence of God hath placed us, and which we believe His own right hand to have planted? These inquiries may not unaptly conclude the design which has been taken in hand, and may furnish matter for grateful contemplation.

I. In the first place, what further insight

do the Scriptures afford us into the Divine intentions in this respect?

In so stupendous a work as that of man's Salvation, designed for the universal good of mankind, and extending from age to age, it is not to be supposed that means would be unprovided, ordinary or extraordinary, for carrying it on from its first commencement to its final close. The Church, indeed, in the largest and fullest acceptation of the term, did not originate with our blessed Saviour and his Apostles; but included all the faithful, under every dispensation of Revealed Religion, antecedent as well as subsequent to the coming of our Lord. But its formation and continuance under the Christian dispensation are the points with which we are more immediately concerned, and in which the providential care of the Almighty is most fully displayed.

The design of the Christian Church, both with respect to its first institution and the means ordained for its perpetuity, are thus stated by St. Paul, in his Epistle to the Ephesians. " He gave some, Apostles; and " some, Prophets; and some, Evangelists; " and some, Pastors and Teachers; for the " perfecting of the Saints, for the work of " the Ministry, for the edifying of the body

"of Christ; till we all come, in the unity of
"the Faith, and of the knowledge of the Son
"of God, unto a perfect man, unto the mea-
"sure of the stature of the fulness of Christ:
"that we henceforth be no more children,
"tossed to and fro, and carried about with
"every wind of doctrine, by the sleight of
"men, and cunning craftiness, whereby they
"lie in wait to deceive; but, speaking the
"truth in love, may grow up into Him in all
"things, which is the Head, even Christ:—
"from whom the whole Body fitly joined
"together and compacted by that which
"every joint supplieth, according to the ef-
"fectual working in the measure of every
"part, maketh increase of the Body unto
"the edifying of itself in love[b]."

Here we have not only a statement of the general purpose for which the Church was constituted, but an enumeration of the several offices appointed for the fuller extension of its benefits. In the time of the Apostles, the difficulties being extraordinary, extraordinary powers were bestowed. A great variety of preternatural gifts distinguished those who were first called of God to minister in sacred things, to enable them to spread the knowledge of the Gospel, and to inter-

[b] Ephes. iv. 11—16.

pret its heavenly truths. And thus the intended effect was rapidly produced, that of bringing persons of all nations, and kindreds, and tongues, to an acknowledgment of the truth, and to a participation in the proffered blessing.

After this, the system, of which the Apostles had laid the foundation, was to be carried on through succeeding generations; but with a gradual diminution of that extraordinary aid, which the circumstances of the case rendered no longer necessary. Truth, once revealed by competent authority, once proved by satisfactory evidence to have come from God, ceased to stand in need of those supernatural powers, which were at first requisite to verify its pretensions, and to command the attention of mankind. Human talents, learning, and authority, accompanied only with that ordinary assistance of Divine Grace which is requisite in every thing relating to man's spiritual improvement, were thenceforth sufficient. Yet since the object to be attained was not temporary, but to continue from age to age; the mode, the form, and the instruments to be employed, were still to be conformable to the primitive institution. Accordingly the Apostles ordained successors to themselves, and took measures for perpetuating in the Church a standing ministry of divers orders and gradations. In so doing they shewed in what sense we are to interpret our Lord's assurance, that he would " be with them always, even unto the end of " the world." They shewed also, that, in the work of bringing men to the knowledge of the Truth, and into the way of everlasting life, not only the Scriptures were to be set before them, but also Pastors and Teachers were to be duly appointed to serve as guides to the flock, and to supply them, from the ample stores of the Word of God, with spiritual food and sustenance.

II. But, secondly, what evidence have we, that the Church in general has been thus instrumental to the preservation of Truth, and to the prevention or removal of Error.

The evidences, from the best historical records, to the simple fact that a visible Church of this description has actually subsisted from the time of our Lord and his Apostles to this moment, are too well known to require a detail. Nor is there any defect of similar evidence to shew that, whatever errors or corruptions may have occasionally found admittance into it, the Church itself has proved a successful instrument in the hands of Providence, both of transmitting the unadulterated Word of God from generation to generation, and also of promulgating and maintaining all its great fundamental truths; nay, perhaps, of preserving even the very name as well as substance of Christianity, which, humanly speaking, would probably have been long since extinct, had it not been nurtured and cherished by this its appointed Guardian and Protector.

Here however it is to be observed, that in describing the Church as so eminently instrumental to the preservation of Scripture-truth, and even of Christianity itself, it is spoken of as existing under that Apostolical form of government which from the date of its first institution it has invariably exhibited in the far greater part of the Christian world. It is the Church *episcopally* constituted, which forms our present subject of investigation; not any of those various modes of professing Christianity which may be found in Communions of *other* kinds. For without entering into controversy with those who deny the Divine origin of Episcopacy, it can hardly be disputed, that this form of Ecclesiastical Polity has so generally prevailed, that, in every age from the time of the Apostles until the separations which in some instances unhappily took place at the period of the Protestant Reformation, the Catholic or Universal Church, properly so called, comprising many particular or national Churches, was known and distinguished by its episcopal constitution. Speaking therefore *historically* only, (which is all that is required for our present purpose,) we are warranted in thus defining the Church: and the question now before us is, How far the Church, thus defined, has hitherto proved itself to be " the " pillar and ground of the Truth," or, according to the interpretation of a distinguished Commentator, " that Pillar, on a basis, by " which the Truth is supported?"

Many writers, whether hostile or not to Christianity itself, take a very unfavourable and unjust view of this subject, by directing their whole attention to the *corrupt* doctrines or practices too often engrafted upon the Faith by *particular* Churches; overlooking the many great and fundamental errors which the Church, considered in its *general* and *collective* character, has been the occasion of preventing or removing. But, with respect to Articles of Faith, those only ought to be considered as sanctioned by Church-authority, which are stamped with the concurring testimony of the Church, exhibited, either in the decisions of General Councils convened for the purpose, or in the various Creeds and Confessionals framed by different Churches. According to this criterion, if a candid investigation be made of the points generally agreed upon by the Church Universal, it will probably be found, that at no period of its history has any *fundamental* or *essential* Truth of the Gospel been *authoritatively* disowned. Particular Churches may have added many superstitious observances, and many erroneous tenets, to these essential truths: and in every Church, particular individuals, or congregations of individuals, may have tainted large portions of the Christian Community with pestilential heresies. But as far as the Church Catholic can be deemed responsible, the substance of sound doctrine still remains undestroyed at least, if not unimpaired.

Let us take, for instance, those Articles of Faith which have already been shewn to be *essential* to the Christian Covenant:—the Doctrines of the Trinity, of our Lord's Divinity and Incarnation, of his Atonement and Intercession, of our Sanctification by the Holy Spirit, of the terms of acceptance, and the Ordinances of the Christian Sacraments and Priesthood. At what period of the Church have these doctrines, or either of them, been by any public act disowned or called in question? We are speaking now, it will be recollected, of what in the language of Ecclesiastical History is emphatically called THE CHURCH; that, which has from age to age borne rule, upon the ground of its pretensions to Apostolical succession. And to this our inquiry is necessarily restricted.

If then it should be said that Arianism, (whose claims in this respect are perhaps more plausible than those of any other heresy) was for a time favoured by the hierarchical powers; let it be remembered that it owed its temporary intrusion and ascendency rather to the unwarrantable interference of secular power, than to any authoritative sanction on the part of the Church itself. From the most distinguished defenders and governors of the Church, Hilary, Basil, the two Gregorys, Ambrose, and Athanasius, it met with determined resistance, although fostered by Imperial favour. It stands therefore upon record, not as an evidence of versatility or indecision among the venerable Pastors of the Christian fold; but rather of the untoward and embarrassing circumstances to which they were often subjected, by the overweening influence of the temporal powers and the turbulence of ungovernable factions. Subsequently to that period, even in the darkest times of Popery and amidst the barbarism and corruptions of the middle ages, however the primitive Faith and Worship might be defaced by " teaching " for doctrines the commandments of men[c]," and by greatly invalidating the very terms of acceptance under the Gospel Dispensation, yet we find no actual renunciation of those doctrines which are interwoven, as it were, with the substance of Christianity itself. The pure metal was still existing in the ore, though obscured by extraneous matter: and when by the work of Reformation it was cleared of its superincumbent dross, the truth came forth, undiminished in sterling value, and with unfaded lustre.

But view now, on the other hand, the labours of those who endeavoured to subvert any of these fundamental truths. Observe the parties with whom they originated, and the estimation in which they were holden. No age of the Church has ever been entirely free from attempts to spread pernicious errors. Yet at what period have they ever received its authoritative sanction? Did the Church in primitive times yield one iota of essential doctrine to the Gnostic Heretics?

[c] Matth. xv. 9.

Did it afterwards adopt either the Sabellian, the Arian, or the Macedonian tenets? Did the wild enthusiasm of Manes, or Montanus, and their followers, in any respect influence its Creed? And in later times, when and where have the Socinian notions been recognized by any legitimate authority? Or, what proof can even the disciple of Calvin produce, that his doctrine of arbitrary and irrespective Decrees was ever the received persuasion of the Catholic Church? To say nothing of the multitude of lesser divisions of religious opinion; or of those ephemeral productions, of each of which, as of their authors it might be said, " in the morning it " flourisheth and groweth up, in the evening " it is cut down and withereth[d]."

Surely here is something to arrest attention; something to awaken reflection; something which they who sincerely profess Christianity, and are tenacious of the inviolability of its doctrines, must contemplate with sentiments of awe and veneration. For though a Sceptic may contend that this species of evidence does not amount to a direct and demonstrative proof of the truth of the doctrines; yet if they be not true, how shall we account for their having been so uninter-

[d] Psalm xc. 6.

ruptedly transmitted to these latter times? How have they withstood the assaults of continued opponents? opponents, wanting neither talents nor inclination to effect their overthrow? If these considerations be deemed insufficient, let the Adversary point out by what surer tokens we shall discover any Christian community, duly answering the Apostle's description, that it is " built upon " the foundation of the Apostles and Pro- " phets, Jesus Christ himself being the chief " corner-stone[e]?"

Nor is this all. Our admiration is heightened, and our conviction strengthened, by observing that the Church has not only, in her general professions of Faith, preserved entire the substance of its fundamental truths; but has also shewn an unceasing solicitude to maintain accurate and consistent expositions of them, against the perverse interpretations of conflicting parties. In this respect, many venerable remains of Ecclesiastical Antiquity are of peculiar value. Those public documents of the Church which, in the form of Creeds or Confessions of Faith, not only obtained general currency at the time when they were composed, but have served as models to after-ages, afford, on

[e] Ephes. ii. 20.

many leading doctrines, the most perfect tests of a sound belief. The chief variations to be found in them are such as arise from a greater or less extent of detail respecting some particular points: several of these formularies having been progressively enlarged or reconstructed, according to the prevalence of certain errors which it became necessary to counteract. This appears to have been the case with what is called the Athanasian Creed: in which the respective errors of Sabellianism, Tritheism, and Arianism, are distinctly opposed by explanatory and cautionary clauses. These, though they may now appear to us unnecessarily minute and controversial, could not but be of great importance in discountenancing the heresies then in existence; and, doubtless, very much contributed to check the growing evil. Independently, therefore, of any application of which they may be capable to more recent times, they are highly valuable for the testimony they bear to the primitive Faith. But they are also in themselves of intrinsic worth. For with respect to this Creed in particular, however lightly it may be regarded by persons of little discernment or tinctured with false notions of liberality on religious subjects; it is in truth a composition, which (to them especially who are conversant with the history of opinions in former times) furnishes matter of admiration, from the extraordinary accuracy and precision with which it is framed, and by which the doctrine it contains is guarded on all sides against misinterpretation.

III. But dismissing any further inquiry into these remoter ages, let us consider, thirdly, what obligations of this kind we owe to *our own Church* in particular; and more especially with reference to the principles which it has been the object of this series of Discourses to elucidate.

It may be safely affirmed, that no Church now in existence has better established its character for *moderation* in doctrine and in discipline, than our own;—moderation, in its pure and genuine sense; not denoting an indulgence to Error or an indifference to Truth, but a sound and correct judgment, carefully steering betwixt opposite errors. By the confession, indeed, of her adversaries, the Church of England is eminent in this respect; some having candidly acknowledged this as an honour justly due to her; while others endeavour to turn it to her reproach, as if it indicated her lukewarmness in maintaining the truth.

But, confining our observations at present to such topics as have already been discussed, it will be found, in the first place, that our Church on every occasion makes the fullest and most unreserved declarations of her submission to the *paramount authority of the Holy Scriptures*. By establishing this as a fundamental principle, she avoids with equal care the error of those who would add to the Scriptures, and of those who would take away from them :—of those who would call in some higher authority to which appeal shall be made, and of those who would admit of no extraneous help for the exposition of their contents. She does not, with the Romanist or with the sectarian Fanatic, virtually supersede the preeminent claims of Scripture by the arbitrary dictates of the Church or the no less arbitrary suggestions of a private Spirit; but expressly declares in her sixth Article, that " Holy Scripture con-
" taineth all things necessary to Salvation:
" so that whatsoever is not read therein, nor
" may be proved thereby, is not to be re-
" quired of any man, that it should be be-
" lieved as an Article of the Faith, or be
" thought requisite or necessary to Salva-
" tion :"—and again, in her twentieth Article, that " although the Church be a Witness

" and a Keeper of Holy Writ, yet as it ought
" not to decree any thing against the same,
" so besides the same ought it not to enforce
" any thing to be believed for necessity of
" Salvation." Nevertheless, as she exemplifies in her own public documents, so she inculcates also upon the Clergy and Laity of her Communion, the necessity of resorting to the aids of human learning in fixing its interpretation, and of reasoning out of the Sacred Word, in order to attain to a clear and correct apprehension of its instructions in matters either of Faith or Practice.

But while our Church is thus careful not to set up her authority as an unerring standard of truth, she omits not to testify her deference to the judgment of the Church Catholic, when it can be duly obtained. She every where shews her readiness to abide by that judgment, and to reverence it in proportion to the evidence of its antiquity and its uninterrupted continuance. She assumes to herself no more than to be regarded as a true branch of the Universal Church; not denying that particular Churches may err; nor asserting any claim of infallibility either for herself or others.

Conformably with these principles, her Clergy are admonished in the Ordination

Service, to be " diligent," not only " in prayer " and in reading of the Holy Scriptures," but also " in such studies as help to the know-" ledge of the same." Her Articles, Liturgy, and Homilies, evidently suppose the necessity of a previous cultivation of the human understanding, to qualify those who undertake the exposition of Scriptural truth. Equally discountenancing dogmatical arrogance, intellectual pride, and enthusiastic pretences to spiritual illumination, she inculcates that the Divine blessing is only to be expected upon the joint operation of Faith in God's Word, sound learning, and due deference to ecclesiastical authority.

As a faithful Expositor of God's Word, her caution and judgment are evinced both in *analysing* and *collating* the truths of Holy Writ. The latter rule of interpretation is recognized in her twentieth Article, which declares it to be not lawful " so to expound one " place of Scripture that it be repugnant to " another." Her attention to the former appears in her adoption of those Creeds only into her public formularies, which lay down nothing as absolutely necessary to salvation but the acknowledgment of fundamental Articles of Faith, or the renunciation of fundamental errors: whence the Romish Church, who herself insists upon many doubtful and unnecessary as well as erroneous matters, accuses us of having a merely negative Religion; because nothing which is not *essential* to the Faith is obtruded into our terms of Communion.

Again; as an Interpreter of Scripture, our Church carefully distinguishes between the Jewish and Christian Dispensations, and between the general and special purposes, to which the several arguments and injunctions of the Sacred Writers appear to have been directed. She teaches in her seventh Article, that " the Old Testament is not contrary to " the New, since both in the Old and New " Testament everlasting life is offered to " mankind by Christ:" and then proceeds to state, that although the ritual or ceremonial Law of Moses does not bind Christians, yet no Christian is free from obedience to its moral commandments. Thus, while she recognizes the inseparable connection between the two Dispensations, she points out also the essential distinctions between them; virtually condemning those who, either by confounding them together, or regarding them as at variance with each other, frequently misapply the reasoning of the Sacred Writers, and especially of St. Paul in some of his Epistles, on points immediately connected with these inquiries.

Further; her three last Articles contain a distinct disavowal and censure of opinions contradictory to those regulations of Civil Society, without which neither the authority of the Magistrate to coerce the evil doer, nor of the State to repel external violence, could be carried into effect:—errors, which chiefly originate in the neglect of comparing the precepts of Scripture with each other, or in regarding as of perpetual and universal obligation what was only of a temporary, local, or personal description.

Another instance of the sound discretion and moderation of our Church, appears in her care to discriminate rightly between the *literal* and *mystical* sense of Scripture. Of this, her doctrine of the Sacraments, as contained in her twenty-seventh and twenty-eighth Articles, affords satisfactory evidence. Baptism she holds to be " not only a sign of " profession, and mark of difference, whereby " Christian men are discerned from others " that be not christened; but also a sign of " Regeneration, or New Birth, whereby, as " by an instrument, they that receive Bap- " tism rightly, are grafted into the Church; " the promises of forgiveness of sin, and of

"our adoption to be the sons of God by the
"Holy Ghost, are visibly signed and sealed."
—In the other Sacrament, she rejects *Transubstantiation*, because "it is repugnant to
"the plain words of Scripture, and over-
"throweth the nature of a Sacrament;"
maintaining, however, that "to such as right-
"ly, worthily, and with Faith receive it, the
"Bread is a partaking of the Body of Christ,
"and the Cup a partaking of the Blood of
"Christ;"—which are taken "only after an
"heavenly and spiritual manner." These
expressions, again, are exactly conformable
with her general definition of Sacraments,
that they are "effectual signs of Grace, by
"which God worketh invisibly in us, and
"doth not only quicken, but also strengthen
"and confirm our Faith." Accordingly, in
her Communion Office, although the very
words of Scripture are adhered to in the Consecration and the Administration of the Elements, yet they are so applied in other parts
of the Service, as to make it impossible to understand them in any other than a *metaphorical* sense: and while the doctrines of Transubstantiation and Consubstantiation are virtually disclaimed, that of the *real Presence*,
spiritually, mystically, and sacramentally understood, is no less clearly implied.

But notwithstanding this care to avoid Error on her own part, and to discountenance it in others, no uncharitable invectives, no bitter anathemas are fulminated against those who separate from her Communion: nor is any unwillingness manifested to give the right hand of fellowship to any other Churches with whom it is possible to hold lawful Communion. Her thirty-fourth Article declares, " it is not necessary that Tra-
" ditions and Ceremonies be in all places one,
" and utterly alike; for at all times they
" have been diverse, and may be changed ac-
" cording to the diversities of countries, times,
" and men's manners, so that nothing be or-
" dained against God's Word." Such differences, therefore, are not allowed by her to break the bond of Christian Unity. Great, too, have been her concessions towards those who have stirred up dissensions among her members: concessions, not made for the sake of popularity, or to enlarge her pale for the admission of them who are unsound in the Faith, but that Separatists might hereby be rendered more willing to listen to her instructions upon essential points, and to examine with candour the lesser matters on which such differences existed. Utterly disclaiming, therefore, the notion that " every

"man shall be saved by the Law or Sect "which he professeth;" she nevertheless shews a disposition to approximate, as nearly as truth and sincerity will allow, to tenets not entirely accordant with her own. To this disposition has been attributed that caution and forbearance in framing her Articles, which still leaves room for slight shades of difference as to their interpretation: and hence she has been regarded, even by those not of her own Communion, as the fit medium of reconciliation between other Churches. It is well known, indeed, that some of her most distinguished members have expressly aimed at forming, upon the model of her constitution, some plan of union, which, without a sacrifice of fundamental principles, might unite foreign Churches with our own, and bring contending parties to something like mutual agreement. But the failure, hitherto, of every such attempt only serves to shew the impracticability of the thing; and may teach us to be so much the less sanguine in our expectations that the purpose will ever be accomplished.

If then the appellation of Catholic could without a solecism be applied to any national or particular Church, our own might perhaps lay better claim to it than any that has ap-

peared since the first establishment of Christianity. She is Catholic in her actual communion with every pure and genuine branch of the Christian Church, and in her desire to extend that union wherever it can be done without a violation of essential principles. She is Catholic in the soundness of her Creed, and in the care she has taken to restore, and to preserve uncorrupted, "the Faith once de-
" livered to the Saints." She is Catholic also in the real liberality of her sentiments towards those who refuse to unite with her; a liberality shewing itself, not in affected indifference to the truths she has espoused, nor in an unworthy suppression of her own belief; but in disclaiming any external coercion to compel assent, and in forbearing harsh or offensive conduct towards the members of other Churches, or of other Congregations, at variance with herself.

The contrast, indeed, in this respect, betwixt our Church and some of her most irreconcilable opponents is very striking. From Romish bigotry and from Sectarian virulence she has alike experienced the effects of an intolerant spirit; and has been severely taught how necessary it is, in any attempts at conciliation with such adversaries, to unite the wisdom of the serpent with the innocence of the dove. She has been taught likewise another important lesson; that, in proportion as these adversaries recede from her pure and moderate principles, they appear, though without any specific bond of union betwixt themselves, to assimilate, in some respects, as to their general ground of dissent. Thus while the Church of England maintains inviolate the supremacy of Scriptural authority; Papists, Libertines, and Enthusiasts, agree in setting up each some other authority *above* that of the Written Word. They agree in arrogating pretensions to something like *infallibility*. They agree in exacting from their disciples an almost *implicit Faith* in their leaders. And they agree in magnifying their own special privileges, to the exclusion of all who are not of their own persuasion. Whatever discordance therefore may be found between their respective opinions, they are in general equally separated from ourselves by one strong line of demarcation not easily to be mistaken.

In retracing then the extensive ground which has been gone over in the course of this inquiry, it is gratifying to have come to this conclusion, that between those principles of Scripture-interpretation which it has been the object of these Lectures to establish, and those on which our own Church grounds her Faith and Practice, there appears to be the most entire correspondence. And we may regard it as an undoubted token of the Divine favour, that this our Zion has hitherto been preserved to us, through innumerable perils and difficulties, and through severe trials and temptations, under which any Church less free from error, or less tenacious of the Truth, must probably have sunk.

But our trust in the continuance of this blessing is still to be regarded as dependent upon our own earnest endeavours to preserve it unimpaired. The purity of our Church in doctrine, discipline, and worship; its exemplary moderation; its faithfulness as a guide to Scripture; these well entitle it to be regarded as a sound portion of " the " Church of the living God, the pillar and " ground of the Truth." If to " hold fast the " faithful Word[f];"—if to be " willing to do " the Will of God[g]," and to " speak as the " Oracles of God[h];"—if " rightly to divide " the Word of Truth[i]," " comparing spiritual " things with spiritual[k]," and having due regard both to the "letter" and the "spirit[l]" of

---

[f] Titus i. 9.   [g] John vii. 17.   [h] 1 Peter iv. 11.
[i] 2 Tim. ii. 15.   [k] 1 Cor. ii. 13.   [l] 2 Cor. iii. 6.

its Divine instructions;—if these be sure characteristics of the Interpreter on whom we may most safely rely;—then is it our bounden duty to uphold the venerable Church of which we are members, and by means of which, with the blessing of the Almighty, we may secure to ourselves, and extend to others, these invaluable benefits.

It would discover, indeed, a great want of due reverence for the Word of God itself, could we betray so sacred a trust. It has evidently been the design of the Almighty, that, from the very first promulgation of the Gospel, the Word and the Ministry should cooperate for the edification of mankind. Both were ordained of God. Both have hitherto been wonderfully preserved by His protecting providence. And since He who said, " Heaven and earth shall pass away, " but my Word shall not pass away[m]," said also to his Apostles, " Lo, I am with you al-" ways, even unto the end of the world[n];" we have the same assurance that both shall be perpetual. It is not, therefore, for us to separate what God hath thus united, unless it could be clearly proved, that the particular Church to which we belong has been unfaithful to her trust. Let not the clamours

[m] Matth. xxiv. 35.   [n] Matth. xxviii. 20.

of party spirit, nor the fluctuations of popular opinion, be suffered to prevail over sober judgment and integrity of principle. Let it not be said, that we know not " whom we " have believed°," or that we are heedless " how" and " what we hear^p."

These are cautions which concern the Fold, as well as the Pastors of Christ's flock. But to those who are here preparing for the Sacred Office, by which they are to become Expositors of the Word of God and to dispense the knowledge of it to others, something additional, in the way of exhortation, may be allowed.

If there be any sentiment which, from their connection with this seat of Religion and Learning, may be expected to predominate in their affections; it is surely that of filial reverence towards the Church in which they have been bred up and nurtured, and of which, we trust, they are soon to go forth the support and ornament. This sentiment they are bound to cherish, in subordination only to that veneration which is due to Scripture itself. Amidst the variety of conflicting opinions which on every side beset them, it is doubtless first of all necessary to be well grounded in the knowledge of the Sacred

° 2 Tim. i. 12.   P Mark iv. 24. Luke viii. 18.

SERMON VIII.

Writings. But, for the attainment of this knowledge, slight and perfunctory endeavours will not suffice. It requires the best preparations of the heart and of the understanding; dispositions conformable to the Divine will; acquirements suited to the weight and importance of the research. It presupposes an unreserved submission to the Word of God, the only infallible Oracle from which there is no appeal; accompanied with the use of all subsidiary means for its right interpretation. Among these means, the authority of the Church, building her Faith upon the Scriptures, and professing to be the Keeper and Witness of Holy Writ, claims our chief regard. No inquiry therefore can be more important, than that which is to ascertain whether *our own* Church has in this respect faithfully discharged her duty. And here we confidently challenge inquiry. We contend, that her moderation is no less conspicuous than her fidelity and firmness; that her Doctrine is Scriptural; her Discipline Apostolical; her Worship pure and primitive. With unceasing care she trains her children in the true faith and fear of God, and " has " no greater joy than to hear that they walk " in the truth q." Her authority is parental,

---
q 3 John 4.

not despotic. She seeks not to " have do-
" minion over their Faith, but to be helpers
" of their joy^r."

Shall we not then be wanting in gratitude to God for so great a blessing, and in due regard for the best interests of ourselves and others, if we shrink from maintaining the just ascendency of this our venerable Parent? May we not endanger, rather than promote the cause of Sacred Truth, if, in our desire to disseminate it far and wide, we neglect that model of sobriety and sound discretion in the work of spiritual instruction, which is set before us in her Creeds, her Articles, her Liturgy, and all her public Formularies? When we look around us, and see how widely the seeds of error and disunion are scattered, and what pernicious fruits they continually bring forth; can we require a stronger argument to shew the necessity of blending with our zeal for the unlimited circulation of the Scriptures, an equal zeal for guarding so sacred a deposit from perversion and abuse? And where shall we find a more unexceptionable pattern for our guidance, in administering to the spiritual exigencies of mankind, and feeding them with the bread of life?

If these considerations be of any weight,

[r] 2 Cor. i. 24.

they will lead us uniformly to acquit ourselves as steadfast members of the Communion to which we belong; desirous to perpetuate its blessings in this our highly-favoured land, willing to communicate its benefits to others, and vigilant to protect its ancient and well-established foundations against all who would endeavour its overthrow, either by open violence, or by undermining subtlety. This vigilance and this fidelity we shall best evince, by thoroughly examining wherein the strength of our fortress lies, and on what support, Divine and human, it principally depends; by cautiously guarding against specious plans of union or alliance, where the true principles of union are wanting; and by acting up to the full measure of our duty as faithful soldiers and servants under the great Captain of our Salvation.

" Walk about Zion" then, "and go round
" about her, and tell the towers thereof.
" Mark well her bulwarks, set up her houses,
" that ye may tell them that come after. For
" this God is our God for ever and ever: He
" shall be our guide unto death[s]."

[s] Psalm xlviii. 11, 12, 13.

APPENDIX.

APPENDIX.

SERMON I.

PAGE 2. l. 23. *This would be a circumstance very discouraging,* &c.] To the objections against Christianity grounded on these divisions among professed believers, satisfactory answers have been given, both by ancient and modern Apologists. Such objections, indeed, come with a somewhat ill grace from the opponents of our Religion, who are generally strenuous advocates for allowing the utmost latitude and diversity of opinion, and are jealous of every attempt to restrict mankind in this respect. Nor do such persons seem to be aware, that the very existence of these divisions removes one objection of a more formidable kind, which cavillers might otherwise allege against it. For, it has been well observed, " the different opinions which have at all times obtained in the Church are a direct and full confutation of that foul aspersion cast upon us by our adversaries, that a Christian is in his belief merely passive: they are a proof that the doctrines of our Religion are examined, sifted, and canvassed by its professors; that they make use of their understanding; and though, like other men, liable to prejudices, do not give their assent without consulting the Reason with which God has, for this purpose, endued every man." *Bandinel's Bampt. Lect.* p. 210. Respecting the great argument from the declarations of Scripture itself, the same Author observes, " the writings of the Evangelists and Apostles abound with exhortations to unity and concord, the spirit of Christianity breathes nothing but love, peace, and charity: yet the Author of our Religion, by his prophetic spirit, declared that he was *not come to give peace on earth, but rather division.*

APPENDIX.

The doctrines of Christianity are laid down in Scripture with a plainness and perspicuity, sufficient and satisfactory to every well-disposed mind: yet we are every where cautioned against *false doctrines* and *false prophets* who were to arise, against *men of corrupt minds who raise perverse disputings*. These disputings and divisions in a Religion whose doctrines and precepts are so averse to them, are surely proofs of the Divine inspiration of those who foretold them; and therefore so far from being an objection against their Religion, they are, on the contrary, a strong confirmation of its truth and Divine original." Ibid. p. 212.

To the same effect are the remarks of Fabricius. " Neque vero desunt vel apud Ethnicos, vel in communione et religione aliqua quacunque, multiplices pugnæ, vitio humani ingenii animique corruptione:—nec Philosophi, nec ipsi Athei aut Sceptici inter se conveniunt. Itaque cum inter Christianos etiam zizania vitiorum reperiantur, quid mirum si inter eos hæc quoque opera carnis, hæreses et schismata, διχοστασίαι, ἔριδες, μάχαι, proveniant? Neque culpa hæc est eorum, qui constanter, ut debent, resistunt erroribus et abusibus, contra disertam formulam sanorum verborum stylo Prophetico et Apostolico conceptam, Ecclesiæ et Christianorum saluti minantibus; sed vero eorum qui, per καινοφωνίας suas et perversæ doctrinæ pertinaciam, pacem Ecclesiæ turbant, atque ita crimen committunt vix martyrii sanguine, ut ait Chrysostomus, expiandum. Quod autem scandalum hoc Christianæ Religionis veritati obesse non possit, vel inde patet, quod a Christo et Apostolis prædictum fuit, et ab eo ut sibi caverent sæpius commoniti sunt Christiani. Matth. xxiv. 5. id. 23, 24. 1 Cor. xi. 16. Itaque Tertullianus: *Non oportet nos mirari super hæreses, sive quia sunt, futuræ enim prænunciabantur: sive quia fidem quorundam subvertant, ad hoc enim sunt, ut fides, habendo tentationem, habeat etiam probationem.*" J. A. Fabricius de Ver. Rel. Chr. p. 672.

Respecting the answers given by ancient Apologists to this objection, see a variety of authorities quoted by Lardner in his Hist. of Heretics, book i. sect. 14.

P. 4. l. 3. *More information perhaps is now to be ob-*

APPENDIX. 253

tained from polemical than from merely didactic treatises.]
—Theology owes most of its valuable stores to the labours of controversial writers; especially in the earlier ages of Christianity. Elementary or didactic treatises were then almost unknown. Even the inspired Writers do not appear to have framed such treatises; and for their expositions of Christian doctrine we are chiefly indebted to the exertions they were compelled to make in dispelling error. In its mode of publication, Christianity itself may be regarded as an unceasing controversy with Jewish and Gentile prejudices, with moral corruption and intellectual pride. Every Apostolical Epistle indicates more or less of this intention. The same necessity for thus unfolding the truths of the Gospel continued long afterwards; nor was it till its doctrines had thus undergone the most ample discussion between contending parties, that systematic views of Theology were generally introduced. And may we not suppose this to have been providentially designed by the Divine Author of our Religion; that, the minds of men being thus incited to a more diligent examination of its contents, and of the purpose for which it was revealed, permanent benefit might be derived from such dissensions, far more than commensurate to the temporary evils they produced?

To assist in forming our judgment on this point, let us call to mind some of the chief controversies which have, from time to time, engaged the attention of the Christian world.

The points in dispute, to which the Apostles chiefly directed their labours, were such as concerned either fundamental articles of Faith, or the terms of Salvation and Acceptance. St. Paul opposed the proud self-righteousness of both Jew and Greek:—St. James, the Solifidian and Antinomian Heretics:—St. John, the oppugners of our Lord's twofold nature, Divine and human. In the two succeeding centuries, the various sects of Gnostics, with the heresies of Marcion, Praxeas, Sabellius, and others, and the enthusiastic notions of Montanus and his followers, gave occasion to very full discussions of points on which the whole system of the Gospel is founded. In the three next centuries were carried on the great contests with Manicheans, Arians, Macedonians, and Pelagians; involving likewise the very essentials of Christian doctrine. After this, the rage of controversy, on points of such magnitude, abated. But during the long interval which ensued of cessation from these disputes, little of real value was added to the stores of theological knowledge. Systems were formed, elaborate, subtle, and voluminous: but for what they contained of sterling worth they were chiefly indebted to the works which had preceded them. And for want of better occupation, new and frivolous topics of disputation were started; corruptions innumerable were engrafted upon the pure and simple Faith; and the human mind retrograded rather than advanced in its knowledge of Sacred truth. With the Reformation, revived again the spirit of inquiry. The advocate of truth had fresh provocations from Error and Falsehood (from bigotry and corruption on the one hand, and from false Philosophy, Fanaticism, or Imposture on the other) to buckle on his armour and take the field. Papal Scholastics were to be driven from the strong holds, in which they had entrenched themselves, of Church-authority. Christian Worship was to be purged of idolatries and superstitions scarcely exceeded by Pagan abominations. The great fundamental points of the sufficiency of Scripture as the Rule of Faith, of Original Sin, of Free-will and Grace, of Faith and Works, and of the nature and efficacy of the Sacraments, were to be cleared on the one side from many of the grossest errors, and guarded on the other side against the efforts of perverse disputers entirely to overthrow them. Here commenced the labours of the wise and good, the learned and the pious, to restore the truth to its primitive lustre, and to retrace the ground already gone over by its first defenders. To the light thus continually shed upon Scripture-doctrine, we of the present day are chiefly indebted for whatever of more accurate or more extensive information we may have obtained. And were we to dismiss from the mass of our theological stores that portion of it only which is purely controversial in form and substance, so great would be the defalcation, that its loss could not but be instantly felt as a general calamity. To say nothing of the Sacred Writers themselves, we should sacrifice, of ancient times, all or many of the best works of Justin, Tertullian, Clement of Alexandria, Irenæus, Origen, Cyprian, Gregory Nazianzen, Augustin, Jerome, and Cyril;—in the beginning of the Reformation, those of Luther, Melancthon, with a host of powerful associates;—and in more recent times the labours of Stillingfleet, Leslie, Waterland, Law, and Horsley. Where is the student who would be content to forego these treasures?

In speaking therefore of Polemical Divinity, Dr. Hey very justly observes, " the right method of conducting debates or controversies seems to be one of the subjects which every man should attend to, who means to study all things useful for a Divine. Suppose him never to engage in controversy himself, yet in reading with a mere view to acquiring knowledge, he must peruse many-controversial writers. But if he at any time engages in the defence of religious truth (what he thinks such) against error and heresy, he will want right notions of controversy still more: without them, he will be sure to hurt the general interests of Religion, if not the particular interests of that cause which he undertakes to defend." *Divinity Lect.* Vol. i. p. 390.

" If," says Dr. Powell, " the objections of Infidels have called forth the best defences of Religion, the errors of Christians have produced the best explications of it. Whilst its doctrines are variously interpreted, every interpretation is curiously examined. Thus a strict search into the genuine sense of Holy Writ has arisen from our divisions and contests." See his *Charge on Religious Controversies*, in his volume of Discourses, p. 296. See also Bandinel's Bampt. Lect. Serm. VI. p. 205—212. and indeed the whole Discourse on 1 Cor. xi. 19.

P. 5. l. 22. *If it spring from a mere spirit of contention*, &c.] " Sunt quos sola eaque pervicax *contendendi libido* in arenam protrahit, quorum inquies animus primum et jugiter *ipsos* vexat, inde et *alios:* quod hîc quidem eo perniciosius, quo conscientias hominum et religionem turbare res est pessimi exempli. Atque hinc immensa illa undequaque seges, non oblata sed indagata et multa vi protracta. Ne nihil agerent homines, quæsierunt de rebus *futilibus*, non in scholis literatorum tantum,—sed in scholis quoque Theologorum hujusmodi: ubi quanta curiositate *Scholastici* qui vulgo appellantur se immiserint in quæstiones multum inutiles, audaces, ἀνεξερευνήτους, omnibus notum. Inde illæ quas Apostolus nominat βεβήλους κενοφωνίας, 1 Tim. vi. 20. et ejusdem cap. vers. 4. qui languent περὶ ζητήσεις, καὶ λογομαχίας."—" Magni refert in disputatione, præterquam ad *rem*, attendere etiam ad disputantis *animum*; quo animo sua agat, quid respiciat, quo collimat: sæpeque discernenti apparebit, unam thesin ab illo teneri, non adeo propter se ac propter aliam. Unde discrimen controversiarum sequitur, in *primarias* et *secundarias*, vel principales et consequentes, quæ ex præcedentibus oboriuntur."— " Deinde ex illis sequitur aliud hîc etiam discrimen observandum, inter *controversiam* et ejus *momentum*: illic qualitas, hîc controversiæ quantitas attenditur. Nam prout grave aut leve est momentum, ita controversia æstimatur, et vel incitanda est vel remittenda. *Pro veritate* ut respondeatur, *ipsa* exigit: sed *quantum* responderi debeat, ex ejus dijudicandum est *momento*; præsertim quando veritati vindicandæ jam factum satis videri queat, et observari ultra debet, ne a charitate latius quam a veritate discedatur."—*Hoornbeck Summa Controv. Relig.* 12mo. 1653. p. 28—31.

P. 6. last line. *Religious controversy is maintained, because agreement in the truth is not otherwise to be effected.*]— " Postquam eo tandem religionis res devenere, ut disputationibus præcipue agi videatur, peculiare et non minimum Theologici studii argumentum fuit hoc quod in tractandis ejus occupatur *controversiis*. Siquidem non instituere jam solum, et tradere dogmatica Theologiæ, vel solam praxin præscribere, prout nunc res sunt, sufficit; nisi et in singulis etiam Theologiæ capitibus adversarios denotemus, et movere controversiam aut discutere, disputationem instituere, et vel corroborare argumentis veritatem, vel falsitatem et errores redarguere etiam, atque diluere queamus." *Hoornbeck, ut supra*, p. 2.

" Occasions," says bishop Horsley, " will from time to time arise, when the truth must not only be taught, but defended. The stubborn Infidel will raise objections against the first principles of our Faith: and objections must be answered. The restless spirit of Scepticism will suggest difficulties in the system, and create doubts about the particulars of the Christian doctrine: difficulties must be removed, and doubts must be satisfied. But above all, the scruples must be composed, which the refinements of a false Philosophy, patronised as they are in the present age by men no less amiable for the general purity of their manners than distinguished for their scientific attainments, will be too apt to raise in the minds of their weaker brethren. And this is the service to which they, whom the indulgence of Providence hath released from the more laborious offices of the Priesthood, stand peculiarly engaged. To them their more occupied brethren have a right to look up, in these emergencies, for support and succour in the common cause. It is for them to stand forth the champions of the common faith, and the advocates of their order. It is for them to wipe off the aspersions injuriously cast upon the sons of the Establishment, as uninformed in the true grounds of the doctrine which they teach, or insincere in the belief of it. To this duty they are indispensably obliged, &c." See *Tracts in Controversy with Dr. Priestley*, pp. 4, 5.

P. 7. l. 9. *Nevertheless, there prevails, in the present day, a spurious kind of liberality*, &c.]—A disposition of this kind has, indeed, been manifested in former ages of the Church, as well as in the present. " All agree," says Dr. Puller, " that Moderation is an excellent virtue: as they said of Hercules, Who ever dispraised him?—St. Austin tells us, (contra Gaudentium, l. 2.) that the Donatists, though both they and the Circumcellions were intolerably severe to the Catholics when they had power, yet were great advocates for liberty of conscience in the free practice of it: which because Julian the Apostate granted them, in crafty design to confound Christianity, how did they magnify him as a mighty moderate Prince, and set up his image?

And Ecclesiastic History abounds with instances of Heretics, who invaded the Church by this serpentine way of insinuation, entering in by all supple accommodation to the innocence and mildness of the dove: but afterwards they appeared of another spirit." See *Moderation of the Ch. of England*, p. 3—7.

Dr. Jackson has also shrewdly observed, that " it was when men grew weary of the religious broils and dissensions in the primitive Church, and became, in consequence, slothful in the search of the Scriptures, that Satan himself, who had sown the seeds of the former dissensions, was content to turn peacemaker for his own advantage; and laid the foundation of that modern Babel, the Church of Rome, which was ready to incorporate itself with barbarous Heresies, Heathenish rites, and several kinds of Paganisms, to please the gross palates of the Goths, Vandals, Huns, Alans, Franks, and Saxons; who all were content to embrace this mixture or new confused mass."—" And to speak properly," says he, " that Unity whereof the adversary so much boasts, since that flourishing age of Fathers, wherein contentions were so rife, and the Roman Church no better esteemed than some of her Sisters, was not a positive consent in the sincere truth, wrought by the Spirit of God, (as a perfect homogeneal mixture by true and lively heat,) but rather a bare negation of actual dissension, caused by a dull confusion of the dregs of error, coagulated and congealed together by ignorance, carelessness, sloth, negligence, and want of zeal for the truth." *Jackson's Works*, vol. i. p. 278.

Hoornbeck too has remarked, that no persons are more impatient of opposition to their own opinions, than those who clamour most for peace and concord with all Christian Sects:—" Verum ita videmus vulgo, nullos magis homines impotentius ferre dissentientes a se, et suis reprehensoribus inclementius dicere, quam qui pacem clamitant cum omnibus sectis inter Christianos ineundam, nullasque hîc dissentiones spectandas invicem esse." *Summa Contr. Rel.* p. 430.

With respect to the prevalence of this lukewarm spirit in

our own times, the following animated passage occurs in Whitaker's Origin of Arianism. It was published in 1792, but is not inapplicable to the present time.—" In this kingdom, and at this period, we may mark a rising aversion to theological controversy. We see it stealing upon the minds of scholars, and giving a tincture to their sentiments. It is only *beginning* at present. It carries, therefore, a faint and dubious appearance with it. But it *is* beginning. And the operations of it, if not checked, will speedily shew themselves in a frigid apathy of moderation, concerning all the fundamental articles of our Religion.

" This new and dangerous sort of Stoicism may be attributed perhaps by some, to the surfeit which the nation has taken of such controversy; from the long and sharp disputes, that have been maintained among us for more than a century past. The human mind is very apt, in its weakness, to be influenced by accidents, to catch the colour of the objects passing beside it, and to reflect them back in its practice. But this is evidently not the cause of that aversion to theological controversy, which is beginning to shoot up in the nation, at present. The disputes about *civil* points during the same period of time, have been as sharp and as long, as concerning articles of Theology. Liberty, in particular, has been even more earnestly contended for, by the three or four last generations of Britons, than any one doctrine in the creed of Christianity. Yet we can discover no aversion to such disputes, starting up in the mind of the nation, and preparing to betray the cause it has so firmly supported. We see indeed the very reverse. The flame of liberty, which has burned so fiercely in the bosom of this kingdom, still keeps up its ardours there; while the warmth for the leading doctrines of Religion is gradually cooling in the heart. And this striking contrast, in the two parts of the national character, serves strongly to shew us the real reason for the latter. Religion is losing its weight, in the scale of the public opinions. A rectitude of sentiment in Religion, therefore, is no longer considered of so much importance as it was. Where the substance is sinking in its efficacy upon the heart, the incidents must necessarily fall off in their consequence with the mind. And political objects still appear momentous in the eyes of our people, still agitate their understandings, and inflame their spirits; because temporal interests still retain their original hold upon their affections.

"While there is any life of Religion actuating the great body of this island, there must and will be controversies in Theology. While the grand code of Christianity exercises the attention, and fastens upon the passions of our people, there will be weakness of intellect to be set right, and perverseness of conduct to be corrected, by the Clergy. These are to stand around the altars of the Gospel, to keep up the fire of Religion there in all its power, and to maintain it in all its purity. Nor will they be found unfaithful to their charge, while there is any spring of theological activity in the clerical mind, and while there are any energies of religious zeal in the clerical heart. When they come to nod beside the altar; to slumber over the dying flame; or to look on with a stupid unconcern, while wretched men are heaping false and unhallowed fuel upon it; then irreligion has finished its course among us. A spiritual frost has spread its influence through the body. It has benumbed the extremities. It is come to the heart. And, like a poor man stretched out upon the snows of the Alps, the nation will then be angry at those, who disturb its rest in order to save it; will then beg to be allowed a little longer repose upon its bed of ice; and feel a kind of pleasing serenity, gliding gradually through all its veins, stopping up one by one all the avenues of life, and hastening on to quench the last spark of vitality, by seemingly lulling it into a gentle sleep." P. 1—4. See also another splendid passage on the special duties of the Clergy in this respect, in Bp. Horsley's Tracts in Controversy with Priestley, p. 72—75.

P. 18. l. 15. *We must nevertheless examine it, as it is delivered to us, clothed in the language of men,* &c.] Dr. Waterland observes, "When we say that Scripture is *perfect*, we mean generally as to the *matter* of it, which is full and complete to be a rule of life and manners, without taking in any *additional* rule to join with it. But if we speak of Scripture being *perfect* in regard to *words* or *style*, we can mean only that it is as perfect as *words* can be, and words, to us now, of a *dead* language. Whatever imperfection necessarily goes along with *all* languages, must of course go along with *Scripture*-language; which though dictated from Heaven, and conducted by the Spirit of God, is yet adapted to the manner of men, and must take its construction from the common rules of interpretation agreed upon among men." *Importance of the Trinity*, p. 397.

On the general subject of this Discourse, the reader is referred to the following works :—Hey's Divinity Lectures, b. ii. c. 1, 2, 5. Powell's Charge on Religious Controversy, in his Volume of Sermons. Puller's Moderation of the Church of England, 1679, chap. 1, 2. Brett's Sermon on True Moderation, 1714. Clagett's Sermons, 1699, vol. i. Serm. ii. iii. viii. Bandinel's Bampton Lectures, Serm. vi. Hoornbeck, Summa Controversiarum, 12mo. 1653, Dissertatio prooemialis, p. 1—58. Hoornbeck, Socinianismus confutatus, 4to. 1650, tom. i. Apparatus ad Controversiam.

SERMON II.

P. 28. l. 4. *But though this censure was specially applied to the Jews, it is not to be restricted to them alone.*]
" The promise is universal in respect to the *object*, being made to all, *If any man will do His will;* no man who is capable of being sincere and honest is excluded. It is also universal in respect of the *matter* of it;—*he shall know of the doctrine*, i. e. of the whole doctrine, whatsoever is necessary or greatly profitable to the end of knowledge. He shall not therefore only learn in general that the doctrine of Christianity is of God, but the particular doctrines that are so: so likewise he shall know the same things better than he did before." *Clagett's Sermons*, vol. ii. p. 272. ed. 1699. Dr. South also observes, " Our Lord states the whole argument upon this issue, that the arguments by which his

doctrine addressed itself to the minds of men were proper, adequate, and sufficient to compass their respective ends in persuading or convincing the persons to whom they were proposed; and moreover that there was no such defect in the natural light of man's understanding, or knowing faculty, but that, considered in itself, it would be apt enough to close with and yield its assent to the evidence of those arguments duly offered to and laid before it. And yet, that after all this, the event proved otherwise, and that notwithstanding both the weight and fitness of the arguments to persuade, and the light of man's intellect to meet this persuasive evidence with a suitable assent, no assent followed, nor were men thereby actually persuaded, he charges it wholly upon the corruption, the perverseness, and the vitiosity of man's will, as the only cause that rendered all the arguments his doctrine came clothed with unsuccessful. And consequently he affirms here in the text, that men must love the truth before they thoroughly believe it; and that the Gospel has then only a free admission into the assent of the understanding, when it brings a passport from a rightly-disposed will, as being the great faculty of dominion that commands all, that shuts out and lets in what objects it pleases, and, in a word, keeps the keys of the whole soul." *South's Sermons*, vol. i. p. 217, 218.

P. 29. l. 17. *It implies a readiness to abide by such a knowledge.*] " It was a custom generally received in the schools of the ancient Philosophers, to spend some time in trying and examining the genius and disposition of their scholars before they admitted them to their ἀκροάματα, the more abstruse and sublimer parts of their philosophy; and the Platonists particularly laid down several rules for the purgation of the soul, for refining and purifying it from the contagion of the body, the infection it might have contracted from the sensitive life, in order to fit and prepare it for the contemplation of intellectual and abstracted truths: and in like manner our Lord and Master here instructs his disciples and followers, what frame and temper of mind to bring along with them when they apply themselves to the study of His most excellent Philosophy. They must live in conformity to the will of God so far as it is made known to them, walk according to their present light, and be ready and willing to improve in their obedience in proportion to the knowledge they shall have of what He requires of them." *Dr. W. Pearson's Serm.* p. 227, 228. ed. 1718.

P. 40. l. 25. *Ask and ye shall have,* &c.] Dr. Pearson, after quoting other texts to the same purpose, observes, " Though these promises of supernatural assistance made to good men do not reach to an exemption from all errors, or give them any assurance of a security from making any mistakes in matters of Religion; yet this they may be assured of, that while they continue so, they shall not fall into any such errors as shall be destructive of their salvation. For supposing that they believe the Scriptures to be the Word of God and the infallible rule of Faith; that the sense of them which God intended is certainly true, whatever it is; and that they use their best endeavours to find out that true sense, and live and practise according to the light and knowledge they have;—we may safely conclude, first, that it is impossible but that they should believe all those things which relate to the Covenant between God and man in Christ Jesus; because they are so plainly delivered and so frequently inculcated, that men of the meanest capacities, with their own care and diligence, in conjunction with the aids and assistances that God hath appointed, and in the due use of them, may attain to a sufficient knowledge thereof:—And secondly, as for those Scripture verities which are not so intrinsecally necessary in themselves, but to be believed upon the account of God's veracity, because they are revealed; I think we may likewise safely conclude, that if any good Christian, after he has used his best endeavours, that is, has taken such pains and care as ordinary prudence and discretion shall advise him to in a matter of the highest importance, to find out the true sense of them, fail, notwithstanding all this, of attaining to it; either God in his Providence will find out some way to convince him of his error, and bring him to the acknowledgment of the Truth, or else that error will not be fatal to him. . . . For, God can never be supposed to punish any good man eternally, that is desirous above all things to do His will, for such mistakes as, with all his care and diligence, he could not perceive or discover to be so." *Serm. ut supra,* p. 237, 239.

P. 41. l. 17. *The main source of all contentions. . . . may be traced to some reluctance to renounce prepossessions.*] " Alius sequitur [sc. morbus,] cujus contagium et longe latius serpit et multo funestiorem stragem in re exegetica edit, *præconceptarum opinionum lues.* Hæc uti in veritate invenienda deterrimas intellectui tenebras offundit, ita quin ad eandem e sacris literis eruendam ineptissimum reddat animum, nemo ad rem attentior pernegabit. *Is enim demum,* ut recte judicat Hilarius, [lib. i. de Trin. p. xi. ed. Par. 1652.] *optimus Scripturæ lector* (adde et interpres) *est, qui dictorum intelligentiam exspectet potius ex dictis, quam imponit; et retulerit magis, quam attulerit; neque hoc cogit videri dictis contineri, quod ante lectionem præsumpserat intelligendum.* At enimvero in contraria potius quævis abripitur interpres præjudicatis opinionibus occæcatus. Non ille Spiritus Sancti mentem e verbis eruere et in apricum proferre satagit, sed suam potius aliorumve clarorum virorum sententiam in Scripturis quærit, quasque jam antea mente conceperat ideas, ex oraculorum cælestium verbis extundit. Quo vitio num quid inveniri queat quod magis interpretis muneri adversetur, ipsi judicent prudentiores." *Rambachii Exerc. Hermeneut.* p. 10, 11. ed. Jenæ. 12mo. 1728.

P. 42. l. 23. *Rashness.*] " Neque tamen minus absit intempestive sedula *temeritas,* omnisque in definiendo dictorum sensu *præcipitantia*[a], fœcunda pravarum interpretationum mater. Recte Comicus, τὰ πολλὰ τολμᾶν, πολλ' ἁμαρτάνειν ποιεῖ. *Qui multa audet, multa peccat.* Quod qui ad interpretem temerarium applicaverit, nihil dixerit cui experientia refragetur." *Ibid.* p. 31.

---

[a] Præcipitantia illa ex variis causis oritur, ut ex philautia, ex impatientia laboris, ex animo novaturiente, ex ambitione et famæ cupiditate, ex pudore illegitimo, ex vivaciore ingenio gratia divina nondum subacto, ex rerum denique quæ similes videntur confusione.

Ibid. l. 24. *Self-conceit.*] " Ante omnia, fertilis iste radix, *arrogantia* et *vanæ gloriæ cupido*, ex animo interpretis extirpanda, imisque, si pote, fibris refellenda est. Illa enim illum ubi semel in transversum egit, dici non potest quanta malorum, ineptiarumque seges inde efflorescat. Neque enim de eo amplius solicitus erit, ut genuinum cujuslibet loci sensum et reperiat ipse et repertum aliis ostendat; sed ut ex doctis suis ingeniosisque scripturarum expositionibus laudem ac gloriam aucupetur. Hinc molitur interpretationes de quibus ante ipsum ne per somnium quidem quisquam unquam cogitavit. Prætervehitur ea loca ex quibus maxima ad se aliosque pervenire utilitas queat: ad obseptos difficultatibus nodos, ad dubia vexata, ad cruces criticorum, arrogantiæ stimulis impulsus, provehitur. Nunquam aut tu ab ipso, aut ipse à se impetrare poterit, ut se non omnia pernoscere, verum hinc inde hærere nihilque certi definire posse fateatur. Nihil est in Scripturis quod nesciat, &c." Ibid. p. 36—38.

P. 43. l. 19. *We are not to wonder then*, &c.] " Poscitur hic *simplex* et *humilis* animus. Vis in doctrina Christi proficere? primam hujus lectionem bene imbibe et in succum et sanguinem converte, *Discite a me, quia sum mitis et humilis corde*. Nullus hic ad judicandum aptior est, quam *simplicitate et humilitate puerulis* similis; ingenuis illis puerulis, sine artificio, sine fastu. Nullus aptior, quam qui *omnem altitudinem, extollentem se adversus scientiam DEI, in captivitatem redigere didicit, omnemque intellectum in obsequium Christi*. Sed ista herba num in doctorum præcipue hortulis crescit? Inter eos, quos plerumque *scientia inflat?* Inter illa gloriæ animalia, ad quæ potissimum directa sunt verba, *Quomodo vos potestis credere, cum gloriam alii ab aliis captetis, et gloriam illam quæ a solo DEO proficiscitur non quæratis?* Quoties hujus ordinis hominibus contingit, quod Augustinus sibi in lectione S. Scripturæ contigisse confitetur; *Tumor meus*, inquit, *refugiebat modum ejus, et acies mea non penetrabat interiora ejus. Verumtamen illa erat quæ cresceret cum parvulis. Sed ego dedignabar esse parvulus, et turgidus fastu mihi grandis videbar.* Confess. lib. iii. cap. 5. Adde, quod tumor ille, qui plerumque ex sublimi de sapientia sua opinione oritur, necessario plurimorum errorum causa sit. Reddit enim homines in judicando præcipites, in decidendo audaces, in sententia semel lata immobiles, in ea aliis obtrudenda violentos, rationes aliorum superbe fastidientes, ad eorum monita surdos, monitoribus asperos, in erroribus denique vitandis incautos, et, sicubi errarunt, corrigi nescios." *Werenfelsii Opusc.* tom. i. p. 29, 30. ed. Lugd. Bat. 4to. 1772.

P. 44. l. 16. *They who, to a grasp of intellect above their fellows, have united the profoundest humility and reverence, in exploring the depths of heavenly wisdom.*] There is an admirable passage in Bp. Horsley's Letters in Controversy with Dr. Priestley, where he relates the progress of his own inquiries into the doctrine of the Trinity. It occurs in the seventeenth Letter, from p. 276 to 296, and affords a striking instance of the happy effect, produced upon a manly and ingenuous mind endowed with uncommon powers, by the influence of those principles and sentiments by which every investigation of Revealed Religion ought to be directed. This the following extracts will sufficiently evince. " I believe, Sir, that few have thought so much upon these subjects as you and I have done, who have not at first wavered. Perhaps, nothing but the uneasiness of doubt, added to a just sense of the importance of the question, could engage any man in the toil of the inquiry. For my own part, I shall not hesitate to confess, that I set out with great scruples. But the progress of my mind has been the very reverse of your's. It was at first my principle, as it is still your's, that all appearance of difficulty in the doctrine of the Gospel must arise from misinterpretation; and I was fond of the expedient of getting rid of mystery by supposing a figure in the language. The harshness of the figures which I sometimes had occasion to suppose, and the obvious uncertainty of all figurative interpretations, soon gave me a distrust of this method of expounding; and Butler's Analogy cured me of the folly of looking for nothing mysterious in the true sense of a Divine Revelation. By this cure I was prepared to become an easy convert to the doctrine of Atonement and Satisfaction; which seemed to furnish incentives to piety that no other doctrine could supply. I soon perceived how the value of the Atonement was heightened, and what a sublimity accrued to the whole doctrine of Redemption, by the notion, clearly conveyed in the Scriptures literally taken, of a Redeemer descending from a previous state of glory, to become our Teacher, and to make the expiation. Thus I was brought to a full persuasion of our Lord's pre-existent dignity. Having once admitted his pre-existence in an exalted state, I saw the necessity of placing him at the head of the creation..... Being thus convinced that our Lord Jesus Christ is indeed the Maker of all things; I found that I could not rest satisfied with the notion of a Maker of the universe *not God*. I saw that all the errors of the Gnostics hung upon that one principle: and I could have little opinion of the truth of a principle, which seemed so big with mischief. I then set myself to consider, whether I knew enough of the Divine Unity, to pronounce the Trinity an infringement of it. Upon this point, the Platonists, whose acquaintance I now began to cultivate, soon brought me to a right mind." p. 279—281. Contending, nevertheless, for a free exercise of the reasoning powers, unfettered by implicit deference to human authority, he proceeds, " There is in most men a culpable timidity; you and I perhaps have overcome that general infirmity; but there is in most men a culpable timidity, which inclines them to be easily overawed by the authority of great names: and much as we talk of the freedom and liberality of thinking and inquiry, it is this slavish principle, not, as it is pretended, any freedom of original thought, which makes converts to infidelity and heresy. Fools imagine, that the greatest authorities are always on the side of new and singular opinions; and that, by adopting them, they get themselves into better company than they have naturally any right to keep: and thus they are secretly worshippers of authority in that very act in which they pretend to fly in the face of it. They worship private authority, while they fly in the face of universal. They deride an old and general tradition, because they have not sagacity to trace the connection of its parts, and to perceive the force of the entire evidence: and while they thus trample on the accumulated authority of ages, with an ideot simplicity they suffer themselves to be led by the mere name of the writer of the day, a Bolingbroke, a Voltaire, a Gibbon, or a Priestley; as if they thought to become wise and learned, by taking a share and an interest in the follies, or the party views, of men of abilities and learning. And where a secret consciousness of ignorance is not accompanied with the vain ambition of being thought wise, still an undue deference to private authority in prejudice of established opinion, seems to be the side upon which even modest men are liable to err. Insomuch that every man may be supposed to partake of this infirmity, in subjects in which he feels himself unlearned." P. 282, 283.

P. 45. l. 5. *Rather misled by weak and erroneous judgment, than by deliberate and intentional opposition to the Divine will.*] " I am hopeful," says Bishop Horsley, " that there is more folly in the world than malignity; more ignorance than positive infidelity; more error than heretical perverseness." *Ut supra*, p. 284. It deserves however to be considered, that heresy and schism may be more dangerous, in one respect, than sins of moral turpitude; because the latter have a tendency, as soon as they are reflected upon, to awaken shame and humiliation; while the former are wont to inflate the mind with pride and self-sufficiency, and thus operate to preclude any disposition to relinquish them. " It is sometimes pleaded," says Dr. Waterland, " that *a wicked life is the worst heresy;* intimating as if breaches made in our most holy Faith were of slight consideration, so long as a man lives a good moral life in other respects. I readily allow that a wicked life is the worst thing imaginable; but I conceive further, that the spreading and propagating of corrupt doctrines is leading a *wicked life* in the strictest sense. I speak not of mere mistakes in judgment, but of *espousing* and *propagating* them; corrupting the Faith in important articles, and diffusing such corruption. A life so spent is a wicked life, if opposing Divine truths, undermining the Gospel, and subverting souls, be wicked attempts; as they undoubtedly are."——" We will allow that an heretic in matters of mere *Revelation* is not so bad a man, generally speaking, as an heretic in *morality:* but still he may be a much worse man, or, to speak plainer, may do a great deal more mischief by his *doctrine*, than the immoral man by his *example*. For, besides his propagating dangerous errors, subverting souls, it is further to be considered, that he sets himself up as a *rival* teacher, in opposition to the faithful Ministers of Christ."——Again: " To advance falsehoods, and in points very material, tending to create infinite disturbances here, as well as to betray many to perdition hereafter, these are crimes unpardonable, if the authors *see* what they do; and if they do not, yet their guilt remains, if they *might* see, and will not. However, the nature and the quality of the thing is not altered by their seeing, or not seeing. For, heresy is still heresy, though a man intends well, as much as persecution is still persecution, though a person thinks and believes that he does God service in it." *Importance of the Doctrine of the Trinity*, p. 143, 146, 147. ed. 1734. See also p. 154—170.

" Vario autem modo circa Veritates fundamentales errari potest: vel enim aliquis bona fide errat ex ignorantia, qui tamen capitur amore cognitionis Veritatis et sincera Pietate imbutus meliora scire desiderat, et mansueta convictione facile in veram viam reducitur, dum non pertinaciter sententiæ suæ insistit, sed veritati demonstratæ lubens manus victas præbet. Vel secundo aliquis errorem fundamentalem ita propugnat, ut, pensitata bene utraque doctrina et ponderatis utrorumque argumentis, tamen falsis ratiociniis deceptus, se ipsissimam tueri veritatem arbitratur, et officii sui esse censet contra quosvis dogma suum defendere et disseminare. Dantur denique, qui pravis affectibus imbuti atque impietatis vi ducti, adeoque ex voluntate plane corrupta, hæreses disseminant. Ex his patet, tres fundamentaliter Errantium esse ordines, qui omnes eodem censu haberi non possunt. *Primi* enim, in veritate informandi et convincendi, dum in erroribus non persistunt, Hæreticorum nomen non merentur. *Secundi* et *Tertii* ordinis vero, dum falsas propositiones suas acriter defendunt et maxima cum pertinacia, omni veritatis demonstratione posthabita, in placitis suis persistunt, Hæretici characterem habent..... Quorum dissensus fundamentalis est, iisdem Sacris uti nequeunt, sed ab Ecclesiastica illorum communione abstinendum est." *Stapferi Inst. Theol. Polem.* tom. i. p. 558—561.

" Non enim nunc *quodcunque adversus veritatem sapit*, Hæresin voco cum Tertulliano. *Non omnis error Hæresis est; quamvis omnis Hæresis, quæ in vitio ponitur, nisi errore aliquo Hæresis esse non possit;* scite alicubi observat Augustinus. Sed errorem intelligo gravem, ab hominibus veræ Ecclesiæ fidem profitentibus, contra Ecclesiæ veræ doctrinam Scripturis conformem, in capitibus præcipue necessariis et fundamentalibus, introductum et defensum. Qualis haud ineleganter *Hæreseos*, sive *Electionis* et *Optionis* nomine venire solet, si ad originem et communiorem vocabuli Græci significationem spectes : siquidem nobis, ductum Magistri unici in verbo divinitus inspirato loquentis sequi jussis, nihil in Religione ejusque doctrina nostro arbitrio indulgere licet; sed nec eligere quod alter de arbitrio suo induxerit." *De Moor, Comment. in Marckii Compendium*, tom. vi. p. 858, 859. ed. Lugd. Bat. 4to. 1771.

See also, on the general subject of this Discourse, Aug. Pfeifferi Hermeneut. Sacr. cap. 4. Buddei Inst. Theol. lib. i. cap. 1. sect. 54. Hoornbeck, Summ. Controv. p. 35—51. Fabricii de Verit. Rel. Chr. p. 491—499. Jackson's Works, vol. i. p. 238—249.

SERMON III.

P. 51. l. 2. *Their sufficiency is the controverted point.*]
" Tradit Scriptura res Religionis *perfecte* et *sufficienter*. Bellarminus, lib. iv. de Verbo Dei, cap. 4. probare satagit, *Quod Scripturæ non omnia ita contineant, ut sufficiant ipsæ sine alia traditione,* vide tom. i. Controv. col. 211.

Nos ex adverso tenemus Scripturæ *perfectionem*, per quam illa sola sit regula totalis et adæquata fidei et morum. Non requiritur ad hanc perfectionem ut contineat *omnes res gestas aut sermones Salvatoris et Apostolorum cunctos*, cujusmodi plura in S. Scriptura non reperiri ultro agnoscimus.—Non requirimus quoque ad hanc perfectionem, ut Scriptura complectatur *ritus temporarios aut externos quosvis*, quorum ordinatio prudentiæ Præfectorum Ecclesiæ relicta est; et circa quos sufficere potest, si communis Apostoli observetur regula, ut *omnia decenter atque ordine fiant*. Eam solum volumus Scripturæ *perfectionem*, *per quam contineat omnia ad salutem necessaria, tum creditu, tum factu:* ut nihil opus sit extra Scripturam ad verbum quoddam ἄγραφον confugere, quod traditiones aliquas dogmaticas vel ethicas suppeditet, quæ ubi deficit Scriptura non minus atque illa pro norma fidei et morum sint habendæ. . . . Nec necesse est, ut omnia creditu factuve necessaria legantur in Scriptura *explicite*, αὐτολεξεὶ, κατὰ τὸ ῥητὸν, totidem verbis; sufficit si reperiantur illic vel *implicite*, κατ' ἰσοδυναμίαν, *per æquivalentiam*, κατὰ διάνοιαν, *secundum sensum*, κατὰ συνακολούθησιν, ita ut per legitimam consequentiam ex Scriptura deduci queant." *De Moor, Comment. in Marckii Compend.* tom. i. p. 342, 343.

P. 51. l. 26. *There are indeed texts both in the Old and New Testament, which, if understood as relating to the whole Sacred Canon, might seem to put the question beyond dispute.*] " It is on all hands granted, that there must be some Authority which Faith is resolved into: for Faith is no other than an assent to some proposition or propositions upon authority: and according as the Authority is, such is our Faith, human or Divine. So that Divine Faith must have Divine Authority; and Divine Authority is no other than Divine Revelation, delivered *at sundry times, and in divers manners*, written or unwritten. And where there is no verbal Revelation by Persons divinely inspired, the written Word is the only Authority that Faith can be resolved into; which our Saviour appeals to, [bidding the Jews *search the Scriptures*,] and propounds as a means sufficient, and in their circumstances the only means for ending the dispute.... In like manner did the Apostles proceed to convince the Jews of their incredulity: so St. Paul *reasoned with them out of the Scriptures, opening and alleging, that the Christ must needs have suffered and risen again from the dead, and that this Jesus is the Christ.* So Apollos *shewed by the Scriptures, that Jesus was the Christ.* To this they always remitted them, as to a rule certain and sufficient, and without which nothing was to be received as an article of Faith. To a rule certain, called therefore by St. Peter *a more sure word of Prophecy,* and which he prefers before a voice from heaven. And a rule sufficient; that is, as St. Paul saith, *able to make wise unto salvation,* and *thoroughly to furnish* even *the man of God,* the Teacher, *unto all good works.* And when these were spoken at that time more immediately of the *Jewish* Canon of the *Old Testament,* they may equally as well be applied to the *New;* which is not only as much the *Scripture,* as St. Peter calls it, (2 Pet. iii. 16.) but also by the addition of it renders the *Old* more intelligible and complete. Now there can be no imaginable reason assigned, why the Scripture, which was then sufficient in all points necessary to salvation, and for resolving of Faith, should now be insufficient after the Revelation made by Christ: that is, that we should be more at a loss with the more clear, full, and perfect Revelation, than they were under the less perfect; that what in the *last days* God delivered and revealed by *his Son,* should be less sufficient to direct us, than what he spake *at sundry times, and in divers manners, in times past,* to the Jews, *by the Prophets.* And especially, considering that there was a time when their circumstances were much the same with ours, which was in the long interval of 400 or 450 years, between the finishing of the Jewish Canon in the prophecy of *Malachi,* (with whom Revelation ceased,) and the appearance of *John Baptist:* in which time they were left, as we are, wholly to the written Word of God for their direction, and the sole Authority they were to rely upon." *Bp. Williams's Boyle's Lect.* Serm. 10.

De Moor, above quoted, in his Commentary on Marckius, observes on the text, Ps. xiv. 8. " Perfectio autem et

Sufficientia illa *Legis* intelligenda est pro ratione Œconomiæ istius, ut additis reliquis libris Vet. et Novi Test. ad illos qui tum extabant, præsens Scripturæ Perfectio, argumento a minori ad majus liquido adstruatur." tom. i. p. 344. This argument, however, has often been contested : and, perhaps, its real force is sometimes misconceived: which rests not, as I apprehend, upon any enlarged application of this or other particular texts to the entire Canon of the New Testament now extant; but upon the analogy between the circumstances of the Jews, or the primitive Christians, and our own. The expressions used by the Sacred Writers, whether of the Old or New Testament, in speaking of the Word of God, evidently go to the extent of asserting its perfection in itself, and its sufficiency for those on whom it was bestowed. The appeal to it also, whenever such appeal is made either by our Lord or his Apostles, is no less clearly grounded on the supposition that it was sufficient for the conviction and satisfaction of the persons whom they addressed. The Old Testament was sufficient to bring the Jews to the knowledge of the Messiah when he should appear, and to the reception of the Gospel when it should be promulgated to them. The Jews, whom our Lord conversed with, are considered, on this ground, as without excuse. The persons, to whom the Apostles addressed their discourses or writings, are also pressed by them with arguments drawn from the Scriptures then extant, which are always appealed to as fully sufficient to enable them to judge of the reasoning set before them. What writings of the New Testament, whether Gospels or Epistles, might be in circulation among the primitive Christians at the time when these references to Scripture were made, it is not material to inquire. Their gradual increase arose out of the immediate exigencies of the Church : and so long as the Evangelists and Apostles lived, accessions were made to the Written Word; and, by the good providence of God, so many of them as might be necessary for the edification of the Church in after-times, have been preserved and transmitted from generation to generation. The argument, therefore, stands thus: that if the *fewer* portions of Holy Writ then extant; if the Old Testament alone, or accompanied with only certain portions of the New; were spoken of by the inspired preachers of that day as full, perfect, and sufficient for general edification; we may, with unhesitating confidence, affirm the same, κατ᾽ ἐξοχὴν, of the *entire* collection as it now exists. Nay, we may no less confidently argue, that, since no evidence is adduced, nor even pretended, that there are any *other* books now extant, stamped with the same seal of Divine authority, we have, in the very cessation of these extraordinary means of instruction, an indubitable token of the Divine purpose in this respect. We learn from it, that God, in His infinite wisdom, designed these to be a complete, entire, and sufficient Revelation of His Will, without any ulterior communications of a similar kind. Nothing can invalidate this conclusion but clear evidence from Scripture itself, that unwritten Traditions were afterwards to be admitted as supplementary to the Sacred Writings, and to be placed upon the same level with them in point of authority.

P. 56. l. 6. *The proposed expedient by no means obviates the alleged difficulty.*] " I acknowledge," says Bishop Williams, " the Church of Rome hath put this matter into a far more compendious course, if it were as true as it is short, by an Infallible Judge, who, by an *ipse dixit*, without giving any reason, stamps upon all he saith an uncontrollable authority: but that must be, if a person is so near the Papal Chair as to have the infallible Ear to apply himself to, and immediately receives the dictate from the infallible Oracle. For if he be remote from him, and receives all by written Decrees, or the oral Tradition of others, it issues then into a kind of fallible Rule, and fails to be the sentence of the Infallible Judge. For, words and writings, if they once fall into fallible hands, according to these, cease to be infallible, and are as much subject to difficulties, and about the sense of which have often happened as endless contentions and misunderstandings, as ever they can pretend have happened to an infallible Rule. Therefore, they are no safer, nor less subject to err by the having an infallible *Judge*, than we by an infallible *Rule*." *Boyle's Lect*. Serm. 10.

APPENDIX. 275

The authority of Scripture itself is, however, alleged by Romanists for the Infallibility of the Church. Their chief arguments on this point are drawn from texts in the Old Testament relating to the peculiar circumstances of the Jewish Church, wherein the authority of its Priesthood, and the whole administration of the Government, Civil and Ecclesiastical, were upholden by a miraculous agency. Thus, the Urim and Thummim were to be consulted as infallible Oracles; the responses given by them being the immediate dictates of Divine Inspiration. In matters of controversy also, respecting temporal as well as spiritual concerns, the people were required, on pain of death, to submit to the judgment of the Priests and Levites: and there was a continual interposition of Divine agency to maintain them in that authority. But to argue from hence to the Infallibility of the Christian Priesthood, or to any similar extent of authority in the Christian Church, is altogether irrelevant. See this point fully discussed, and the several texts supposed to relate to it particularly and accurately discussed, by Dr. Bennet, in his *Confutation of Popery*, part i. ch. iv. p. 22—36.

P. 57. l. 11. *The interpreter and the author can never stand upon one and the same footing of authority.*] "When we affirm that the Scriptures are the only infallible rule in matters of Faith and Christian Obedience, we understand such a rule in these matters as Aristotle's Organon may be said of Logic; supposing it were sound, and free from all suspicion of error in every point, and contained in it all the general and undoubted principles, from which all true forms of argumentation must be deduced, and into which all must finally be resolved. To illustrate this truth by a known practice. Our younger students are bound to yield their absolute assent to Aristotle's authority in matters of Logic; but not unto any Interpreter that shall pretend it, save only when he shall make evident unto them that this was Aristotle's meaning. And while they so only, and no otherwise, yield their assent, they yield it wholly and immediately unto Aristotle, not to the Interpreter, although by his means they came to know that this was Aristotle's meaning:

which, once known, without any further confirmation of other testimonies or authority, commands their obedience and assent. But ere they can fully assent unto this their great Master, or thoroughly perceive his meaning, they must conditionally assent unto their private Tutors, or other Expositors, and take his sense and meaning upon their trust and credit. In like manner (say we) in all matters, doctrines, or controversies of Faith and Christian Obedience, we are bound to yield our assent directly, absolutely, and finally, unto the authority of Scripture only, not unto any Doctor, Expositor, or other, whosoever he be, that shall pretend authority out of Scripture over our Faith; save only when he shall make it clear and evident unto us, that his opinion is the true meaning of the Scriptures. And thus yielding our absolute assent unto the Truth explained by him, we yield it not to him, but unto the Author of Truth, whose words we hold to be infallible in whose mouths soever; and once known to be His words, they need not the testimony or authority of him that did bring us to the true knowledge of them." On the other hand, " If we yield the same absolute and undoubted assent unto his authority, which we would do unto God's Word immediately known, in itself and for itself, or rely upon his infallibility in expounding God's Word, as fully as he doth upon the Word, (which it is supposed he knows immediately in itself and for itself,) by doing thus we rob God of his honour; giving that unto man, which is only due to HIM." *Dr. Jackson's Works*, vol. i. b. ii. ch. xi. pp. 224, 225.

P. 61. l. 13. *To them is to be assigned no more than a secondary rank.*] "There are many things of excellent use in themselves, which come to be suspected and reproached, because of the abuse they have had in the Roman Church: of which, *Tradition* may be a great instance. Because the Church of Rome hath made Tradition equal, if not superior, to Holy Scripture; therefore, others run to the other extreme of undervaluing all kind of good and lawful Tradition, not considering that Holy Scripture is Tradition recorded; and forgetting that in the Church of God, one great proof of the integrity of the Canon of the

Holy Scripture itself hath been always Tradition, which these men so confidently despise. There are also some Traditions not contrary to the Holy Scripture, which, if they be rightly qualified, have and ought to have great authority with us. Wherefore upon all occasions is celebrated among us that famous passage of Vincentius Lirinensis, *quod ubique, quod semper, quod ab omnibus creditum est.*" Dr. Puller's *Moderation of the Church of England,* pp. 91, 92.

Many important observations on the degree of attention due to unwritten Traditions occur also in Dr. Hey's Divinity Lectures, b. iv. art. 6. sect. 5. In summing up his judgment upon the question, he makes the following observations: " Whatever particular Traditions we may think it right to set aside, it does not seem as if we ought to entertain any *general* prejudice against every thing that is *unwritten.* For some considerable time, there were comparatively very few written records in the Christian Church: during that time, a good deal must go on Tradition. If we had any verbal directions which had been really given, by Christ or his Apostles, to the newly-formed Churches, we should value them very highly: these indeed seem advantages not to be expected in any degree; but very early *customs* and *practices,* in such Churches, afford so strong a presumption of their having been owing to such *directions,* as to demand our highest respect. And writings of *Fathers* and decrees of *Councils* are to be considered in the same light; that is, as conveying an evidence of something *unwritten:* early *comments,* also, are esteemed, as telling us *received* Interpretations. All these ought to have weight, whenever there is no appearance of *indirect* motives; and when the persons, whose accounts we receive, were competently qualified to inform us. But, whenever we have any reason to distrust, we should be at full liberty to reject every thing of this kind: which is a very different thing from its being held " necessary to salvation." Vol. ii. pp. 468, 469. See also Berriman's L. M. Lect. Serm. i.

P. 62. l. 5. *Unsupported by any solid foundation.*] To these considerations may be added that of the practical evil which appears to have arisen, in the first ages of the Church, from the too ready admission of unwritten Traditions. The proneness to receive these as of equal authority with the Scriptures, probably gave occasion to many spurious and apocryphal productions, and greatly favoured the growth of heretical opinions. Upon such Traditions, either fabricated for the purpose, or erroneously believed to be genuine, some of the earliest Heresies appear to have been founded. Of this, frequent complaints are found in the writings of the Fathers. Lardner, in his History of the Heretics of the two first Centuries, b. i. sect. 11, 12, cites several passages to this effect. He also remarks, "perhaps none of the sects were free from the fault;" and, " most of those apocryphal pieces, whether gospels, or acts, or circuits and travels, or revelations, went under the names of Apostles, or Apostolical men." He adds, " Tertullian writing against the Heretics assures us, that they could not deny, and even owned, that the Apostles knew all the doctrines of the Gospel, and agreed with one another in what they taught. The most they could presume to assert in favour of their peculiarities was, that the Apostles did not declare the whole truth to all:—*sed, ut diximus, eadem dementia est; cum confitentur quidem nihil apostolos ignorâsse, nec diversa inter se prædicâsse; non tamen omnia volunt illos omnibus revelâsse : quædam enim palam, et universis ; quædam secreto, et paucis demandâsse.* De Præscript. Hæret. c. xxv." *Lardner*, ut supra, ed. 4to. 1780.

P. 62. l. 20. *If the Church were judge of faith, it would set her above God.*] In the tract, from which some of these expressions are taken, Leslie has fully argued this point in the form of a Dialogue between the Church of England, the Church of Rome, and the Protestant Dissenter. To the Romanist he observes, " Where any thing is determined by authority, that authority must be superior to what it determines. And thus the Church (supposing it such a judge of Faith) would have an authority above God, or Christ, or any thing contained in the Creed. And therefore I think it is plain, that we receive not the *Creed* upon the authority of the Church. *Rom. Catholic.* You had never had the Creed but by the Church. *Church of*

England. That may be. The Church taught it me; proposed it to me; and convinced me of the truth of it: but not by way of authority; for I could not believe the authority of the Church, till I was first convinced by the Scriptures that Christ had established such a Church, and vested her with such authority. So that I receive the Scriptures upon the testimony, not authority, of the Church: and I examine that authority, as I do other facts, till I have satisfied my private judgment: there is no other way. As suppose an Atheist to be convinced by me of the being of a God: he then believes it, and I may be said to be an instrument in this. But how foolish would it be in me, nay, blasphemous, to assume authority over him for this, and say that it was by my authority that he believed a God, and therefore that he was obliged to believe every thing else I told him, without examining; because if my authority was taken for the being of God, then nothing surely of lesser consequence could be excepted from it. This is the manner of argumentation for receiving the Faith from the authority of the Church: this is that Circle, from which you can never rid yourselves, of believing the Scriptures upon the authority of the Church, and then, back again, of believing the Church upon the authority of the Scriptures. This makes each of them of greater authority than the other, and each of them of lesser! *Dissenter.* You have run down the authority of the Church: I see no authority you have left her. *Church of England.* Because I do not allow her an absolute, unconditional, infallible authority, and that in matters of Faith; you think she has no authority at all. *Dissenter.* Your Twentieth Article (so much contested) says she has *authority in controversies of Faith. Church of England.* Yes, but far from infallible. You see how it is there limited, not to be repugnant to Holy Scripture, &c. She has authority as a Witness and Keeper of Holy Writ, as the Article words it: to determine Controversies of Faith only ministerially, as the ordinary dispensers of the Word, as servants of Christ, and ministers of the Gospel; not absolutely and authoritatively, as lords of our Faith, and infallible interpreters of Scripture." Again, " The Church is the Interpreter of Scripture, as the Judges are of the Law; and they have authority so to interpret; and they judge authoritatively. Yet they are but the ordinary dispensers of the Law, to which an ordinary interpretation of the Law is necessary. But the ultimate interpretation of the Law is only in the Legislative authority; according to the maxim, *cujus est condere ejus est et interpretari*, that is, it belongs to the same power which enacts to interpret. For the makers of the Law best know their own meaning. Thus the Church is the ordinary dispenser, and so far the interpreter of Scripture. But the ultimate decision is in God, and we may still appeal to Him; and must make use of our own private judgment for our understanding it and governing our practice accordingly, in the great points of Faith and Worship."

The above Extracts are from Leslie's Tract, entitled *Of Private Judgment and Authority in Matters of Faith:* and notwithstanding their length, I cannot forbear adding his happy illustration of the whole subject, in the case of a Traveller and his Guides.—" I suppose a man on his road to such a place; and coming where there are three or four different ways, he knows not which to choose. But he finds there several Guides standing, who all pretend to be appointed Guides of that road, and offer their service with equal assurance; each saying that the way he points is the right, and none other. But the Traveller has a chart or plan of the way in his hand, which all the Guides allow to be just and right, and would have him walk by it. Only one tells him he may mistake his plan, therefore desires he would give it up to him; and moreover, that he should be blindfolded, because otherwise he might be disputing the way, which would retard his journey, and besides imply a distrust of his Guide. But another Guide tells him he should keep his plan in his hand, and he would give him leave to examine every step he led him by the plan, and then his own eyes should be judge whether he led him right or not; and he would not desire it should be left in his power to lead him over a precipice with his eyes shut. The Holy Scriptures are the Plan; and the Church of

Rome takes them from the people, lest they dispute about it, and requires them to trust absolutely and blindly to her guidance. The Church of *England* shews her commission to be a guide upon the road to Heaven, derived by succession from the Apostles, with a competent, though not an infallible authority. The *Dissenters* have no commission nor succession to shew; they have thrust themselves as Guides upon this road, of their own heads, not above 150 years ago. And they have no authority either to preach the Word, or to sign and seal the Covenant which God has made with man, in the Holy Sacraments of His institution, nor to bless in His name. This honour they have taken to themselves, which the Apostle says, *no man can take unto himself, but he that is called of God, as was Aaron.*" *Leslie's Works*, folio, vol. i. p. 180—188.

Much more upon this and other topics connected with it may be found in another Tract by Leslie, in the same volume, entitled, *The Case stated between the Churches of Rome and England*. But a small volume recently published by the Margaret Professor of Divinity in Cambridge under a similar title, *A Comparative View of the Churches of England and Rome*, comprises within a short compass so much extensive research, forcible reasoning, and perspicuous illustration of the subject, as almost to supersede the necessity of further investigation. If to this work, however, be added a careful perusal of the two pieces of Leslie just mentioned, together with his *Case of the Regale and of the Pontificate stated*, in the same volume; a clearer view may, perhaps, be taken of some points, upon which it did not fall within the scope of Dr. Marsh's design to dilate. The reader will thus be enabled to form a correct notion of all the principal matters at issue between the parties, and may be effectually guarded against the numberless sophistries with which they are generally obscured and perplexed by the advocates of the Romish Church.

Upon the particular subject of Traditions see also Dr. Hey's Divinity Lectures, article xxxiv. vol. iv. p. 437—456.

P. 67. l. 4. *Gnostics*.] " Sic dicti quotquot ex Simonis, Menandri, Saturnini, Basilidis, Carpocratis, Valentini disciplina prodierunt. Variis quidem inter eos *differentiis*, sed communi *nomine*, quo semet ipsos, statim ab initio, distinxerunt, eodemque superbo, sc. a γνώσει, vere ψευδωνύμῳ, quasi καταξιωθέντες τῆς γνώσεως sublimioris ac mysteriosæ sapientiæ cognitione præcellentes." *Spanhemii Introd. ad Eccl. Hist. N. T.* Sæc. 2. §. 6—" Omnes ætatis illius Sectæ in duas dividi possunt classes; *alii* disciplinam Christi ad normam Philosophiæ, cui dediti erant, sive γνώσεως revocabant, illique accommodare studebant; *alii* vero Religionem Judaicam cum Christiana commiscere moliebantur. Priores communi Gnosticorum nomine complectuntur, quod omnibus illius temporis sectis, quæ ex Gentilismo prodiere, commune fuisse constat. Vox γνῶσις subinde bono sumitur sensu, et significat accuratam mysteriorum fidei cognitionem, qua ii gaudent qui exercitatos in verbo divino sensus habent. Malo autem sensu sumta significat cognitionem illam Supremi Numinis, quam Philosophiam illi crepabant, et rerum a materia secretarum quæ contemplando tantum intelliguntur." *Stapferi Inst. Theol. Pol.* tom. v. p. 332. See also Mosheim, cent. i. part 2. ch. v. §. 5—8.

P. 67. l. 12. *It is remarked by Mosheim.*] *Eccles. Hist.* cent. 3. part 2. ch. iii. §. 1. Lardner also observes, that " some, if not all the ancient Heresiarchs, or leaders of sects, were men of letters:" and he confirms the observation by several testimonies from Jerome, Augustin, Tertullian, and Origen. See his *Hist of Heretics*, b. i. sect. 13. " Some," says Bp. Horsley, " thought that they gave a clear solution of the dark question about the origin of evil, when they maintained that the world is the work of one or more intelligences, far inferior to the first Mind. Some, to account for some circumstances of contrariety, that may appear upon a superficial view of the Old and the New Testament, taught that the God of the Jews was a distinct being from the Father of our Lord Jesus Christ. Some, to solve the difficulties in the great doctrine of the Incarnation, indulged in a most criminal wantonness of speculation concerning the person of Christ. Some, affecting a deep mysterious wisdom, endeavoured to explain, in obscure and ill-imagined allegories, the procession of the different orders of intellect and life from the Divine Mind, and the production of the visible world. Some, the most profane and hardened, artfully availed themselves of certain mysterious points of the Christian doctrine, to give personal consequence to themselves, and to gain credit among the vulgar to the most impious pretensions." *Tracts in Controv. with Priestley*, p. 436.

P. 64. l. 27. *Many of the early Heretics rejected large portions of Holy Writ.*] " The Heretics so charged," says Dr. Waterland, " are Cerinthus, Ebion, Saturninus, Carpocrates, Cerdon, Marcion, Lucian, Apelles, Tatian, Ptolomæus, Theodotus, Artemon, Manichæus, the Ophitæ, Cainites, Sethites, Alogi, Pepuzians, Severians, and perhaps some others." *Importance of the Trinity*, p. 364. Lardner's statement differs from this, with respect to some of the Heretics and Sects here mentioned, though it confirms it as to many of them, and speaks of others not here named as liable to the same censure. The Gnostics in general entirely discarded the Old Testament.

P. 68. l. 19. *Vain attempts to explicate points which, to our present apprehensions, must ever remain enveloped in a certain degree of mystery.*] It were well if all who attempted such discussions would prosecute their researches under such impressions as appear to have influenced the mind of that profound and luminous reasoner, Bp. Horsley. " In a subject," says he, " so far above the comprehension of the human mind, as the doctrine of the Trinity must be confessed to be in all its branches, extreme caution should be used to keep the doctrine itself, as it is delivered in God's word, distinct from every thing that hath been devised by man, or that may even occur to a man's own thoughts, to illustrate it, or explain its difficulties. Every one, who hath ever thought for any length of time upon the subject, cannot but fall insensibly and involuntarily upon some way or other of representing the thing to his own mind. And if a man be ever so much upon his guard to check the licentiousness of imagination, and bridle an irreverent curiosity upon this holy subject, yet if he read what others have written, Orthodox or Heretics, he will find opinions proposed with too much freedom upon the difficulties of the subject; and among different opinions, he cannot but form some judgment of the different degrees of probability with which they are severally accompanied; nor can he so far command himself, as not in some measure to embrace the opinion which seems the most probable. In this manner, every one who meddles at all with the subject, will be apt to form a solution for himself of what seem to him the principal difficulties. But since it must be confessed, that the human mind in these inquiries is groping in the dark, every step that she ventures to advance beyond the point to which the clear light of Revelation reaches; the probability is, that all these private solutions are, in different ways, and in different degrees, but all in some way, and in some degree, erroneous: and it will rarely happen, that the solution invented by one man will suit the conceptions of another. It were therefore to be wished, that, in treating this mysterious subject, men would not, in their zeal to illustrate, what after their utmost efforts must remain, in some parts, incomprehensible, be too forward to mix their private opinions with the public doctrine. Many curious questions were moved by the Heretics of antiquity, and are now revived by Dr. Priestley, about the nature and the limit of the Divine generation. Why the Father generates but one Son? Why that Son generates not another? Why the generation is not infinite? Instead of answering such questions, it seems to me, that, except when the necessity may arise, as indeed it too often will, of " answering a fool according to his folly," it should be a point of conscience with every writer, to keep any particular opinions he may have formed, as much as possible, out of sight; that Divine truth may not be debased with a mixture of the alloy of human error, and that controversies may not be raised upon points in which no man, or set of men, can be authorized or qualified to prescribe to the belief of others. . . . . Upon such points, the evidence of Holy Scripture is, indeed, the only thing that amounts to proof. The utmost that reasoning can do, is to lead to the discovery, and, by God's grace, to the acknowledgment of the weakness and insufficiency of Reason; to resist her encroachments upon the province of Faith: to silence her objections, and cast down imaginations, and prevent the innovations and refinements of philosophy and vain deceit. Had philosophical reasoning upon points of express Revelation been held as cheap by Dr. Priestley as they are by me, the present controversy never had arisen." *Tracts in Controv. with Priestley*, pp. 458—461.

P. 70. l. 17. *Socinians.*] Mosheim, speaking of the main principle of Socinianism, observes, " Although the Socinians profess to believe that all our knowledge of Divine things is derived solely from the Holy Scriptures; yet they maintain in reality, that the sense of Scripture is to be investigated and explained by the dictates of right reason, to which, of consequence, they attribute a great influence in determining the nature and unfolding the various doctrines of Religion. When their writings are perused with attention, they will be found to attribute more to Reason, in this matter, than most other Christian Societies. For they frequently insinuate artfully, nay, sometimes declare plainly, that the Sacred Penmen were guilty of several mistakes, from a defect of memory, as well as a want of capacity; that they expressed their sentiments without either perspicuity or precision, and rendered the plainest things obscure by their pompous and diffuse Asiatic style; and that it was therefore absolutely necessary to employ the lamp of human reason, to cast a light upon their doctrine, and to explain it in a manner conformable to truth. . . . According to this representation of things, it is not the Holy Scripture which declares clearly and expressly what we are to believe concerning the nature, counsels, and perfections of the Deity; but it is human Reason, which shews us the system of Religion that we ought to seek in, and deduce from, the Divine Oracles. This fundamental principle of Socinianism will appear still more dangerous and pernicious, when we consider the sense in which the word *Reason* was understood by this Sect. The pompous title of *Right Reason* was given by the Socinians to that measure of intelligence and discernment, or, in other words, to that faculty of comprehending and judging, which we derive from nature. According to this definition, the fundamental rule of the Socinians necessarily supposes, that no doctrine ought to be acknowledged as true in its nature, or Divine in its origin, all whose parts are not level to the comprehension of the human understanding; and that whatever the Holy Scriptures teach concerning the perfections of God, his counsels and decrees, and the way of Salvation, must be modified, curtailed, and filed down, in such a manner, by the transforming power of art and argument, as to answer the extent of our limited faculties. . . . In consequence of this leading maxim, the Socinians either reject without exception, or change and accommodate to their limited capacities, all those doctrines relating to the nature of God and of Jesus Christ, the plan of redemption, and the eternal rewards and punishments unfolded in the Gospel, which they either cannot comprehend, or consider as attended with considerable difficulties." *Eccles. Hist.* cent. xvi. ch. iv. sect. 3. part 2. §. xv. xvi.

Stapfer, in his *Inst. Theol. Polem.* tom. iii. p. 364, quotes from Smalcius, a Socinian writer, these expressions: " Etsi Scriptura pluries dixisset Christum esse Deum, se id tamen non crediturum, quia Ratio nempe ipsi dictet, illud omne quod ea assequi non potest, pro absurdo esse habendum." But for a full exposition of the Socinian mode of reasoning on divine subjects, let the reader consult Dr. Edwards's Preservative against Socinianism, in four parts, 4to. 1698. Also Leslie's Socinian Controversy discussed, in six Dialogues, contained in his works, vol. i. p. 195—283, and Ashwell de Socinianismo, 8vo. 1693.

P. 73. l. 20. *This is, in effect, transferring from the Church to individuals a privilege of a similar kind.*] Werenfels, speaking of those who contend for such an immediate act of the Holy Spirit influencing and persuading, without any concurrence of the reasoning faculty, observes, " Nescio num Theologi, ita statuentes, satis attenderint ad naturam persuasionis, quæ, ubi nulla prorsus argumenta persuadentia sunt, vera persuasio esse nequit. Nescio, quo pacto hanc persuasionem discernere velint a tot vanis persuasionibus, quibus homines pertinaces, sine ullis rationibus, manent addicti. Nescio, qua ratione persuasionem hanc modo tam extraordinario a Deo in mente productam, distinguere possint ab *Enthusiasmo*. Nec video, ex quibus criteriis cognoscant, hujus DEUM potius, quam *Spiritum* quendam *deceptorem*, causam esse. Non denique invenio, quid Doctoribus Ecclesiæ Romanæ responsuri essent, si isti faterentur quidem se Ecclesiæ suæ ἀναμαρτησίαν sine ulla ratione credere, id tamen minime impedire, quo minus hæc persuasio divina sit, et ab ipso DEI Spiritu in omnibus genuinis Ecclesiæ Catholicæ membris immediate producta." *Opuscula Theologica*, tom i. pp. 159, 160.

" This doctrine," says Dr. Hickes, " differs from the preceding (that is, from the Pope's Infallibility) only in this, that that makes only the Bishop of Rome, but this makes every private Christian a Pope; and as it utterly overthrows the authority of the Scriptures, and makes them an useless Rule of Faith, so hath it already cashiered the use of the Sacraments, and annulled the ministerial orders, contrary to the precepts and precedents in the Gospel, and the practice of God's Universal Church. And when time shall serve, it can as effectually convert the professors of it into downright Papists, consistently with their own principles: for they have nothing more to do, than to say that the Spirit, or Light within, hath told them that the Church of Rome is the One Holy Catholic Church, and that *supra hanc Petram* belongs to the Pope. As this doctrine was first privately sowed among us by Popish emissaries, so hath it been published in our and other countries, by those who were bred among the Papists, as by Robert Barclay, who was for some time educated in the Scottish Convent at Paris, and Labbadie a Jesuit defrocqued." *Enthusiasm Exorcised*, p. 62.

P. 75. l. 7. *Appears to rest on an assumption, that the knowledge of Divine truth cannot be perpetuated*, &c.]
" Fanatici sensum Spiritus Sancti comprehensum sacris literis immediata demum revelatione arbitrantur innotescere: at falli eos, partim ex eo constat, quod nusquam ad istiusmodi immediatam illuminationem remittimur exspectandam,

sed ad scrutandas potius Scripturas, 2 Pet. i. 19. John v. 39. partim etiam ex absurdo consequente: nisi enim ex ipsis Scripturæ verbis liceret justa interpretandi via in cognitionem veri sensus pervenire, sed peculiari opus esset manifestatione, quid intelligatur sub verbis patefaciente; sensum hujus revelationis denuo declaratura alia revelatio præstolanda esset, quæ sibi novam iterum præstrueret, nec ipsam sine priore quadam sufficientem, quod quidem sic progressui in infinitum viam sterneret, quo nihil deprehenditur alienius a veritate." *J. E. Pfeifferi Inst. Hermeneut. Sacr.* pp. 2, 3.

P. 77. l. 6. *Known by the general title of Pneumatics.*]
" All the sorts of *Montanists*, both of the *Proclian* and *Æschinist* schools, or the *Lucians*, the *Tertullianists*, the *Artemonists*, the *Priscillists*, the *Quintillists*, together with the *Theodotians* and the *Helcesaites*, did also consent, with one accord, to quit every such name as distinguished them by their leaders, and to call themselves all by the one common name of πνευματικοί, or the *Inspired*, as those that had received the Holy Ghost, that was to lead them further on into all truth." *Hist. of Montanism, by a Lay-Gentleman*, published together with Hickes's Enthusiasm Exorcised, and Spinckes's New Pretenders to Prophecy examined. Lond, 1709. Jablonski mentions this work with high commendation.—" Anonymi cujusdam, qui se Laicum profitetur, *Historia Montanismi*, accurata imprimis, lectuque digna, multis etiam observationibus ad recentiores Montani Sectatores applicandis referta, quam Anglice scriptam, ob eximium qui inde capi potest usum, operæ pretium esset cultu Latino vel Germanico induere." *Inst. Hist. Chr. Antiq.* p. 71. ed. 8vo. Frank. 1754. The work is undoubtedly very curious and interesting, and shews great research; though it were to be wished that the Author had been more frequent in his reference to the *authorities* on which he relies. I cannot trace his authorities for this classification of Enthusiastic Sects under the denomination of *Pneumatics*, though the assertion is followed by a specification of several reasons why they appropriated this name to themselves at that particular juncture. There is no doubt, in-

deed, that all Enthusiastic Sects were wont to consider themselves as πνευματικοὶ, or spiritual, and all others as ψυχικοὶ, or carnal: but they do not appear to have been so generally recognized under that denomination, as the philosophical Sects were under the title of *Gnostics*.

P. 77. l. 27. *Many texts have been pressed into their service*.] A detailed exposition of these may be found in Dr. Bennet's Confutation of Quakerism, a very able and satisfactory treatise, applicable to the tenets, not of Quakers only, but of other fanatical Sects who contend for the necessity of *immediate* revelations from God to individuals, for their salvation. Respecting their mode of expounding Scripture, and the texts on which they chiefly insist, see ch. 4, 5, 6, 7, 8, and 12. Several of these are also distinctly examined and refuted by Buddeus in his Treatise de Fide Naturali. See his Misc. Sacr. tom. ii. part. iii. p.137—145.

SERMON IV.

P. 81. l. 4. *To beware that in refuting one error he give no encouragement to another*.] Archbishop Laud observes, " A man is apt to think he can never run far enough from that which he begins to hate; and doth not consider therewhile, that where *Religion corrupted* is the thing he hates, a *fallacy* may easily be put upon him. For he ought to hate the *corruption* that depraves Religion, and to run from it; but from no part of *Religion* itself, which he ought to love and reverence, ought he to depart."—Speaking of the confusion occasioned in his times by such extremes, he also remarks, " While the one faction cries up the Church above the Scripture; and the other, the Scripture to the neglect and contempt of the Church, which the Scripture itself teaches men both to honour and obey; they have so far endangered the *belief* of the one and the *authority* of the other, as that neither has its due from a great part of men. Whereas according to Christ's institution, the Scripture, where 'tis plain, should guide the Church; and the Church, where there's doubt or difficulty, should expound the Scripture; yet so as neither the Scripture should be forced, nor the

Church so bound up as that, upon just and further evidence, she may not revise what hath slipt by her."—*Conference with Fisher, Epist. Dedic.* p. 9. See also Dr. Jackson's Works, vol. i. b. 2. ch. iv. p. 187.

P. 87. l. 1. *Assuming to themselves a denomination expressive of their being purely Scriptural Divines,* &c.] It appears from Mosheim, that in the twelfth century " an important distinction was made between the Christian Doctors, who were divided into two classes. In the first class were placed those who were called by the various names of *Biblici,* i. e. Bible-Doctors, *Dogmatici* and *Positivi,* i. e. didactic Divines, and also *Veteres,* or Ancients; and in the second were ranged the *Scholastics,* who were also distinguished by the titles of *Sententiarii,* after the *Master of the Sentences,* and *Novi,* to express their recent origin. The *former* expounded, though in a wretched manner, the Sacred Writings in their public schools, illustrated the doctrines of Christianity without deriving any succours from reason or philosophy, and confirmed their opinions by the united testimonies of *Scripture* and *Tradition.* The *latter* expounded, instead of the Bible, the famous *Book of Sentences;* reduced under the province of their subtle philosophy whatever the Gospel proposed as an object of faith, or a rule of practice; and perplexed and obscured its Divine doctrines and precepts by a multitude of vain questions and idle speculations."—These metaphysical Divines, however, " were attacked," as Mosheim adds, " from different quarters; on the one hand, by the ancient Divines or Bible-Doctors; on the other, by the *Mystics,* who considered true wisdom and knowledge as unattainable by study or reasoning, and as the fruit of mere contemplation, inward feeling, and a passive acquiescence in Divine influences. Thus that ancient conflict between *faith* and *reason,* that had formerly divided the Latin Doctors, and had been for many years hushed in silence, was now unhappily revived, and produced every where new tumults and dissensions." This controversy between the Biblicists and the Mystics on the one side, and the Scholastics on the other, was carried on through the next century; and the union of the former in opposition to the latter appears to have given occasion to a systematic neglect of human learning, as if necessarily hostile to Revealed Religion, and thus to have facilitated the introduction of many enthusiastic extravagancies by which this æra of Christianity was disgraced. See Mosheim's Eccl. Hist. cent. xii. part ii. ch. iii. §. 5—12. and cent. xiii. part 2. ch. 3. §. 7—12.

P. 87. l. 25. *Nor was even the Protestant Reformation wholly unsullied by fanaticism of this kind.*] " There still remained," says Mosheim, " some seeds of that ancient discord between Religion and Philosophy, that had been sown and fomented by ignorance and fanaticism ; and there were found, both among the friends and enemies of the Reformation, several well-meaning, but inconsiderate men, who, in spite of common sense, maintained with more vehemence and animosity than ever, that vital Religion and Piety could never flourish until it was totally separated from learning and science, and nourished by the holy simplicity that reigned in the primitive ages of the Church." *Eccl. Hist.* cent. xvi. sect. 2. §. 6. The effect of this long neglect of learning he states in the preceding section, ch. i. §. 14. where he observes, " any Commentators, that were at this time to be found, were such as, laying aside all attention to the true meaning and force of the words of Scripture, which their profound ignorance of the original languages and of the rules of criticism rendered them incapable of investigating, gave a loose to their vain and irregular fancies, in the pursuit of mysterious significations."

P. 90. l. 3. *One demands absolute assent,* &c.] " Infallible assent, and illimited, *unreserved obedience we may not perform to the present Church*, or any visible company of men ; but to the Scripture only, made known and evident to our consciences. This assertion is directly and fully contradictory unto the Papists. Conditional assent and *cautionary obedience we may and must perform to our Spiritual Pastors*, Overseers, and Governors, albeit we see not express commission out of Scripture, to warrant those particulars whereunto they demand assent or obedience. It is sufficient that they have their general commission for obedience, expressly contained in Scripture. This assertion directly contradicts the other extreme, or contrary assertion, and of all the three only doth not contradict the Word of God, which expressly teacheth that *some peculiar obedience is due unto spiritual Governors."* Dr. Jackson's Works, vol. i. b. 2. sect 1. ch. iv. See also ch. ix. x. on the Nature and Properties of conditional Obedience, and wherein it differs from implicit Faith.

P. 90. l. 10. *Heresies at first sprang up from want of due respect and subordination to ecclesiastical powers.*] Tertullian's Treatise, de Præscriptione Hæreticorum, is grounded chiefly upon their wilful departure from the authority of the Church: and Scultetus considers the title given to it as intended to convey that meaning. " Scopus Tertulliani in hoc libro est, docere, hæreticis nihil esse causæ, cur ab Ecclesia Catholica deficerent, nulliusque esse momenti ea omnia, quæ ad insaniam suam prætexerent: Ac proinde ad Ecclesiæ authoritatem revocandos esse, quæ ut interpres est et custos veritatis, sic in illius sinu fideles veram salutaremque doctrinam debeant discere, et ex illius doctrinæ auspicio omnium hæreticarum peregrinarumque doctrinarum adulteria dignoscere atque detestari. . . . Utitur autem Vir juris peritissimus vocabulo in jure civili usitato. Præscribere enim est excipere, et præscriptio est usucapio. Cum enim vindicanti rem suam Domino possessio longi temporis objicitur, præscribi ei dicitur: eaque præscriptio longi temporis, præcisa locutione, pro præscriptio ex longi temporis possessione appellatur. Sic præscriptionem hæreticorum et Ecclesiæ vocat Tertullianus illud omne, quod juris cujusdam specie hæretici Ecclesiæ, et contra hæreticis orthodoxi opponebant." *Sculteti Medulla Patrum*, part. i. lib. 7. cap. 5. p. 153. ed. 4to. Francof. 1634.

P. 91. l. 15. *Yet is he bound, in prudence and in conscience, to look to such authorized Teachers for necessary information.*] This is forcibly urged by Dr. Jackson. " *God's written Word, then, is the only pure fountain and rule of Faith:* yet not such immediately unto all as it is written, but the learned, or spiritual Instructors only, whose hearts and consciences must be ruled by it, as in all other spiritual duties, so especially, as they are Instructors, in this, that they may not commend any truths or principles of Faith unto the illiterate, but such as are expressly contained in God's written Word, or, at least, are in substance the self-same with these written truths. If the unlearned, through God's just judgment, absolutely admit of other principles, and equalize them with these; such shall lead them into error, and pervert their Faith. If they doubt of any man's doctrine, whether it be truly spiritual, or consonant to the foundation of Faith, they may appeal to Scriptures, as they shall be expounded to them by others. Finally, they are tied to no visible company of men, whom they must under pain of damnation follow: but for their soul's health, they may try every spiritual Physician. If they will be *humorous*, they may; but at their own peril, both for temporal punishment in this life, and for eternal in the life to come." Vol. i. b. 2. ch. xi. p. 226.

P. 93. l. 16. *The responsibility on either side is great.*] This is certainly a point of great nicety and of difficult adjustment. If it be asked, What is to be done when the individual thinks the doctrine of the Church evidently *unscriptural* in *essential* points, and the Church forbids him to depart from it,—whether he ought not, in that case, to depart from it?—the answer must surely be in the affirmative. And, on the other hand, if the Church has, after due deliberation, determined, that the doctrine of the *individual* is unscriptural, must not the decision be the same? Must she not eject him from her communion? The peril, on either side, may be great: but, supposing each party to act conscientiously, although one must necessarily be in error, we may confidently hope that neither is chargeable with *wilful* error. But that is not left to human judgment. To his own Master each must stand or fall.

P. 94. l. 4. *Much discussion has from time to time arisen respecting the deference due to the writings of the primitive Fathers of the Church.*] This subject is very clearly and succinctly stated by Dr. Waterland in his Importance of the Doctrine of the Trinity, ch. vii. on the Use and Value of Ecclesiastical Antiquity in controversies of Faith.

To a general prejudice against the use of the Fathers, as if it derogated from the perfection and supreme authority of Holy Writ, he answers, " that we produce not *Fathers* to superadd *new* doctrines to Scripture, but only to secure the *old;* not to *compleat* the Rule, but more strongly to assert and maintain both its *true* sense and *whole* sense."— " Many," he observes, " would exclude the *ancients,* to make room for *themselves;* and throw a kind of slight upon the *received* interpretations, only to advance their *own.*" But, he adds, " the *perfection* of Scripture is a point allowed, and is no part of the question between us: the main question is, how we may be most secure of reaping the full *benefits* of that perfection; whether with the light of antiquity before us, or without it? . . It might be shewn, that those who have least indulged their own fancies, but have adhered strictly to antiquity, in the prime things, have done most honour to the *perfection of Scripture,* and have kept the Rule of Faith entire." p. 395—397. Leigh, in his Body of Divinity, p. 134, quotes an excellent saying from Roger Ascham;—" Patres libenter amplector, et recipio: doctrina enim ex veteri memoria plena antiquitatis, plena dignitatis existit: sed recipio patres, ut ipsi jubent se recipi, hoc est, si contineant se in sua ditione, et non migrent in possessionem verbi Dei."—See also Berriman's L. Moyer's Lect. p. 2—15, and the Preface to Knight's L. Moyer's Lect.

P. 94. l. 24. *Against any such deference being paid to these our spiritual forefathers,* &c.] These objections are taken from Daillé's Treatise de Usu Patrum, written originally in French. This work was very ably answered by Matthew Scrivener, in a Latin Dissertation adversus J. Dallæum de Usu Patrum. Lond. 1672.

P. 97. l. 1. *Descending still lower in the scale of history, this authority rapidly diminishes.*] " Quo usque extendenda sit illorum ætas atque ordo, non omnium una eademque est sententia: alii enim millesimo a Christo anno, sive seculo decimo, alii sexto, alii etiam quinto sive anno quingentesimo eam terminant: neque negari potest observatio Danæi aliorumque, qui in Oriente post CYRILLUM ALEX. in Occidente autem post AUGUSTINUM, doctrinam et cultum

Religionis evidenter declinasse notarunt. Constat imprimis, quod post annum sexcentesimum puritas doctrinæ et cultus, augescentibus, Dei justo judicio, erroribus et superstitionibus, magnam labem passa sit: quodque libertas ministerii in asserenda religione exinde fuerit minor, stabilita mox ab initio Sæc. vii. tyrannide Papatus in Bonifacio III. per Phocam Imperatorem." *De Moor, Comment. in Marckii Compend.* tom. i. p. 438.

P. 98. l. 18. *If, in addition to these special grounds of confidence*, &c.] The particular gift, called the "discerning of spirits," Bp. Horsley considers as "bestowed for the better government of the Church, and as corresponding to the office or station of those who held governments" in the Church, comparing 1 Cor. xii. 10. and 28. See Append. to his Ordination Serm. in vol. i. p. 358. Dr. Hickes, in his Enthusiasm Exorcised, discusses the peculiar nature of this gift more at large, and considers it as extending to the discrimination of miracles or prophecies wrought by evil spirits, from those which were wrought in confirmation of the truth. In whatever it consisted, the exercise of it would unquestionably give an extraordinary weight of authority, in matters of doctrine as well as of discipline. But any pretensions of this kind alleged for the primitive Fathers, will necessarily involve the great question respecting the continuance of miraculous powers in the Church; on which it is not within the scope of these Lectures to dilate.

Ibid. l. 15. *They illustrate the diction and phraseology of the inspired Penmen.*] See Waterland's Import. of Trin. p. 365.

P. 99. l. 22. *They assist in fixing the sense of controverted texts*, &c.] See Waterland, *ut supr.* p. 366—371 also 380—382.

P. 100. l. 21. *No man, says Bishop Bull, can oppose Catholic consent*, &c.] The passage occurs in his Apologia pro Harmonia, sect. i. §. 6. " In dogmatis Theologicis, a novaturiendi prurigine adeo alienus sum, ut quæcunque Catholicorum Patrum et veterum Episcoporum consensu comprobata sunt, etiamsi meum ingeniolum ea non assequatur, tamen omni reverentia amplexurus sim. Nimirum non paucis experimentis monitus didiceram, cum adhuc juvenis *Harmoniam* scriberem, (quod mihi jam confirmata ætate persuasissimum est,) neminem Catholico consensui repugnare posse, quin is (utcunque ipsi aliquantisper adblandiri videantur Sacræ Scripturæ loca nonnulla perperam intellecta, et levicularum ratiuncularum phantasmata) tandem et divinis Oraculis, et sanæ rationi repugnasse deprehendatur." *Bulli Opera*, ed. Grabe, fol. 1703. The deference, however, which the Fathers always paid to the Holy Scriptures, as the sole authoritative Rule of Faith, is sufficient to guide us in the deference which they would have admitted to be due to themselves. " The ancient Fathers," says Abp. Laud, " relied upon the Scriptures, no Christians more; and having to do with *Philosophers*, (men very well seen in all the subtleties which natural reason could teach, or learn,) they were often put to it, and did as often make it good, that they had sufficient warrant to rely, so much as they did, upon *Scripture*. In all which disputes, because they were to deal with *Infidels*, they did labour to make good the authority of the Book of God, by such arguments as unbelievers themselves could not but think *reasonable*, if they weighed them with indifferency." *Conference with Fisher*, p. 49.

P. 101. l. 8. *What degree of deference is due to the authority of human reason.*] " Ita vero res hæc intelligenda est, ut Rationi usus suus in dijudicandis rebus theologicis minime denegetur; absque ratione enim nihil confici potest: et Rationis usum rejicere velle, esset oculos sibi eruere. Uti autem illa veritatum revelatarum norma ac principium esse negatur, ut non secundum suum placitum et sententiam decidere possit, ita ipsi instrumenti functionem adjudicamus, hoc est, facultatem dignoscendi, inferendi, et conferendi, circa objectum. Non ceu lex et norma in dijudicandis rebus fidei, sed ceu organum dijudicandi, illa adhibenda est. Hoc vero tenendum, quod Ratio aliter se habeat postquam pravis habitibus corrupta, et usu et consuetudine peccandi: concedentibus ipsis adversariis, præjudiciis imbuta, æquum ac justum de omnibus rebus judicium ferre non amplius queat. In rebus theologicis distinguenda sunt ea quæ ex ipsis Rationis principiis constant, ab iis quæ sunt supra Rationem: in prioribus dijudicandis et nos Rationem normam facimus, in posterioribus non nisi instrumentum. Nec negamus in S. Literis omnia *cum* Ratione concilianda esse, quidquid enim Rationi contradicit illud ceu falsum rejicimus; sed hoc negamus, omnia *ad* Rationem exigenda esse. Per Rationem dijudicare possumus num aliquid possibile esse possit, an vero contradictionem involvat; sed modum quo aliquid esse potest, illam in omnibus assequi posse plane negamus: licet ergo illa sit judicium *falsi,* minime tamen sequitur illam normam et principium omnis *veri* esse." *Stapferi Inst. Theol. Polem.* tom. iii. p. 450, 454.

"Fateor me non alia facultate pollere, qua aut de sensu S. Scripturæ, aut de dogmatis alicujus contradictione judicem, nisi illa quæ nos homines a brutis animantibus distinguit, quam Rationem vulgo appellamus. Huic an nimium tribuam ut judicari possit, libet hic subjicere *corollaria* quædam de *usu Rationis.* I. Controversiæ generales de usu et auctoritate Rationis in Theologia, plerumque in Logomachias abeunt. II. In genere enim omnes, quotquot revelationes agnoscunt, in duobus his principiis conveniunt:—1. credendum esse, quicquid a Deo vere revelatum est, etsi nobis id creditu difficillimum videatur:—2. quod Rationi contrarium et revera contradictorium est, pro Revelato non est habendum. III. Peccatur tantum in horum applicatione." *Werenfelsii Opusc.* tom. i. p. 200.

P. 102. l. 22. *This is the legitimate province of Man's Reason.*] It can hardly be necessary to observe, that Reason is also presupposed to have been duly exercised in determining the great previous question, respecting the Divine authority of the Religion proposed to its consideration. This privilege necessarily belongs to it. "Deus O. M. ne homo perpetuo in vita aberraret, ducem illi actionum Rationem indidit. Hæc cum a peccato corrumpi se passa esset, factum est, ut in miserrimum statum homo conjiceretur. Deus, qua est bonitate, hominis misertus, videns rationem homini lapso erigendo atque ex miseria liberando non sufficere, mittit Revelationem, Rationique mandat ut huic se subjiciat, atque in homine regendo nullas sibi partes vendicet, nisi a Revelatione concessas. Quid hic agit Ratio? ante omnia examinat, num hoc, quod revelatio divina dicitur, revera a Deo sit; quod nisi cernat, sine insigni temeritate imperium hominis ab ipso Deo sibi concessum illi tradere non potest: hoc vero quamprimum videt ex indubitatis divinæ revelationis criteriis, sine mora paret, totamque, si modo rationalis est ratio, Dei verbo se submittit. Quis hic dicat revelationem rationis auctoritati niti, quæ nihil aliud agit, quam quod agnoscit ejus auctoritatem, quam sine summa cæcitate non potest non agnoscere?" *Werenfelsii Opusc.* tom. i. p. 161.

" Patet Rationis non parvum circa Revelationem usum esse. Illa nimirum Veritates juxta notiones communes sive universales examinat, neque quidquam pro vero agnoscit, nisi vel ostendatur illud ex principiis suis demonstrari posse, vel saltem ut illis non contrarium sese approbare; unde etiam convinci nequit Veritates revelatas divinas esse, nisi illud externum Veritatis principium sese illi certis argumentis et characteribus insitis adprobet. Primus ergo ejus usus versatur circa Revelationis acceptionem. Et quoniam Revelatio stylo humano est expressa, illa sensum ejus ex regulis hermeneuticis disquirit, illumque non ex suis principiis infert, sed ex verbo revelato deducit, et illum scrutatur et illustrat, ad dicentis porro scopum attendit. Et cum illius sit ratiocinari, etiam Veritatem cum Veritate confert, antecedentia cum consequentibus, legitimas inde deducit consequentias, Veritates etiam in Verbo revelato detectas in systema redigit, et errores veritati revelatæ oppositos ex veritate refutat, illamque ad conscientiam hominum demonstrat. Tandem quia Ratio novit Deum infinite plura revelare posse quam per Rationem nota sunt, Mysteria eam ob causam quod ex Rationis principiis demonstrari nequeant, neque secundum Rationis principia ut normam examinari possint, non rejicit; sed ipsi sufficit illa principiis non contrariari; et propterea, de Revelationis necessitate convicta, etiam de Mysteriorum necessitate facile convincitur." *Stapferi Inst. Theol. Polem.* tom. i. p. 297, 298.

P. 105. l. 3. *There are indeed, in every branch of human knowledge, certain principles and certain facts,* &c.] " Inter rationes omnes quibus obscuris locutionibus lux potest afferri, una ex præcipuis est, ad rei naturam attendere; quæ regula, cum palmaria sit, paulo distinctius est exponenda. Igitur in libris sacris supponi possunt ideæ rerum pæne omnium quas vel sensibus percipimus, vel ratione apprehendimus, cœli et astrorum, terræ, &c. qualia ab hominibus concipiuntur, et eo tempore concipiebantur quo libri sacri scripti sunt. Sic supponuntur communes notiones tum metaphysicæ, tum physicæ, tum mathematicæ; velut quod totum majus sit sua parte, &c. His enim principiis omnis ratiocinatio nititur, ac proinde quicumque scribunt, ista et ejusmodi principia supponunt. Supponuntur etiam a scriptoribus sacris axiomata practica, ut neminem esse lædendum, gratum animum benefactoribus deberi, aliaque id genus; atque hoc est opus legis, seu lex hominum cordibus inscripta, &c. Speciatim circa Deum multa supponunt, ut ejus existentiam, potentiam, misericordiam, bonitatem, &c. uno verbo supponunt lumen naturale. Itaque cum rerum illarum notitia a scriptoribus sacris supponatur, sæpe fit ut locutiones obscuræ circa verba ex rei natura possint illustrari, et ad verum sensum adducantur... Recte statuunt Theologi, ea quæ de Deo dicuntur ἀνθρωποπαθῶς, θεοπρεπῶς intelligenda esse, quia scilicet rei natura id suadet... Atque hæc est regula maximi et perpetui in Scripturæ interpretatione usus, sed quæ prudenter et perite adhibenda est: non supponenda sunt ut natura nota, quæ revera non sunt: sed si perite hæc regula adhibeatur, difficultates circa res momentosissimas evanescant." *J. A. Turretin de S. S. Interpr.* par. ii. cap. ii. p. 249—251. ed. Frankf. 12mo. 1776.

P. 106. l. 22. *That our sufficiency is of God.*] "Equidem quum humani sermonis similitudini Deus verbum suum accommodavit, lubentes concedimus, posse hominem, usu rationis præditum ac regulis hermeneuticis instructum, sine peculiari gratiæ lumine, sacri sermonis sensum adsequi passim, atque in criticis, historicis, geographicis dubiis enodandis satis feliciter versari. At trade illi istiusmodi dicta, ubi agitur de regni Dei mysteriis, quæ nec oculus hominis sibi relicti videt, nec auris audivit, tum hærebit in tenebris, nec pedem nisi in præcipitia promovebit. Adde alia loca quæ depravatis ipsius adfectibus moribusque perditissimis refragantur; ibi vero id serio aget, ut illa aliovorsum, vi illata, inflectat, eaque veluti injecta equuleo hermeneutico excruciabit tamdiu, donec quod ipse volet fateantur. . . Vides igitur quam necessarium sit interpreti divinum lumen quod ex verbo Dei mentem illapsum ac intra præcordia admissum, collustret ac calefaciat animum, pulsisque præjudicatarum opinionum tenebris ita disponat, ut quæ scripturis continentur vera, sancta, salutaria, vere, sancte, salutariter cognoscat. Quanquam enim per se clara sint sacra oracula, lucemque sibi divinitus insitam quoquoversus spargant; tamen si interpretis animo veluti velum oppansum sit, quod serenissimos illos verbi divini radios intercipiet, parum is inde capiat emolumenti; homini similis qui oculis captus, in ipsa meridie, et inter medium quo circumfusus est solis splendorem, pedem usquequaque allidit." *Rambachii Exerc. Hermeneut.* p. 127—130. ed. Jenæ. 12mo. 1728.

"Non negamus magnas esse Dei Spiritus partes in hoc negotio. 1. Enim dum *Scripturam* intelligimus, eo ipso Spiritus mentem percipimus, et ab eo illustramur. 2. Dotes et dispositiones, quarum ope possumus verum *Scripturæ* sensum detegere, quemadmodum attentio, docilitas, veritatis amor, affectuum compositio et sedatio, aliaque id genus, sunt indubie dona Spiritus Sancti. 3. Speciatim dum practico modo *Scripturæ* sensum cognoscimus, id est, tali modo ut ad praxin ejus præcepta revocemus, ita in nobis agit Dei Spiritus; nam qui non divino aguntur Spiritu, eo se modo non gerunt; theoretice quidem Evangelii veritates possunt noscere, sed iis non moventur: qui vero iis moventur, eo ipso a Spiritu Sancto moventur, sanctitatis et obsequii spiritum habent. Itaque magnæ hic sunt Spiritus partes. Sed vero, quod dentur afflatus interni, quibus doceamur de *Scripturæ* sensu absque ratiocinationibus quibus ille demonstretur, id est quod negamus et pernegamus." *Turretin de S. S. Interpr.* p. 104.

P. 107. l. 24. *Is not to be expected as a special or extraordinary gift.*] "Donum interpretandi Scripturas statim ab ascensione Domini in cœlos se exseruit in Apostolis... Quemadmodum vero post Ecclesiam Christi plantatam generatim dona miraculosa desierunt: ita habitum quoque infusum interpretandi sacras literas expetere, nusquam jussi sumus vel in ecclesia plantata exspectare. Adquisitus potius iste est habitus, quo nunc gaudere licet, sub assistente quidem Spiritus sancti gratia, non tamen sine studio ac labore, sed opera nostra intercedente pedetentim obtinendus: fere ut linguas nobis ignotas, cum ad intelligentiam verbi divini tum ad præconium ejus forte opportunas, adhibita diligentia sensim nunc discimus, quarum habitum totum simul Apostolis effusio Spiritus sancti largiebatur." *J. E. Pfeifferi Inst. Herm. Sacr.* p. 22. This important distinction between the *common* gifts of the Spirit, the gifts of *Sanctification*, which all Christians are bound to pray for and to expect; and the *special* gifts, the gifts of *Edification*, which men are not ordinarily bound to expect, and which have been vouchsafed only in cases of special exigence; is considered at large by Dr. Hickes, in his discourse, entitled, The Spirit of Enthusiasm Exorcised; the whole of which deserves attentive consideration, as striking effectually at the root of all fanatical pretensions, and being applicable to many of the delusions of the present day.

P. 108. l. 16. *The light of human learning, bearing some faint analogy to the light of inspiration.*] See Bp. Horsley's admirable sermon on this subject, preached at an Ordination at Gloucester. Vol. i. Serm. 14.

Ibid. l. 23. *While therefore we entirely reject*, &c.] "Falso accusamur a Pontificiis, quasi privatum cujusque spiritum in interpretatione sacri codicis sequeremur: eas potius interpretandi regulas sequimur, quæ ex communi orationis vel ex peculiari Scripturæ, rerumque in illis propositarum, indole repetuntur. Enthusiastis hoc objiciant, non nobis. Nos talem ἰδίαν ἐπίλυσιν improbamus, cum maxime atque ἀποτόμως negamus in dijudicandis doctrinæ cælestis capitibus, ad arbitrarium proprii cordis dictamen remitti quemquam posse, nisi omnia destinato consilio velimus reddere incertissima, aut omnino in hominum Fanaticorum somnia incidere." *J. E. Pfeifferi Inst. Herm. Sacr.* p. 24.

"Non est igitur, quod segnes expectemus nescio quam illuminationem nobis oscitantibus in pectora delapsurum, quæ nobis divinam Scripturæ auctoritatem persuadeat; utendum est ratione, quam Deus nobis dedit: hic in primis intendenda est ejus vis: nusquam melius illam impendere possumus. Regat modo Deus rationem Spiritu suo sancto, ut hæc facultas ab ipso sanctificata, et liberata a servitute peccati pravarumque cupiditatum, a quibus misere sæpe excæcatur, a quibus pessima principia sæpe mutuatur, quibus operam toties commodat; ratiocinetur hic pro Auctore suo, ex principiis ab eo datis, secundum leges ab eo præscriptas; eoque, Duce Deo, veniat, ut videat eundem esse auctorem suum, et ejus libri quem sacram Scripturam vocamus; eundemque Deum, qui rationi subjecit hominem, rationem subjecisse revelationi quam hoc libro comprehendere voluit." *Werenfelsii Opusc.* tom. i. p. 162.

SERMON V.

P. 114. l. 25. *The critical meaning of the word ὀρθοτομοῦντα.*] See Schleusner's and Biel's Lexicons, Elsneri Observ. Sacræ, Wolfii Curæ Philologicæ, and Poole's Synopsis in locum.

P. 115. l. 16. *The Scriptures themselves are not presented to us in a systematic form.*] " Nothing seems to have been less the intention of any of the Evangelists, than to compose a system of fundamental principles. Instruction in fundamentals in that age was orally delivered. The general design of the Evangelists seems to have been nothing more, than to deliver in writing a simple unembellished narrative of our Lord's principal miracles; to record the occurrences and actions of his life, which went immediately to the completion of the ancient prophecies, or to the execution of the scheme of man's redemption; and to register the most interesting maxims of Religion and Morality, which were contained in his discourses. The principles of the Christian Religion are to be collected neither from a single Gospel, nor from all the four Gospels, nor from the four Gospels with the Acts and the Epistles; but from the whole code of Revelation, consisting of the canonical books of the Old and New Testament: and for any article of Faith the authority of a single writer, where it is express and unequivocal, is sufficient." *Horsley's Tracts in Contr. with Priestley*, p. 253.

Stapfer thus combats the objections brought against Christianity by unbelievers, from the want of systematic method in the Sacred Writings. " Succedunt his nonnullæ quæ contra N. T. libros afferuntur *objectiones*. Primo quidem hoc Naturalistæ desiderant, quod doctrina Evangelica non in Systema aliquod redacta sit, sed quod Articuli Religionis hujus passim in Apostolorum scriptis nullo ordine ac nulla methodo tradantur; quodque momentosissima hujus Religionis capita hinc inde ex Epistolis ad communiones sive Ecclesias, imo ad homines privatos exaratis sint colligenda. Contra vero, divinæ Sapientiæ, si immediate ab ea hæc provenisset disciplina, longe convenientius fuisse, ut omnia ea quæ ad disciplinam hanc necessaria erant in unum redigerentur Systema.—*Primo* quidem, systematicam methodum non contemnimus, et præcipue respectu eruditorum insignem potest habere usum; cum omnes Christianæ disciplinæ veritates juxta methodum hancce in certum disponatur ordinem, illarumque connexio, harmonia, sive consensus ostendatur, atque quomodo una Veritas ex altera fluat, uno quasi conspectu videri possit: ipse propterea Apostolus Paulus commendat Ὑποτύπωσιν ἔχειν τῶν ὑγιαινόντων λόγων, ut bene aliquod disciplinæ Christianæ Systema nobis formemus.—*Secundo*, libri sunt vel *historici* dogmaticis mixti, vel pure *dogmatici*; posteriores prioribus quasi superstructi sunt: hic ergo N. T. librorum ordo est, ut *primo* historia quædam fundamenti loco ponatur; ut *deinceps* Christianæ disciplinæ dogmata illi superædificentur. Prius in *Evangeliis* continetur, posterius in *Epistolis*. In Historiæ recensione Evangelistas elegantissimum observasse ordinem et modo simplicissimo omnia proposuisse, nemo est qui neget. Si vero reliqua Apostolorum scripta consideramus, ea vel integrum tradunt doctrinæ Christianæ compendium, vel controversias ac difficultates circa Articulos nonnullos motas dirimunt. Ad priora pertinent ex. gr. Pauli ad Romanos et Ephesios Epistolæ, in quibus Religionis Christianæ capita, neminis non consensu, methodo hominibus ad veritatem adducendis concinna maxime tradita sunt. In iis autem, in quibus controversiæ dirimuntur, semper observari ordinem a Sacrorum Oraculorum Interpretibus, sæpissime ostensum est.—*Tertio,* non inficiamur doctrinam Christianam tunc temporis nondum in artem fuisse redactam, uti hodie; neque tot tricis ac inutilibus quæstionibus ac distinctionibus fuisse refertam. Inveni in Theologi cujusdam celeberrimi Systemate ultra nonaginta solum de Christi persona distinctiones: at Christus et Apostoli modo simplicissimo, omni humanæ scientiæ apparatu vacuo, totam illam disciplinam tradiderunt... *Quarto,* Christus ac Apostoli in concionibus suis auditoribus ac discipulis sese accommodabant, methodoque illis temporibus familiari usi sunt, methodo ad persuadendum et convincendum efficacissima." *Stapferi Inst. Theol. Polem.* tom. ii. p. 1173—1175.

P. 117. l. 5. *It is not every truth clearly deducible from Scripture, or manifestly necessary to be believed, that can with propriety be called fundamental.*] " Articulus fidei est talis veritas ad quam credendam homo vel per Religionem naturalem vel revelatam obligatur. Fundamentale vocatur, quod ad ipsam rei essentiam pertinet, ut illo sublato ipsa rei forma atque essentia pereat. Unde articulus fidei fundamentalis est talis veritas quæ ad ipsam Religionis Christianæ essentiam pertinet, ut illa sublata ipsa etiam vera Religionis forma atque essentia pereat." *Stapferi,* ut supr. tom. i. p. 513.

" Dogma fundamentale est tale, *quod est necessario credendum ut quis dicatur habere fidem illam salvificam, a qua Evangelium salutem hominum suspendit.* Error fundamentalis est, *qui prorsus impedit, quominus aliquis de dogmatibus fundamentalibus possit esse persuasus,* aut qui tollit ex animo errantis fidem quæ debetur dogmati fundamentali. Non dico, qui *pugnat* cum dogmate fundamentali, aut illi oppositus est, sed qui *tollit* fidem, quæ debetur tali dogmati." *Werenfelsii Opusc.* tom. i. p. 461.

P. 117. l. 28. *The number of those which are to be regarded as fundamental will be too much circumscribed,* &c.]

"Non debent articuli fundamentales nimium multiplicari, uti fit a *Papistis*, pro proprio lubitu; sed nec cum *Socinianis* adeo minui, ut *sex* tantum de Deo sint creditu necessaria, et *de Christo vix quidquam*... Non sufficit Articulorum fundamentalium verba tenere, sed et sensum genuinum accipere decet. Unde *Pontificii*, cum aliis *hæreticis*, *Apostasiæ* recte insimulantur ex 2 Thess. ii. 3. etiamsi Symbolum et Decalogum externe retineant. Quando autem Articulus aliquis unus vere creditur, et alius additur per quem priorem destrui credentes utrumque non vident, uti in Omnipræsentia humanæ naturæ Christi Lutherana locum habere id observamus, non debet his hominibus propterea Apostasia tribui." *Marckii Chr. Theol. Medulla,* cap. iii. §. xv. xvi.

P. 120. l. 13. *All which are but ambiguous or defective criteria.*] De Moor, in his Commentary on Marckius's Compendium, thus animadverts on some of these uncertain tests of fundamental doctrines.

"Non sunt Articuli necessarii æstimandi, a. Ex *Universali omnium Christianum nomen profitentium consensu:* sic tamen vult Smalcius contra Smigl. Hobbes libro de Cive; Edv. Herbert Baro de Cherbury in genere, *unicam Veritatis normam in necessariis facit Consensum ipsum universalem.* Sed, 1. *Fides,* adeoque necessitas Articulorum Fidei, æstimanda est non ex consensione hominum aut sectarum, sed ex Verbo Dei. Rom. x. 17, &c. 2. Christianum nomen adoptarunt sæpe hominum monstra, quibus pro Fidei articulis fuere somnia delirantium et quidvis statuendi vel oppugnandi licentia: horumne requireretur consensio, ut quid sit Articulus fundamentalis statuatur? 3. Nisi hæc nota fallit, non habuerunt Apostoli pro Fundamentalibus, Adventum Christi in carne, Resurrectionem mortuorum, Justificationem per fidem Jesu, &c. quibus aliisque capitibus jam olim fuit contradictum. 4. Imo sic vix ullum datur caput Christianæ Fidei, cui non uno alterove tempore contradictum fuit. 5. Sic soli illi libri habendi pro Canonicis, qui ab omnibus Christianorum sectis semper tales habiti fuerunt; at nullus fere datur Liber, cui non fuit contradictum. 6. Hoc ipsum perquam dubium est, quinam sint illi Articuli qui omnium consensione Christianorum probantur: imo quot Articulus ille Hobbesianus, Jesum esse Christum illum qui venturus erat, non implicat controversa?

β. Neque ex *Explicita Revelatione totidem Literis in Scriptura Sacra*, quod voluerunt olim *Manes, Arius, Eutyches*, &c.; sic hodie *Sociniani, Ostorodius*, alii; sic ex parte quoque *Methodistæ recentiores*. Hoc enim nec necessariis omnibus commune, neque etiam his solis proprium: in iis quippe quæ in Scripturis revelantur consideranda veritas, utilitas, et necessitas: priora duo ubique obtinent; at non putandus salute excidisse, qui non explicite noverit cuncta in toto S. Codice literis consignata.

γ. Neque ex argumento *Practico*, cum non sola praxi absolvatur Religio. Cum itaque *Sociniani* hoc Articuli necessarii et fundamentalis dicunt Criterium quod directe spectet ad Obedientiam Deo Christoque præstandam, seu studium pietatis ac bonorum operum; Criterium ponunt non adæquatum rei, . . . quia non solum præcepta faciendorum, sed etiam dogmata credendorum ad salutem sunt necessaria: imo non per operum obedientiam, sed per fidei assensum justificari dicitur peccator.

δ. Non ex complexu *Symboli Apostolici* vulgo dicti: quia 1. hoc de Cultu Dei non agit, sed habet tantum Articulos theoreticos, qui spectant ad Fidem. 2. Articulos omnes Fidei explicite non continet, licet, præter expresse illic memorata, per consequentiam plura inde elici queant: sic nihil habet explicite de Providentia, de Satisfactione Christi. 3. Nec ab Apostolis, sed ab Ecclesia antiqua successive pro ratione crescentium hæresium, profectum est.

ε. Neque tandem *ex mera Ecclesiæ determinatione*, uti fit in *Papatu*. . . . Inter errores propter quos Leo X. Lutherum anathemate feriit, in Bulla *Exsurge* hic quoque refertur: "Certum est, in manu Ecclesiæ aut Papæ prorsus non esse statuere Articulos Fidei." Ast hoc pacto, 1. petitur τὸ ἐν ἀρχῇ, et priusquam Ecclesiæ determinatio pro Criterio habeatur Articulorum Fundamentalium, probandum foret Ecclesiæ, in specie Romanæ hodiernæ, deferendum esse Fidei Catholicæ et Salutis arbitrium: cujus contrarium visum fuit. 2. Non tolluntur per hanc notam difficultates circa formationem Articulorum Fundamentalium, sed augentur potius." *De Moor, Comment. in Marckii Compend.* tom. i. p. 475—477. See also Dr. Waterland's Charge on Fundamentals, p. 30—60. 8vo. 1735. where he enumerates ten of these exceptionable tests, and refutes them at large.

P. 120. l. 24. *Among the many directions which have been given for our guidance in this respect*, &c.] No subject, perhaps, has more generally occupied the attention of systematic Theologians, than this of ascertaining what are *fundamental* truths in Revealed Religion. The general principle here laid down is adopted from Dr. Waterland's Discourse on Fundamentals, in which he enters largely into a review of what had been done by other Divines preceding him in the inquiry; and his references to authors who had expressly written on the subject are very copious. He has also incidentally touched upon the same topic, in his Importance of the Trinity, ch. 1, 2, 3. where he shews upon what grounds that doctrine ought to be received as a fundamental article: and in ch. 4. he urges many arguments to shew, that no communion ought to be held with those who openly reject the fundamental doctrines of Christianity. To these two excellent works, which are so full of matter as not easily to admit of abridgment, I must refer the reader for more particular information. These will lead him also to a variety of the best authors, didactic or controversial, who have pursued the inquiry to its utmost extent: among whom are Mede, Chillingworth, Hoornbeck, Hammond, Stillingfleet, Dean Sherlock, Clagett, Frederic Spanheim the younger, Puffendorf, Witsius, Turretin, &c. To these may be added Werenfels, in his Dissertation de Ratione uniendi Ecclesias Protestantes, cap. 3—6. Buddei Inst. Theol. Dogm. lib. i. cap. 4, 5. De Moor, Comment. in Marckii Compend. tom. i. p. 475—485. and two short tracts by Abp. Synge on Catholic Christianity, and on the Fundamentals of Christianity, in the third volume of his works, 12mo. Lond. 1744. There is also a valuable Discourse de Fundamentalibus, delivered as a Concio ad Clerum, by Dr. J. Burton, Fellow of Eton, and printed at Oxford, 1756.

P. 122. l. 14. *The points thus assumed are to be regarded as forming the basis of the Christian system.*]
"Necessarii et fundamentales dicendi sunt Articuli, 1. quorum necessitas expressis Scripturæ testimoniis asseritur, sive denunciatione mortis facta non tenentibus eos, sive Salutis cum illis conjunctione: ita, pro necessaria Fide Trinitatis, seu pluralitatis Personarum divinarum, vide negative 1 Joh. ii. 23. positive Joh. xvii. 3. pariter de Christo, Eph. ii. 12. 1 Cor. iii. 11. Act. iv. 12. de Justificatione, Rom. iii. 24. de mortuorum Resurrectione, 1 Cor. xv. 2. Illi dicendi sunt necessarii, absque quibus *Salutis nostræ opus consistere non potest*; quorum adeo certus cum Salute nostra juxta Scripturæ normam deprehenditur nexus; sive considerandi sint ut causæ Salutis magis vel minus principales, dum sublatis causis tollitur effectus; sive ut media ad fidem ducentia, dum negatis mediis neque finis expectari potest. Ita Causæ Salutis principales sunt Gratia Dei, Rom. iii. 24. meritum Christi et Justificatio per illud, Rom. iii. 24, 25. Sanctificatio Spiritus regenerantis, Joh. iii. 5. Tit. iii. 4—7. Causa instrumentalis est Fides, Joh. iii. 16. 36. Act. x. 43. Hebr. xi. 6. medium ad finem eundem Salutis tendens est quoque Resipiscentia, Luc. xiii. 3, 5.—Possunt Articuli hi ad aliqua capita reduci, quæ inter Fundamentalia numeranda esse, ex Criteriorum modo datorum applicatione sponte liquet. 1. Ad *principium* credendi, ceu Scripturam pro θεοπνεύστῳ habendam. 2. Ad *cognitionem Dei Triunius* ut *perfectissimi*, ac perfectiones suas declarantis, (tum in operibus *Creationis, Conservationis* ac *Redemtionis*, tum in horum Proposito æterno,) illiusque Perfectionibus dignum ac convenientem *cultum*. 3. Ad *hominis miseriam*, quæ *peccatum* et *pœnam* in se continet, ad omnes extensam. 4. Ad *cognitionem Christi Mediatoris*, respectu *Naturarum*, respectu *Munerum*, respectu *Statuum*, respectu *Beneficiorum.*" De Moor, ut supr. tom. i. p. 477—479.

Concerning the doctrine of the Trinity, as a fundamental article, nothing more full or satisfactory can be desired than Dr. Waterland's elaborate work, already referred to, on the *Importance* of the doctrine. A more concise view of it is taken in his Familiar Discourse on the Trinity, a single sermon, 8vo. 1720. See also Bp. Horne's Sermon on the same subject.

That it is no less necessary to entertain a right apprehension of the condition of man, in the relation he generally bears to God, and particularly as a fallen creature, is thus illustrated by Stapfer, in his Chapter de Articulis Fundamentalibus. "Fundamentum Religionis est *certa quædam hominis ad Deum relatio*, quæ fluit ex opere aliquo Dei circa hominem, ex quo officium Deum ad Salutem cognoscendi et colendi oritur, ut et modus quo id fieri debeat. Alius vero est status hominis integri, alius peccatoris: qua Peccator enim, amplius ad Dei gloriam vivere nequit; unde alius salvandi modus est hominem integrum, alius Peccatorem, qui iterum illi statui restituendus est, in quo ad Dei gloriam vivere possit cum Salute propria. Unde aliud fundamentum est Religionis Naturalis, ad quam homo Peccator qua homo obligatus est; aliud Revelatæ, ad quam qua Peccator obstringitur. Ergo Religio Peccatoris utramque Religionem Naturalem et Revelatam complectitur.

Fundamentum Religionis Naturalis est, *Creatio* et *Providentia*. Finis, ut homo cum propria Salute ad Dei Gloriam vivat. Unde Religionis hujus Veritas primaria et maxime fundamentalis hæc est, Hominem per dependentiam suam a Deo, ut omnium rerum causa prima et fine ultimo, et propter finem ad quem creatus est, obligatum esse ad actiones suas secundum Voluntatem Dei dirigendas et in Dei Glorificatione æternam Salutem quærendam.

"In hac autem immediate sequentes continentur Veritates, quæ adeo non minus ac hæc ipsa fundamentales sunt: —a. Deum existere. β. Eundem esse omnium rerum Causam primam et finem ultimum. γ. Adeoque omnes in se continere Perfectiones, quæ ad id requiruntur. δ. Hominem omniaque reliqua a Deo creata fuisse. ϵ. Cum omnia ad sapientissimum finem dirigantur, *dari Providentiam*. ς. Hominem sui juris non esse, sed a Deo in omnibus actionibus suis dependere. ζ. Voluntatem Dei esse actionum ejus normam. η. Dari Religionem. θ. Deum ipsum quærentibus esse Remuneratorem, cum in ipsius Glorificatione æterna Salus obtinetur. ι. Animam esse immortalem.

" Si nunc ex Articulis hisce, qui cum Religionis fundamento immediate connexi adeoque *primarii* sunt, tanquam ex principiis alii demonstrentur, illi *secundarii* sunt, qui quidem non debent negari, sed possunt ignorari.

" *Finis* Religionis Revelatæ est homini Peccatori medium liberationis ostendere; sive quomodo ex statu moraliter imperfecto liberatus iterum cum propria Salute ad gloriam Dei esse queat. *Fundamentum* est aliquod opus divinum circa Peccatorem, quod ex ipso hujus Religionis fine aliud esse non potest, quam Liberatio sive Redemtio. Unde etiam S. Script. opus hoc ceu Religionis fundamentum proponit, 1 Cor. vi. 20. in quo Peccator totus a Deo pendet. *Medium* autem illud, quod homini revelatur, est Jesus Christus, qui factus est unica atque perfectissima Salutis nostræ causa. Fundamentum enim aliud nemo potest ponere, præter jactum, quod est Jesus Christus, 1 Cor. iii. 11. Ex his patet, Veritatem Religionis Revelatæ primariam et maxime fundamentalem hanc esse: Jesus Christus ceu unica atque perfectissima Salutis Causa ab homine Peccatore agnoscendus et recipiendus; Deusque propterea a toto homine, hoc est, Anima et Corpore, glorificandus est. Ad hoc enim mysterium inculcandum et explicandum tota tendit Revelatio, et omnia Religionis Revelatæ dogmata ad Veritatem hanc cognoscendam vel supponuntur, vel in ea continentur, vel ex ea fluunt et derivantur. Et quæcunque alia in S. Script. dicuntur, vel historiæ, vel typi, vel prophetiæ, vel exempla, omnia huc faciunt, ut Doctrina hæc illustretur et declaretur. Unde si fundamentum hoc et Veritas primaria reliquarum omnium et fons et scopus inconcussa manet, etiam Religionis Revelatæ essentia salva manet atque inconcussa; hac vero vel negata vel impugnata, simul tota Revelata Religio in complexu suo negatur vel impugnatur. Quicquid ergo immediate ex hac Veritate fluit, illud ad Articulos fundamentales primi ordinis pertinet, et ad Deum cum propria Salute cognoscendum et colendum requiritur, sive ad Salutem creditu factuque absolute necessarium est." *Inst. Theol. Polem.* tom. i. p. 540—545.

P. 123. l. 3. *The acknowledgment of our Lord Jesus Christ as the Mediator between God and man, combining in his person the twofold nature, human and Divine,* &c.] Dr. Priestley acknowledges, that "if the doctrine of the Trinity be true," (in which that of our Lord's Divinity is necessarily included,) "it is no doubt in the highest degree important and interesting." See *Horsley's Tracts,* p. 306.

"In the sound and solid view of theological controversies," says Mr. Whitaker, "the first object of all controversy is the doctrine of the Trinity. This concerns the very foundation stone of our Religion. This affects the very pillar and ground of the truth. If this doctrine be *false,* then nine tenths of the Christians through every age and in every country have been guilty of *idolatry;* of an idolatry indeed, not so gross as that of the Heathens, because not the worship of *devils* in the place of God; yet of an idolatry more gross than that of the Papists at present, because not merely the worship of *saints* and of *angels,* in *subordination* to God; but the worship of a *creature* along *with* the Creator, placing him *equally* with God upon the throne of the universe, giving God a partner in his empire, and so deposing God from half his sovereignty. And if the doctrine be *true,* then the opposers of it are bold and blasphemous abusers of the faith; are like the giants of old, brandishing their arms directly against heaven; and are vainly endeavouring to tear down our blessed Redeemer from the throne of the Godhead there." *Origin of Arianism,* pp. 4, 5.

The learned Mede, after defining *Fundamentals of Salvation* to be such Articles as "without the knowledge and belief thereof we can neither invocate the Father aright, nor have that faith and reliance upon Him and his Son, our Mediator Jesus Christ, which is requisite to Remission of Sins and the hope of the Life to come," adds, "How far this *ratio* of a *fundamental Article* will stretch, I know not; but believe it will fetch in most of the Articles of the Apostles' Creed. And by it also those two main errors of the *Socinians,* the one denying the *Divine nature,* the other the *Satisfaction* of Christ, may be discerned to be *fundamental.* For without the belief of the first, the Divine Majesty cannot be rightly, that is incommunicably, worshipped, so as to have *no other Gods besides him:* for he that believes not Christ to be consubstantial with the Father, and yet honours him with the same worship, worships not the Father incommunicably; which is the *formalis ratio* of the worship of the true God, from whom we look for Eternal Life. And without the belief of the Second, the *Satisfaction of Christ*, there can be, I suppose, no saving Faith or reliance upon Christ for forgiveness of Sin." *Epistle* 83. p. 868. ed. fol. 1677. The subject of Fundamentals is touched upon in some other of his letters to Hartlib and Duræus, from Ep. 82. to Ep. 88. inclusive.

P. 123. l. 16. *The same may be said respecting the conditions of salvation.*] "By *a condition of the Gospel-Covenant* is properly to be understood, *not whatever is commanded or required, but that only which is required at the peril of one's soul*, i. e. on which a man's eternal Life and Salvation does so much depend, that the same being performed a man attains Salvation, and not otherwise. Again, such a condition is twofold, either as being *absolutely* required at the peril of our souls, or necessary to Salvation; or only *on a supposition*. The *inward* works of Faith, Repentance, &c. are *absolutely* required unto Salvation. But the fruits, or *outward* works of Faith and Repentance, (under which are comprehended in Scripture all other Christian Virtues, whence the said outward works are wont to be denoted by *a good life* or *holy conversation*,) are required only on a supposition that God grants life and opportunity. This being premised concerning the nature of a Gospel-Condition, it follows, that *one* and the *same* is a Condition properly so called of the *Gospel-Covenant*, and of our *Justification* by the Gospel-Covenant. For first, Nothing is required in the Gospel-Covenant *absolutely*, at the peril of our souls, but what is required to our Justification.—Secondly, Nothing is required in the Gospel-Covenant at the peril of one's soul, even on *supposition*, but what is also so far required to our Justification.—The foundation of both Propositions is contained in this third, that in a man's Justification God confers on him a right to Salvation. Hence arises this clear consequence, that nothing can be required in the Gospel to *obtain* or *retain* our right to Eternal Life or Salvation, which is not also required to *obtain* or *retain* our Justification." *Wells on the Covenants,* part ii. ch. 6. pp. 149, 150.

P. 124. l. 17. *Its efficacy in the work of our Sanctification.*] " The salvation effected for us by the renewing of the Holy Ghost, is represented in the Scriptures as corresponding to every part of our ruin, as an instance of Grace, and to which we had no claim by nature. If our old man be corrupt, through the loss of the Divine image and similitude, by which our Understandings are *darkened* and our Wills *perverted;* by this we are *renewed again in Knowledge after the image of Him who created us,* which is called our *new man, created after God, in righteousness and true holiness.* If the φρόνημα σαρκὸs, or natural concupiscence, hangs a weight on our affections, and inclines them to earth, the φρόνημα πνεύματος, or spiritual desire, is a balance against the carnal mind, and restores the Will to its freedom, which is the *glorious liberty of the Sons of God,*" &c. *Ridley's Sermons on the Divinity and Operations of the Holy Ghost,* p. 203.

P. 125. l. 12. *The Christian Sacraments and the Christian Priesthood.*] The necessity of the Sacraments is largely discussed by Dr. Bennet, in his Confutation of Quakerism, ch. 24, 25, 26. That of the Priesthood is fully investigated in Dr. Hickes's Treatises on the subject, and in Hughes's prefatory Dissertation to his edition of Chrysostom on the Priesthood, 8vo. Cantab. 1710. Both subjects are frequently and copiously enlarged upon by Leslie, in his several controversial writings with the Quakers, particularly in his Discourses on Water-Baptism, and on the Qualifications requisite to administer the Sacraments. See his Works, vol. ii. p. 669—713, and 719—757. See also Scrivener's Body of Divinity, ch. 33. and Sherlock on Religious Assemblies, p. 125—133.

P. 127. l. 18. *Respecting the Covenants entered into by the Almighty with mankind.*] " A Covenant is nothing else but an agreement solemnly made between two distinct parties, with Conditions mutually to be observed, as in that between Laban and Jacob, Gen. xxxi. 52. So likewise between God and Man, a stipulation and re-stipulation is made, that the one should perform the part of a Patron and Lord, and the other of a faithful servant to him. This Covenant is but *twofold* in general, however it be diversified according to the several occasions of revealing the same. The first was properly a Covenant of *Nature;* the second of *Grace.* The Covenant of Nature was first made with Adam at his creation, wherein were bestowed on him, not only such faculties and perfections of being as necessarily tended to the natural perfection of man; but superadded certain supernatural graces which might dispose him with facility to fulfil the Law and the Will of God. Notwithstanding which, he disobeying God, forfeited those more special aids and accomplishments, and so dissolved that Covenant. God proceeded not upon faithless Man according to the rigour of his Justice; but out of his free inscrutable favour inclined to renew a Covenant with him again, and that was in a third Person, not with false Man immediately as before. And this Person, through whom he thus covenanted a second time with Man, was the Man Christ Jesus: and than these are no more Covenants really. Yet because this second, of sending his Son as a Mediator between God and Man, had such different forms and faces upon it, according to the several Oeconomies or Dispensations it pleased God to make to Man, it is often in holy Scripture distinguished into the Old and New: as by St. Paul to the Galatians, saying, *These two are the two Covenants, the one from Mount Sinai; the other from Mount Sion or Jerusalem,* Gal. iv. 24. And to the Hebrews; *If the first Covenant had been faultless, then should no place have been found for the second;* Heb. viii. 7. Where he spake of the Covenant of Moses, and that of the Gospel. . . . But that which is often called the New Covenant, or the Covenant of the Gospel, is, according to the substance, of an ancienter date than that made either with Abraham or Moses; being the same which was made with Adam, the second time in Paradise. But it is called the New Covenant, because it appeared but newly in respect of its dress and clearer Revelation, at Christ's appearing. And therefore St. John excellently expresses this, when he seemeth to speak on both sides, saying, *Brethren, I write no new Commandment to you, but an old Commandment, which ye had from the beginning. Again, a new Commandment I write unto you, which thing is true in him and in you.* 1 John ii. 7, 8. signifying unto us in what sense the Gospel was New, and in what Old. It was New in comparison of the more conspicuous manifestation of it: it was Old in respect of its ordination. For to this end, the Apostle to the Colossians speaking of the Gospel, calleth it *the Mystery which hath been hid from ages and from generations, but now is made manifest,* &c. Coloss. i. 26." Scrivener's Course of Divinity, ch. xxxiv. p. 162, 163. See also Wells on the Covenants, ch. 1, 2, 3, 4.

P. 128. l. 4. *Every intermediate dispensation forms a part only of the second Covenant.*] It is very important, towards an accurate interpretation of the Sacred Writings, to discriminate between what are, strictly speaking, distinct *Covenants,* and what are only different *Dispensations* of the same Covenant. Scrivener, in the chapter just quoted, notices the confusion that is often made in treating of the Old and New Testament, from not observing in what respects these Covenants and Dispensations agree, or differ from each other. The first Covenant terminated with the Fall. The second Covenant commenced immediately after the Fall, and will continue to the end of the world. The different *Dispensations,* however, of this latter Covenant, sometimes called the Old and New Covenants, agree in certain respects, and differ in others. They agree, in that the substance of both is the same: they agree in their Author: they agree in the principal Mediator of both, *Jesus Christ, the same yesterday, to-day, and for ever:* they agree as to their main end, the glory of God and the Salvation of mankind: they agree, in that both were given not immediately from God, but through a Mediator. On the other hand, they differ as to the Persons by whom they were delivered, Moses being only man, but Christ both God and Man: the Law was a type or shadow only, the Gospel the substance: the Law was temporary, the Gospel perpetual: the Law had only temporal promises and penalties; the Gospel, spiritual and everlasting.—But in this twofold division of the Old and New Testaments, the former must be understood to include the Patriarchal as well as the Mosaic Dispensation. Accordingly, some make the division *threefold*, instead of twofold. This is noticed by Marckius in his Christianæ Theol. Medulla, cap. xvii. *de Fœdere Gratiæ*, where he observes, " Fœderis hujus Gratiæ Oeconomia potest dici *triplex*; *a. antelegalis*, sc. a lapsu ad Mosen, quam hodie *promissionis* multi appellant; β. *legalis*, a Mose ad Christum, quam *Vet. Test.* iidem dicunt; γ. et *evangelica*, seu *N. Test.* a Christo ad finem seculorum. Est enim revera magnum discrimen in administratione gratiæ ante et post Mosen, qui verbum scriptum dedit, legem perfecit, unum populum præ aliis omnibus assumpsit, &c." To this division, however, Marckius objects, as tending to obscure the great leading characteristics of the two Covenants before and after the Fall. But if a right discrimination be made between the Covenants themselves and the different dispensations of the second Covenant, local or temporary, no inconvenience can follow from adopting the simple chronological arrangement, by which the several Epochs from Adam to Moses, from Moses to Christ, and from Christ to the end of the world, are marked as distinct from each other in their external circumstances and administration, though one and the same as to their essential purpose.

P. 128. l. 11. *Covenants of Nature and of Grace, of Incorruptibility and the Resurrection, of Works and of Faith.*], Scrivener, as appears from the foregoing extracts, adopts the first of these distinctions. Hingeston, in his Discourses upon the Divine Covenants, 8vo. 1771, speaks of the Covenant of Nature, the Covenant of Incorruptibility, and the Covenant of Resurrection: denoting by the first, that general and universal Law imposed upon man at his creation, and never totally repealed by any subsequent Covenants; by the second, the promise of Eternal Life, before the Fall, upon certain conditions; by the third, the renewal of that promise, upon new conditions, after it had been forfeited. The next distinction, that of Works and Faith, is not

APPENDIX. 317

equally clear; since it is evident that Faith under each Covenant and every Dispensation was necessary to acceptance, and that works suitable to each were also required as an indispensable condition. For, as Scrivener justly observes, (p. 163.) the Covenants made with Abraham and with Moses are termed Covenants of Works, not that they only required working, and the Gospel, believing; (for they supposed Faith in the promised seed;) but that they were as a Codicil annexed to the first solemn Covenant of Faith, conveying special promises and privileges, of a temporal kind, to the seed of Abraham, upon terms not common to all mankind, and which, therefore, no longer subsisted under the Christian Dispensation.

P. 130. last line. *The great variety of subject-matter contained in the Sacred Writings.*] " Præstantissimorum Commentatorum consuetudo est, ut libro quem explicandum sibi sumunt, præmittant dissectionem ejus, quantum fieri potest, accuratam, in partes suas minores. Quæ diligentia, tametsi nonnullis visa est paulo obscurior et molestior, superavit tamen ac prævaluit utilitatis, (addo, et non parvæ necessitatis,) meditatio, ut quo penitius aliquis Scripturæ mentem aut penetravit, aut saltem penetrare annisus est, eo majorem laborem in illarum divisione recte expedienda collocaverit. Quicquid enim conspectu uno, et velut ἐν συνόψει, animo spectandum offertur, etsi alias magnitudine et multitudine præditum velut insuperabile menti facile videri queat, multo facilius imbibitur et intellectui repræsentatur." *Chladenii Inst. Exeget.* p. 532. ed. 12mo. Viteberg. 1740.

P. 131. l. 19. *Have collectively obtained their appropriate appellation, the Bible.*] " Ceterum is librorum θεοπνεύστων complexus modo in singulari dicitur ἡ γραφή, modo in plurali αἱ γραφαὶ, *illud*, quia tanquam corpus revelationis integrum, quæcunque ad salutem nostram pertinent, exactissimo omnium consensu docens, præstantissimus, dignissimus, atque perfectissimus liber est, omnes in orbe libros, quotquot scripti sunt unquam aut scribentur, magno post se relinquens intervallo: *hoc*, quia pluribus absolvitur in unum collectis voluminibus, quæ singulæ partem aliquam divinæ constituunt revelationis." *J. E. Pfeifferi Inst. Hermeneut. Sacr.* p. 51, 52.

P. 132. l. 5. *The Historical Books.*] A series of useful and judicious rules for the interpretation of these portions of Scripture may be found in Turretin's excellent Treatise de S. S. Interpretatione, part. ii. cap. 3. The subject is also very fully illustrated by J. E. Pfeiffer, in his Inst. Herm. Sacr. cap. xi. p. 641—692.

Ibid. l. 24. *The necessity of the greatest care and circumspection,* &c.] " Neque minora sunt commoda, quæ ex *conjectandi* peritia in Scripturæ sacræ tractatorem redundant. Hinc enim non solum felicius versabitur in locis intricacioribus, et quæ sibi invicem refragari videntur; sed in narrationibus etiam historicis quam plurimas rei gestæ circumstantias, quas scriptor sacer silentio pressit, non inepte supplebit. Utrobique tamen caute admodum et circumspecte agendum est, ne φαντασία, quæ optima famula, pessima domina est, extra oleas vagetur. Unde quemadmodum equi, ubi nimis in cursum effusi sunt, in loco proclivi habenis cohibentur; ita ingenium, in conjectando nimium præceps ac rapidum, judicii severitate castigandum, prudentiæque freno reprimendum, et intra rationis gyrum revocandum est. Præstat enim in locis dubiis fateri ignorantiam, quam incertis indulgere conjecturis, aut eas rerum fingere circumstantias, quas si legeret scriptor sacer, exclamaret fortassis, quod de Platone dialogum de se conscribente Socrates dixisse fertur, *O quam multa juvenis ille de me mentitur!" Rambachii Exercit. Hermeneut.* p. 56—58.

P. 133. l. 21. *The Prophetical Books.*] Rules for the interpretation of these are also detailed by Turretin and Pfeiffer, as above; by the former, part. 2. cap. iv. by the latter, cap. xv. §. 232—260.

P. 134. last line. *Doctrinal or practical.*] Similar instructions for the exposition of these portions of Scripture are given in the above-mentioned works. See Turretin, part. 2. cap. vi. vii. and Pfeiffer, cap. x. xii.

P. 135. l. 28. *The several other occasions and purposes, whether general or special.*] " Ubi summa operatur divini Numinis sapientia; ibi nihil fit sine fine certo, et fines peculiares in communem aliquem resolvuntur. Quum finis orationis constituat scopum ejus, non solum scriptum quodlibet Scriptura sacra comprehensum peculiarem habet scopum suum; sed et communis quidam scopus est, in quem scopi isti omnes diriguntur. Scopum hunc *generalem* Scripturæ, illos vero, libris singulis proprios, *speciales* appellare solent. Scopum totius Scripturæ *generalem* esse patefactionem Servatoris nostri, aliunde constat. *Specialis* cujusvis scripti scopus, pro diversitate scriptorum, diversus est, sed generali subordinandus. Ut autem patefactio Domini nostri Jesu Christi cum illustratione perfectionum divinarum et salute hominum connexa est, sic merito tota Scriptura simul ad perfectionum divinarum illustrationem et salutem hominum tendere censetur." *J. E. Pfeifferi Inst. Herm. Sacr.* cap. i. §. 7, 8.

P. 138. l. 7. *Were evidently written to meet the particular exigencies of the faithful in those times,* &c.] Buddeus has an important Dissertation, de Statu Ecclesiarum Apostolicarum, in which he urges the necessity of attending to these circumstances in the interpretation of the Sacred Writings, and particularly in ascertaining the real scope and purport of St. Paul's Epistles. See his Miscell. Sacr. tom. i. part. 2. p. 216—266.

P. 143. l. 13. *The same exercise of the mental faculties.*] Turretin lays it down as a general rule, " non aliam esse Scripturæ interpretandæ rationem, quam reliquorum librorum; attendendum scilicet ad vocum et locutionum sensum, ad auctoris scopum, ad antecedentia et consequentia, aliaque id genus; ac sane hæc est ratio, qua libri omnes imo omnes sermones intelliguntur. Cum autem Deus nos per libros et sermones docere voluerit, non vero alia via, sane eo ipso evidens est, *sacram scripturam* non aliter quam reliquos libros intelligendum." This rule he establishes and illustrates by nineteen distinct propositions, accompanied with a variety of specific instances where its application is most evidently important. See his Tract de S. S. Interpr. part. 2. cap. ii. More errors in the interpretation of Scripture have, perhaps, arisen from neglect of the obvious rules and principles of common sense and correct reasoning, with which other ancient authors are wont to be explained, than from any intentional perversion of its truths.

SERMON VI.

P. 147. l. 13. *The design of the Apostle in laying down this maxim.*] A full explanation of this text, as deducible from its context, may be found in Dr. Felton's Lady Moyer's Lectures, p. 114—116, and p. 170—174. The learned Author applies it chiefly to the assertion of the Catholic doctrine of the Trinity against Deists, Arians, and Socinians. In the course of the discussion, which is among the most elaborate and profound Treatises on the subject, are interspersed many important rules and observations respecting Scripture-interpretation in general, which render it a very valuable work to a theological Student. To the whole is also prefixed a copious prefatory Dissertation concerning the Light and the Law of Nature and the Expediency and Necessity of Revelation, to which I have had occasion, in another work, frequently to refer.

P. 149. l. 19. *Of which we can otherwise obtain no certain or satisfactory information.*] " We must not judge," says Dr. Felton, " *of the things of God* according to the maxims and principles of *human science*, but according to those *revelations* which are given us, concerning the Divine Nature and Attributes; and we must *receive* them, not according to the figurative schemes and language of human wisdom, but according to those plain assertions of fact delivered in the Scriptures. This is the only sure way of proceeding; and the things of God are then truly discerned and judged of, *when spiritual things are compared with spiritual*, and every part of Revelation is received in a sense agreeable to, and consistent with all the other." *L. M. Lect.* p. 393.

Ibid. l. 22. *What Theologians call the Analogy of Faith.*] " Analogia Fidei est tenor sive summa cœlestis doctrinæ de credendis seu articulis fidei, petita e talibus

Scripturæ locis ubi Spiritus Sanctus de iisdem ex professo vel saltem ex omnium confessione agit, idque verbis rotundis, planis, perspicuis, et omni exceptione majoribus. Istam *Analogiam* in explicatione Scripturæ omnino esse attendendam, et, licet ultimo loco proponatur, tamen primo loco esse habendam, aperte innuit Apostolus ad Rom. xii. 6. et 2 Tim. i. 13. Idem porro suadet ipsa *sana ratio,* scilicet, loca specialia et obscura esse interpretanda secundum effata generalia et indubitata. Ex. gr. locus indubitatus est omnique exceptione major, DEUM *non velle peccatum*, adeoque ejus *non esse causam*, Ps. v. 5. Cum proinde hoc effatum omni dubio prorsus careat, nulla omnino ullius loci Scripturæ admittenda erit explicatio quæ illud evertat. Quod si proinde loca quædam occurrant, quæ in speciem videntur continere contrarium, ex. gr. *de induratione Pharaonis,* et similia, illa ita sunt emollienda et commoda quapiam explicatione declaranda, ut illud perpetuo maneat inconcussum, DEUM NON ESSE CAUSAM PECCATI." *Aug. Pfeifferi Hermeneut. Sacr.* cap. xii.—J. E. Pfeiffer subjoins to a similar definition of the Analogy of Faith, a necessary caution as to its application:—" Harmonia Articulorum fidei in nexu suo spectatorum inter se mutua constituit Analogiam fidei. Quum igitur in ea doctrina quæ ad salutem recuperandam pertinet, omnimoda firmitudo consectanda sit; articulos fidei ex locis certæ interpretationis, adeoque et ipsam analogiam fidei determinari opus est. Quodsi vero sic rite determinata est, quidquid eidem adversatur, veritatibus in scriptura propositis non concordat, proindeque dissensus ab analogia fidei characterem falsæ interpretationis constituit. Notandum duntaxat est, *negative* potius quam *positive,* analogiam fidei ad interpretandum valere; nimirum, si qua interpretatio analogiæ fidei rite determinatæ adversetur, falsam eandem esse hinc intelligo; ut autem vera et genuina sit interpretatio, ad id sola nondum sufficit cum analogia fidei consensio." *Herm. Sacr.* cap. xii. §. 184. This is a sound distinction; since though it is evident that no doctrine can be true which is irreconcilable with the Analogy of Faith, yet there may be many erroneous interpretations of Scripture which do not violate that Analogy; and on the other hand, where that Analogy is not violated, there may be room for some variety of interpretation, without incurring the hazard of dangerous error.

Almost every systematic Theologian has treated largely on the Analogy of Faith. See Glassii Philol. Sacr. lib. ii. part. ii. *de Script. Sensu eruendo.* Chladenii Instit. Exeget. cap. iv. sect. 7. Rambachii Exerc. Hermeneut. containing an excellent Tract *de Parallelismo Scripturæ.*

P. 149. l. 28. *To prophesy according to the proportion of Faith.*] " This is that *Analogy*, which St. Paul requireth in his Epistle to the Romans, and we translate the *proportion* of Faith; not meaning thereby the *degree* of it, either in the Teacher or the Hearers, but the *agreement* of their *doctrine* with the *Scriptures* of the Old Testament and all parts of the Gospel preached and delivered by our Lord and his Apostles; and this rule doth now extend to the New Testament as well as to the Old. For there is an entire agreement and consistency of the Scriptures with themselves from one end to the other, from the first dawning of Revelation as a *Light that shineth in a dark place, till it shineth more and more unto a perfect day.*" *Felton's L. M. Lect.* p. 288.

P. 150. l. 3. *That no prophecy of Scripture is of any private interpretation.*] See a Dissertation upon this text by Werenfels, Opusc. tom. i. p. 238—252. Also Turretin de S. S. Interpr. cap. ii. p. 29. and Bp. Horsley's Sermon on the text, vol. ii. p. 13—16.

Ibid. l. 22. *Systems of Divinity.*] Buddeus, after a short historical sketch of systematic Theology, thus vindicates it against the indiscriminate prejudice with which it has been often assailed. " Neque ideo improbanda est, aut rejicienda hæc theologiam tractandi ratio, si caute atque sobrie instituatur. Etsi enim scholastica theologia non sine ratione male audiat, non omnia tamen quæ scholastici doctores aut a majoribus acceperunt, aut ipsi excogitarunt, prorsus rejicienda sunt... Quare et cum opera beati M. Lutheri nostri melioris doctrinæ lux ecclesiæ nostræ adfulgeret, repudiatis atque rejectis scholasticorum quisquiliis, systematicam tamen theologiam retinendam censuerunt nostrates, sed ea lege, ut ex ipsis Scripturæ fontibus hausta sobrie tractaretur, nec ipsius Scripturæ ea quidquam derogaretur pretio; cumprimis autem, ne, quæ in scholasticis Lutherus ipse et alii cum eo damnaverant vitia, postliminio reducerentur... Nec enim video, quid prohibeat, quo minus quæ cognitu ad salutem necessaria sunt, ex Scripturæ S. fontibus hausta, justo ordine disposita, riteque inter se devincta, proponantur, explicentur, confirmentur; modo veritati cuncta sit consentanea, et ad fidei simul et vitæ praxin referantur. Id vero est, quod nos systematicam theologiam vocamus. Nec vocum quarundam, aut terminorum consuetudine receptorum, quenquam offendere usus poterit, cum abusum ipsimet procul esse jubeamus; sobrie autem et caute si adhibeantur, ad perspicuitatem, pariter ac inutiles ambages evitandas, plurimum faciant." *Inst. Theol. Dogm.* tom. i. p. 69.

P. 152. l. 9. *There is no reason to suppose that the Holy Spirit ... should so entirely overrule their natural faculties*, &c.] " Multiplicanda fuissent miracula, nisi Deus per συγκατάβασιν scriptorum sacrorum genio se accommodare voluisset; atque hoc vere factum fuisse, diversitas stili quæ in Scriptura deprehenditur evincit.... Sua nimirum cuique est, quemadmodum dicendi, sic etiam cogitandi peculiaris quædam ratio: aut igitur ad unum aliquod commune cogitandi atque dicendi exemplum conformanda sacrorum scriptorum vis omnis, aut cujusque ingenio attemperandus erat divini Spiritus impulsus.... Quin tanto facilius quæ animo objiciantur concipimus, quanto magis ordo et stilus nobis familiaris servatur; opus autem erat a scriptoribus sacris recte intelligi quæ Deus inspirabat, ut ea aliis explicare uberius et veram edisserere possent sententiam. Varietas stili, quæ istam comprobat Spiritus Sancti accommodationem, per totam observatur Scripturam." *J. E. Pfeifferi Inst. Herm. Sacr.* cap. i. §. 15. pp. 96, 97.

P. 153. l. 1. *But.... there is a general cast of character*, &c.] " Quod ad reliquam attinet stili sacri indolem, majestatem simplicitas comitatur, casta est et verecunda dicendi ratio, nec plenitudini brevitas officit; atque in universum tales eminent virtutes, quæ facile originem ultra hominum vires elevatam arguunt. Simplicitas stili, quam sacræ vindicamus Scripturæ, non est confusum quoddam et naturalis pulchritudinis intelligentiæque expers dicendi genus; sed lenociniis verborum, fucoque eloquentiæ, et iis opponitur artificiis, quibus oratores uti solent, ad occupandos auditorum animos. Gravitas stili generatim negat indignum quidquam perfectionibus divinis in dictione Scripturæ deprehendi; sigillatim, in eo eminet, quod, intuitu credendorum, assensus in veritates gravissimas absolute absque additis rationibus postulatur: intuitu agendorum, irrefragabilis obedientia ab omnibus terræ incolis, ipsis etiam principibus neminem inter mortales superiorem agnoscentibus exigitur." *J. E. Pfeifferi Inst. Herm. Sacr.* cap. i. §. 17. p. 106.

P. 154. l. 12. *An historical as well as critical knowledge of the language.*] " Alteram jam observationem subjungimus; scilicet, in Scripturæ ut et cæterorum librorum interpretatione sedulo attendendum esse, quænam certis vocibus ideæ eo tempore responderint, quo illi libri scribebantur, non vero quænam ipsis nunc respondeant. Neque enim credendum, Hebræis Græcisque vocibus voces Latinas, quibus redduntur, ita semper respondere, ut iis præcise res eædem significentur: sæpe magnum interest discrimen." *Turretin de S. S. Interpr.* part. ii. cap. 2. §. 14. This subject is examined in all its bearings by Chladenius in his Inst. Exeget. cap. iv. sect. 2. de Scrutinio Verborum et Phrasium.

P. 155. l. 10. *The Historical Analogy of Scripture.*] Some useful observations on this point occur in J. E. Pfeiffer's Hermen. Sacr. cap. xi. §. 149, 150. Also in Rambachius's Treatise de Parallelismo Scripturæ, §. xi. xii. xiii. and Chladenius's Inst. Exeg. cap. iv. sect. 6. Aphorism. 2.

P. 157. l. 6. *The Doctrinal Analogy of Scripture.*] A distinction is made by some Divines between the Analogy of Scripture and the Analogy of Faith; the former being necessary to prevent any expositions which may set one part of Scripture at variance with another, either as to verbal or real differences; the latter, to make every particular or subordinate point of doctrine harmonize with general or fundamental truths. Attention to both these is evidently essential to a correct Interpreter of Holy Writ. " Scrutinium *Analogiæ Scripturæ* in eo consistit, ut Exegeta accurate attendat, an interpretatio Scripturæ quam idoneam judicat, *consuetudini et assertis in Scriptura receptis* congruat. Estque talis Parallelismus vel verborum vel rerum... *Analogia Fidei* est constans sibique perpetua, sibique semper similis, articulorum fidei harmonia, in dictis fundamentalibus seu cardinalibus, a Spiritu Sancto perspicue proposita, ex iisque hausta, quæ singulorum credendorum et agendorum, quatenus ex Scriptura eruuntur, adeoque et explicationum ejus, Lydium lapidem regulamque infallibilem et vere catholicam, constituit." *Chladenii Inst. Exeg*. cap. iv. sect. 6. et 7. p. 398 et 406. Marckius makes a similar distinction: " Analogia, tum *Fidei*, quam primo et semper attendere debemus; tum *Contextus* antecedentium, consequentium, scopi, quæ cum Analogia Fidei semper est jungenda, ne ex quolibet loco quidlibet eliciatur." *Christian. Theol. Medulla*, cap. ii. §. 45.

P. 157. l. 17. *Principles to a certain degree recognized in the exposition of other writings.*] " Solent nimirum profanorum auctorum interpretes, ubi in locum aliquem difficilem et obscurum incidant, circumspicere alia loca, ubi scriptor de re eadem sententiam clarius dixit.... Quum sacræ paginæ, quamvis a diversis scriptoribus consignatæ, ab uno tamen eodemque summo auctore, qui omnium animos calamosque gubernavit, profectæ sint, non possunt non in rebus pariter ac verbis exactissime inter se consentire. Recte enim Epiphanius, tom. i. Operum, hær. 73. Οὐκ ἐναντία τὰ ῥήματα τῆς γραφῆς ἀλλήλοις ἐστὶ, κἂν μάχεσθαι δοκῇ παρὰ τοῖς τῇ πίστει μὴ ὑγιαίνουσιν, ἤτοι ἀσθενοῦσι τῇ γνώμῃ." *Rambachii Exerc. Herm.* pp. 209, 210.

P. 158. l. 18. *A reputed saying of Rabbinical Writers.*] " Rabbinorum fertur dictum, *Nulla est objectio in lege quæ non habeat solutionem in latere...* Jurisconsulti dicunt, *Turpe est de lege judicare, tota lege nondum inspecta.*" *Glassii Philol. Sacr.* lib. ii. part. ii. sect. ii.

P. 160. last line. *These several Analogies are intended to cooperate in explaining obscure passages by those which are clearer,* &c.] " Observandum est, cum aliquid clare patet ex tota revelatione, imo ex scopo revelationis, illud ex locis quibusdam obscuris convellendum non est; sed contra, obscura ex clarioribus exponenda. . . . Verbi gratia, nihil in Scriptura frequentius est, adeoque certius in Religione, quam Deum esse bonum, nec solummodo erga quosdam, sed etiam erga omnes:—sic David, Psal. cxlv. 9. et Ezechiel xviii. 23. Sæpe etiam tum in libris legis, tum apud prophetas, testatus est Deus, quanta cum vehementia optet peccatoris ad se redditum. Matt. xxiii. 37. 1 Tim. ii. 4. 2 Pet. iii. 9. Itaque cum loca quædam occurrunt quæ prima fronte Dei bonitati adversari videntur, quasi, verbi gratia, Deus eum in finem homines quosdam creaverit, ut eos damnaret, quemadmodum volunt Supralapsarii; profecto ex obscuris hisce locis convellenda non est certissima de Dei bonitate doctrina, sed contra hæc loca ex clarioribus explananda sunt." *Turretin de S. S. Interpr.* part. ii. cap. 2. pp. 271, 272.

P. 161. l. 10. *Such as in earlier times was comprised in those shorter summaries of Christian Faith to which we may conceive St. Paul to refer,* &c.] " Originem systematicæ theologiæ ab ipsis Apostolis nonnulli derivare adnituntur. Certe, quando Paulus Timotheo suo ὑποτύπωσιν ὑγιαινόντων λόγων commendat, non desunt, qui brevem ac rudem designationem, ceu formulam quandam ac sciagraphiam intelligunt, quam ex præscripto Apostoli in conspectu habuerit, cujusque ductum in docendo sequutus sit Timotheus. Verum, cum etiam typum quendam, seu summam doctrinæ quam quis animo comprehendit, vox hæcce denotare queat, infirmo nituntur fundamento, qui de formula quadam literis consignata eam accipiunt. Hugo Grotius ὑποτύπωσιν per *exemplar* exponit, additque, *sed intellige exemplar in animo fixum, quod* ἰδέαν *Platonici vocant.* Recte etiam Abr. Calovius monet, *non rudem tantum delineationem, uti nec solam docendi formam, notari, verum imprimis ipsam doctrinæ cœlestis substantiam.* Summa autem quædam doctrinæ cœlestis, quam quis animo comprehensam habet, nondum systematis nomen, si adcurate loqui velimus, promeretur." *Buddei Inst. Theol.* tom. i. pp. 66, 67.

APPENDIX. 327

P. 161. l. 27. *The determinate sense of the word Regeneration.*] See Schleusner's and Biel's Lexicons, and the Lexicographers in general.

P. 162. last line. *A new principle of spiritual life.*] "The general doctrine both of our Lord and St. Paul is, that *water* applied outwardly to the body, together with the *grace* of the Spirit applied inwardly to the soul, *regenerates* the man; or, in other words, the Holy Spirit, in and by the use of water-baptism, causes the *new birth.*" Again; "*Regeneration*, passively considered, is but another word for the *new birth* of a Christian; and that new birth, in the general, means a spiritual *change*, wrought upon any person by the Holy Spirit, in the use of *Baptism*, whereby he is translated from his *natural* state in *Adam*, to a *spiritual* state in *Christ.*" *Waterland's Discourse on Regeneration*, p. 3, 5. republished in the first volume of the Churchman's Remembrancer, 1807.

Buddeus has treated the subject of Regeneration with great accuracy and perspicuity. Speaking of the peculiar force and propriety of the term Regeneration, as applied to the Sacramental Rite of Baptism, he observes, " Sicut nempe per generationem naturalem aliquid producitur quod antea non erat, ita regenerati adepti sunt vitam et vires spirituales, quibus antea destituebantur, Rom. vi. 4. Quemadmodum per generationem genitus fit particeps naturæ generantis, sic per regenerationem simile quid præstatur, 2 Pet. i. 4. . . . Non dicimus tamen, quod aquæ virtus regenerationi tanquam subjecto naturaliter insit, nec quod naturali vinculo Spiritus S. gratiam conjunctam habeat: sed quicquid salutis inde concipitur, id ex ordinatione divina fieri, probe novimus. Nimirum per baptismum tanquam ὄργανον bona ista cœlestia Deus operari promisit: hinc quando ad elementum accedit verbum, fit Sacramentum, secundum tritum illum theologorum canonem. Cur vero Deus externos Sacramentorum ritus sua institutione adjecerit promissioni evangelicæ, eleganter explicat B. Martinius Chemnitius, Exam. Conc. Trid. part. ii. p. 18. *Deus ut divitias bonitatis suæ nobis ostenderet et commendaret, non uno tantum modo, per nudum scilicet verbum, gratiam suam nobis exhibere voluit: sed infirmitatem nostram voluit certis adminiculis sublevare, institutis scilicet et promissioni evangelicæ annexis Sacramentis, hoc est, certis signis, ritibus, ceu ceremoniis, in sensus incurrentibus: ut illis commoneret, erudiret, et certos nos redderet, quod foris in specie visibili geri cernimus, illud intus virtute et potentia Dei in nobis effici. Sicut enim verbum incurrit in aures, et ferit corda; ita ritus Sacramentorum incurrit in oculos, ut moveat corda, ut non dubitemus Deum nobiscum agere, et velle juxta verbum in nobis efficacem esse ad salutem,"* &c. *Buddei Misc. Sacr.* tom. ii. pp. 13, 14.

That this was the view generally taken of the subject by the primitive Fathers, is fully shewn by Dr. Waterland, in his notes to the discourse above quoted. Buddeus recites also the following strong passage from Luther to the same effect, on the text Gal. iii. 27. " Non accepistis per baptismum tesseram tantum, per quam adscripti estis numero Christianorum, ut nostro tempore multi fanatici baptisma tesseram tantum, seu nudum et inane signum faciunt; sed quotquot baptizati estis, Christum induistis: h. e. estis extra legem rapti in novam nativitatem, quæ facta est in baptismo: ideo, inquit, non estis amplius sub lege, sed novo indumento, hoc est, justitia Christi vestiti estis." *Lutheri Opera*, tom. iv. Jen. fol. 115.

P. 164. l. 3. *Terms of similar import were in frequent use among the Jews.*] " The name, or the notion of Baptism," says Dr. Waterland, " probably was not altogether *new* in our Lord's time: for the Jews had been used to admit converts from heathenism into the Jewish Church, by a *baptism* of their own; and they called the admission or reception of such converts by the name of *regeneration* or *new birth;* as it was somewhat like bringing them into a *new world.* Such *proselytes* were considered as *dead* to their former state of darkness, and born anew to light, liberty, and privileges, among the children of Israel, and within the Church of God. The figure was easy, natural, and affecting; and therefore our Lord was pleased, in his conference with Nicodemus, to adopt the same kind of language, applying it to the case of admitting converts both

APPENDIX. 329

from Judaism and Paganism into Christianity; transferring and sanctifying the rite, the figure, and the name to higher and holier, but still *similar* purposes. Such is the account given of this matter by many learned and judicious writers." *Discourse on Regeneration*, p. 56. The writers to whom Dr. W. refers are Selden de Jur. Nat. et Gent. Elderfield of Regeneration, Hebrew and Christian; Wall's Infant Bapt. and the Defence; Wotton's Misc. Disc. Vitringæ Obs. Sacr. Abp. Sharpe, vol. iii. Serm. xii. Deylingii Obs. Sacr. Wesselii Dissert. To these may also be added, Buddei Misc. Sacr. tom. ii. pp. 6, 7. and Lightfoot's Horæ Hebr. on Matth. iii. and on John i. 25. The question, however, is amply discussed in Wall's Introduction to his History of Infant Baptism.

P. 164. l. 20. *An instantaneous, perceptible, and irresistible operation of the Holy Spirit.*] This notion so entirely separates Regeneration from any actual connection with the Rite of Baptism, that it cannot consistently be maintained, but by those who altogether discard Baptism as a *Sacrament*. For a Sacrament is an outward sign, or token, of some inward grace, or spiritual blessing, actually conveyed by it: and if Baptism be not the sign or token of Regeneration, it is a sign of nothing: it is unmeaning, as well as inefficacious. Nay, it is fallacious; because it is a token beforehand of what, according to this theory, may never take place. The advocates of this opinion, indeed, perpetually remind us, that multitudes are baptized, who live and die in a wholly unregenerate state. Of what, then, could Baptism ever be a token to such persons? Or, how will it be possible to apply to their case any of those texts of Scripture which connect it with Regeneration? None, therefore, but those who reject this Sacrament altogether, or who, at least, reject Infant Baptism, can consistently hold this doctrine.

Ibid. l. 26. *By others, it is regarded as a continued and progressive work of the Spirit.*] This opinion is maintained by many who do not intentionally undervalue the Sacrament of Baptism; conceiving that they attach to it its full importance, since they acknowledge it to be accompanied with a renovating and sanctifying grace, the principle of that new life which is afterwards to be improved and perfected by further aids of the Holy Spirit. And this is, in truth, the whole purport and effect of this Divine Institution. But the question is, what more than this is meant by *Regeneration?* Regeneration denotes an *incipient* state, not one that is *complete*; the period of *birth*, not the period of *full age*. To represent it as a *continued* work and as denoting our *growth* in grace, and even our attaining to Christian *perfection*, seems not only to destroy the metaphor and to violate the analogy of Scripture language, but in a great degree to disconnect the sign from the thing signified; making that which, as a purely *initiatory* Institution, is complete and certain in its character, significative of that which must, from its very nature and circumstances, be doubtful and incomplete.

P. 165. l. 2. *Others, again, maintain a distinction between Baptismal and Spiritual Regeneration.*] This opinion, though supported by respectable authorities, appears to be liable to a similar objection, that it either invalidates, or misrepresents, the true *sacramental* character of Baptism. For, if *Spiritual* do not accompany *Baptismal* Regeneration, in what proper sense can the latter be called Regeneration? It is only the *Spiritual* change it produces, which can entitle it to that appellation; and divested of such spiritual effect, it is reduced to a lifeless and unavailing ceremony. If it be not the *means* and the *pledge* of receiving that spiritual benefit, of which it is acknowledged to be a *sign* and *token*; what is its inherent value as a sacramental ordinance? The advantage given by such representations of it, to Fanatics, and to all who decry the Sacraments as beggarly elements of Religion, is manifest. The mistake, however, here, as in the preceding case, may, perhaps, be rather *verbal* than *real*. It appears to arise from conceiving the term Regeneration to be equivalent in force and meaning to that of *final* Justification, and to imply an absolute *assurance* of Salvation. If this were its true signification, it must, indeed, be altogether distinct from Baptism, or, at least, subsequent to it as to the period of its taking place.

But is such an interpretation of it supported by the analogy either of Scripture-language or of Scripture-doctrine? Is there any passage of Scripture where a *baptized* Christian is spoken of as *unregenerate ;* or where *Regeneration* is represented as still *necessary* or *wanting,* to those who, having been already made partakers, by Baptism, of the Christian Covenant, forfeit its privileges by walking unworthily of their Christian calling?

P. 166. l. 24. *By identifying Regeneration with the initiatory Sacrament of Baptism, its full importance is assigned to it,* &c.] That this is the view generally taken of the subject by the best primitive Christian Writers, by the chief leaders of the Protestant Reformation, and by our own Church in particular, appears to be a matter capable of substantial proof. Dr. Waterland, in his admirable Discourse above referred to, produces many strong and convincing testimonies from the Fathers, in corroboration of his arguments: and Buddeus, whose sentiments correspond with Waterland's, says, " Sane consentiunt hic atque doctrinæ huic adstipulantur primitivæ ecclesiæ patres plerique omnes, Tertulliano quidem excepto." Luther's opinion has already been quoted. That of our own Church, as expressed in her Articles and Liturgy, gives no countenance to any other view of it. She constantly speaks of Regeneration as spiritually conferred in Baptism, and of those who are baptized as actually regenerate persons, who are bound, in consequence of that act, to lead the rest of their life according to that beginning. It is to be lamented, that some distinguished writers in her communion have not always with equal accuracy and precision expressed their agreement with her on this point, though doubtless with no intention of essentially differing from her opinion. To Dr. Waterland our Church is greatly indebted, for rectifying many current misapprehensions concerning it, and for the many valuable testimonies he has brought forward in its support. The names of Wall, Wotton, Sharpe, Bull, Bingham, Whitby, Stanhope, Beveridge, Hooker, Clagett, and Bennet, may be considered as sufficient guarantees of the soundness of her Faith in this respect.

P. 170. l. 15. *The Jewish converts were slow of belief, and prone to misinterpret its truths.*] Whence these errors originated, and how necessary it is to a right understanding of the Apostolical writings to be well acquainted with the source of them, Buddeus has distinctly shewn in his Treatise de Statu Ecclesiarum Apostolicarum. The three main points of controversy between the Jewish converts and St. Paul, are thus compendiously stated.—" 1. Utrum gentes ad consortium Evangelii admittendæ sint, necne? Qua de re initio ipsimet dubitabant Apostoli, ut patet exemplo Petri, qui cœlesti demum visione rectiora condocendus erat, Act. x. 34. Sed et qui per Judæum et Samariam dispersi erant, non nisi Judæis primum adnuntiasse Evangelium dicuntur. Putabant enim, promissionem de Christo solum ad posteros Abrahami pertinere. . . . 2. Qui adfirmabant gentes omnino ad consortium fidei esse admittendas, in duas iterum scindebantur partes; nonnullis, tum demum admittendas existimantibus si reciperent legem Mosaicam; aliis, ne id quidem ab iis postulandum contendentibus. . . . . 3. Tertia denique controversia erat: an saltem Judæi, utpote quibus lex data esset, Judaica instituta cum Christianorum disciplina conjungere deberent, necne? Prius adfirmabant multi Judæi jam conversi, quibus etiam Jacobus aliquamdiu adstipulatus fuisse videtur, Act. xxi. 18. negabat autem Paulus. Tametsi enim voluntati Jacobi morem gerebat, ipsam tamen legem, ejusque observantiam, ad salutem consequendam non requiri, passim docet. Vitandi equidem offendiculi causa interdum Judæorum imbecillitati aliquid concessit, 1 Cor. ix. 20. necessitatem tamen legem Mosaicam observandi nuspiam, vel Judæis, vel gentilibus imposuit; immo contra eos qui necessitatem hancce urgebant, subinde acriter pugnavit." *Miscell. Sacr.* tom. i. pp. 227, 228.

P. 172. l. 2. *The same species of misapprehension led to heresies the most opposite to each other.*] With reference, probably, to the necessity of viewing the Old and New Testaments in *connection* with each other, our Lord says of a well-instructed Scribe, or Expositor of Scripture, that he " bringeth out of his treasure things new and old." Luther compares the New Testament to the Sun, and the Old to

APPENDIX.

the Moon, enlightened by the Christian Dispensation. And our great Christian Philosopher, Boyle, compares the two Covenants to the Cherubs which overshadowed the Ark, looking towards each other, and jointly supporting the Mercy-seat. Hence the frequent references which the Writers of the New Testament make to those of the Old; embracing every occasion to shew that the doctrine of Christ and his Apostles was not of recent origin, but had a deep and everlasting foundation in the Sacred Oracles, delivered from the beginning by the Omniscient Spirit of God. Accordingly, our Lord continually directs the Jews to Moses and the Prophets: and St. Paul declares, that he said nothing but what Moses and the Prophets had already spoken. Moses, therefore, and the Prophets must be compared with each other; and both with the Apostles and Evangelists; to enable us to form a correct judgment of either. At the same time, the *distinction* between these different Dispensations must be carefully observed; lest local and temporary concerns should be confounded with those of universal and perpetual obligation: an error, similar to that which our Lord reproved under the similitudes of putting new wine into old bottles, and old cloth into a new garment; by which the consistency of each is marred and destroyed. Had these fundamental principles of Scripture Interpretation been duly regarded, neither Jewish nor Anti-Jewish Christians would have fallen into those extravagancies which distinguished many of the primitive Heresies. On this connection between the Old and New Testament some important observations occur in Rambachius's Treatise de Parallelismo Scripturæ. See his Exercit. Herm. p. 213—234.

P. 173. l. 15. *Interpreting what St. Paul says of the calling of the Gentiles and the rejection of the Jews,* &c.] There is an admirable Discourse of Dean Tucker's on the Potter and the Clay, Rom. ix. 21. in which these erroneous interpretations are ably refuted, and shewn to be destitute of any solid foundation. Towards the conclusion of the Discourse is given this general caution against similar misapplications of Scripture. "In all such cases, the best general rules of explication are these: Let the scope, drift, and nature of the argument be more attended to, than the bare Words or literal Expressions :—And where a few single passages seemingly contradict the general Design, let those be reconsidered in connection with the rest: Let us place ourselves in the situation of those who heard the Speaker or Writer himself: And let us endeavour to find out, what were the meaning of the Words *at the Time they were spoken;* not what they may *now* imply at times so far distant, and among people so very different in their manners and customs from the former. Moreover, in all cases of Difficulty, let the plain Texts be the Interpreters of the obscure, not the obscure of the plain. These, I say, are the best and most equitable maxims to proceed on, and indeed are necessary for the Interpretation of all Writings, human or Divine." *Serm.* i. p. 33.

P. 176. l. 15. *Thenceforth, Scripture is divided against itself.*] Dr. Felton observes, that " both Arians and Socinians, departing from the *Analogy of Faith,* depart *from* the *Analogy* of *Language* too. . . . If they assert the *Divinity* of the *Persons,* they make *Three Gods:* if they allow not the *Divinity,* they make the *Son* and the *Holy Ghost mere Creatures.* . . Those who allow the true and proper *Divinity* without acknowledging a *real distinction* of *Persons,* do as expressly contradict the *Revelation,* as those who own the *distinction* and *deny* the *Divinity* of the *Persons.* Now the same way of Interpretation which convinceth the *Sabellians,* and all that hold with them, of the Divinity of the Persons, that, whatever they are, they are truly *Divine;* would, if attended to, convince them of the *distinction* too; that, as they are truly *Divine,* they are also really *distinct.* And the same rule of Interpretation, which convinceth the *Arian* and *Socinian,* and all that any way hold with them, of the real *distinction* of the *Persons,* would, if applied to *that side* of the question, convince them of the *true Divinity* likewise; that the Father, the Son, and the Holy Ghost, as they are really *distinct,* are also *truly Divine.*

" The *Sabellians,* in owning the *Divinity,* understand the Texts which ascribe this Divinity to the *Son* and to the *Holy Ghost* in the same proper and obvious *significa-*

tion of the *Words*, as they understand those Texts which ascribe it to the *Father;* and if maintaining, as they do, the *Unity* of the Godhead, they would take those Texts which reveal a *distinction* of *Persons*, in the *same* obvious *sense* with those which assert the *Divinity*, they must then acknowledge, that in the *Unity* of *Essence* there are *Three Persons* and *One GOD*.

"On the other hand, if the Arians and Socinians, and all that think with them, would reflect upon *what* grounds they acknowledge this *distinction* of *Persons*, they will find there is as strong reason for acknowledging the *Divinity* also: and if all opposers of the Christian Doctrine would, upon the firm *basis* of the *Divine Unity*, consider what is expressly *revealed* concerning the *Divine Nature*, they must acknowledge the *Divinity* and *distinction* of *Persons* to be clearly asserted in the *Unity* of *Essence*. This then is the Catholic doctrine, which owneth the *Divinity* with the Sabellians, and the *distinction* of *Persons* with the Arians, but still in a true *consistent* sense with the *Divine Unity*." *Felton's L. M. Lect.* p. 340, 342.

P. 176. l. 18. *The strange phenomenon of opposite heresies deduced from the same premises.*] Bishop Horsley, speaking of the phrase used by St. John, of "Christ's coming in the flesh," observes, "that in the sense in which the Church hath ever understood it, this phrase refers to two divisions of the Gnostics, the Docetæ and the Cerinthians; affirming a doctrine, which is the mean between their opposite errors. The Docetæ affirmed, that Jesus was not a man in reality, but in appearance only; the Cerinthians, that he was a mere man, under the tutelage of the Christ, a superangelic being, which was not so united to the man as to make one person. St. John says, 'Jesus Christ is come in the flesh;' that is, as the words have been generally understood, Jesus was a man, not in appearance only, as the Docetæ taught, but in reality; not a mere man, as the Cerinthians taught, under the care of a superangelic guardian, but Christ himself come in the flesh; the Word of God incarnate. St. John says, that whoever denies this complex proposition, is of Antichrist. It surprises me, that you should find an improbability, upon the first face of the thing, in supposing that the same expression should be equally levelled at two heresies, which we confess to be opposite. For is it not always the case, that expressions which predicate a truth lying in the middle between two opposite falsehoods, equally impugn both the false extremes?" *Tracts in Controv. with Priestley*, pp. 108, 109.

P. 177. l. 12. *New Versions too of the Scriptures are brought forward*, &c.] The recent attempt made by the Unitarian Sect to introduce an *improved* Version of the New Testament, adapted to their own peculiar tenets, has been fully examined, and its manifold perversions of the Text exposed, by Dr. Laurence and Dr. Nares, by an anonymous Author, understood to be Mr. Rennell, and by an able writer in the Quarterly Review, May, 1809.

P. 179. l. 5. *These rules must be accompanied with certain cautions.*] Werenfels, in his Lectiones Hermeneuticæ, admonishes the interpreter of Scripture to beware of mistaking particular theories of Religion for the Analogy of Faith, or substituting doubtful and controverted points of doctrine for those which are manifestly scriptural, to serve as the test of Truth. "Non enim hic tanquam norma cæterarum interpretationum, sensus Scripturæ, qui ipsi sunt dubii et controversi, sunt adducendi. Quæ distinctio cum non observatur, fit ut S. Scripturam quilibet ita interpretetur, ut sensus suis placitis et suo *systemati*, quod aut ipse excogitavit, aut aliunde hausit, nulla in re contradicat; et hoc quilibet appellat Scripturam interpretari secundum *analogiam fidei*; ita fit, ut ἀναλογία fidei admodum sit *homonyma* vox, et quot sunt *Sectæ*, tot sint *analogiæ fidei*. Sicut itaque rectus regulæ modo dictæ usus saluberrimus est, ita abusus esset perniciosissimus, et causa plerarumque Scripturæ Sacræ detorsionum. Quare etiam atque etiam cuilibet videndum est, ne quid pro ἀναλογία fidei, et consequenter, pro norma omnium cæterarum interpretationum admittat, nisi manifestissime sit verbum Dei." *Opuscula*, tom. ii. p. 346.

The following extract from Rambachius is no less important.

"Denique uti universa res exegetica prudenter et circumspecte tractanda est, ita parallelismi etiam studium ad normam analogiæ fidei instituere, omnemque *abusum*, quo verus locorum sensus pervertitur, evitare decet. Haud immerito magnus theologus, Abr. Calovius, in Præloq. ad Bibl. Illustr. p. 20. inter causas falsarum interpretationum refert, *verborum et phrasium e diversissimis locis collationem. Conferuntur quidem, ita ait, merito loca parallela, ut Scriptura sui ipsius interpres sit, quum ἰδίας ἐπιλύσεως non sit. Sed primo ac præcipuo loco, tum τὸ ῥητὸν verborum textus, tum συνάφεια contextus pensi habenda. Neque parallela quæ censentur loca semper talia sunt, sed sæpe longe alia tractant, et a locis de quibus agitur sunt alienissima. Unde si proprietate verborum, quæ præ manibus, et contextu orationis, antecedentibus item et consequentibus neglectis, ex aliis locis sensus petatur, fieri non potest quin aberremus facillime a mente et intentione Spiritus Sancti....*Tenendum itaque est, nullum locum Scripturæ jus quoddam ac dictaturam in alterum exercere; sed sensum ante omnia ex ipsis sermonis visceribus, verborum scopo ac nexu in consilium adhibito, esse eruendum, deinde locis parallelis magis confirmandum et illustrandum, nisi et ipsi falli, et alios fallere velimus. Jungamus igitur sinceræ industriæ suspirium Augustini; *Sint castæ deliciæ meæ Scripturæ tuæ; nec fallar in eis, nec fallam ex eis.*" *Rambachii Exercit. Hermeneut.* p. 247, 248.

SERMON VII.

P. 183. l. 22. *He distinguishes the two Dispensations by the terms Letter and Spirit.*] Turretin thus explains these terms, in refutation of the sense affixed to them by Enthusiasts:—" Ex variis etiam locis argumentantur Enthusiastæ, ubi litera spiritui opponitur; per *literam* autem meram intelligunt *Scripturam*, ab immediatis revelationibus sejunctam; per *spiritum* vero suas illas privatas revelationes.... Verum ea perpendenti, perperam ab Enthusiastis proponi patebit. In iis quidem Paulus legis literam vel interiori legis sensui, vel Evangelio quod illum exponit sensum, sed non Scripturam revelationibus opponit internis. Scilicet lex spectari poterat respectu vel præceptorum externorum et corticis externi, nempe præceptorum cæremonialium, quæ utramque fere paginam in lege faciebant, vel mentis legislatoris in eorum publicatione, cujus scopus erat interiorem hominibus sanctitatem commendare... Quoniam vero illa mens Dei speciatim fuerat revelata, et clarius etiam in Evangelio, hinc fit ut Evangelio opponatur legis litera, quod legis mentem nobis manifestat; ut ostenditur, Rom. vii. 6. cum dicitur *nos servire Deo non per vetustatem literæ*, &c. hic intelligitur œconomia vetus, nempe lex, quæ erat abolenda; *per novitatem vero Spiritus* intelligitur Evangelium, quod præcepta spiritualia revelat, et non nova œconomia veteri opposita. Vocatur autem Evangelium *spiritus vel ministerium spiritus*, quia præcepta spiritualia tradit, cum præcepta legis essent carnalia. Lex, si exteriorem corticem spectes, præcepta externa tantum jubebat; sed Evangelium res jubet quæ Dei spiritui præcipue placent: deinde, lex destituebatur variis auxiliis quæ traduntur in Evangelio,—verbi gratia, peccatorum venia in eo promulgata, maximum est ad pietatem auxilium, quo lex carebat—præterea varia Spiritus dona maxima mensura concesserat Deus ad confirmandum Evangelium, &c. . . . Dicunt [Enthusiastæ, sc.] Apostolum dicere, *Litera occidit, Spiritus vivificat:* ibi autem immediatis revelationibus, ad vivificandum aptis, opponi *Scripturam*, huic effectui ineptam. Sed perperam: id enim significat tantum ipsam legem, si in se spectatur, nullam promittere peccatorum veniam; sed in Evangelio occurrere peccatorum veniæ credentibus et resipiscentibus promissionem. Hoc itaque sensu lex erat *litera quæ occidit;* sed Evangelium erat *spiritus qui vivificat:* quoniam hæc spiritus lex vitam promittit credentibus. Hic hujus est sensus loci." *De S. S. Interpr.* part. i. cap. iii. pp. 89, 92.

P. 184. l. 23. *The terms literal, figurative, spiritual, and mystical.*] See Turretin, ut supr. part. ii. cap. 2. p. 253—262. Glassii Philol. Sacr. lib. i. part. i. tract. 2. sect. 1, 2. Aug. Pfeifferi Herm. Sacr. cap. iii. Scrivener's Course of Divinity, b. i. ch. 9. Jackson's Works, vol. ii. b. vii. sect.

APPENDIX. 339

2. p. 597—601. Felton's L. M. Lect. p. 202—222. Waterland's General Preface to his third edition of Script. Vindicated, p. ii—viii. and Dr. Marsh's Lectures in Divinity, part iii. lect. 16.

P. 186. l. 20. *The term mysterious has no reference to this mode of interpretation.*] " Per *mysticum* vero *sensum* non intelligimus in genere *fidei Christianæ mysteria*, quæ ex sensu literali in suis sedibus et primariis Scripturæ dictis eruuntur, (quo respectu quodvis dictum, *articulum fidei et mysterium cœleste proponens*, mysticum sensum habere dici posset, juxta 1 Cor. ii. 6, 7. Rom. xvi. 25.) sed *in specie* talem quorundam Scripturæ locorum sensum, *qui non verbis Scripturæ proxime significatur*, sed *in ipsis rebus* (per verba *sensu literali* denotatis) *a Spiritu Sancto, Scripturæ authore, intenditur;* seu, quod idem est, qui alio ex intentione Spiritus Sancti refertur, quam ad id quod verba immediate significant; quo modo vox μυστηρίου Eph. v. 32. Apoc. xvii. 7. accipitur." *Glassii Philol. Sacr.* lib. ii. part. i. tract. 2. sect. 2.

Ibid. l. 26. *But mystic denotes another sense superadded to that*, &c.] It has long been a subject of controversy between Papists and Protestants, whether Scripture in general admits of more senses than one, consistently with truth. The former have almost uniformly maintained, that a great portion of Scripture admits not only of a double sense, the literal and spiritual, but also of a much greater variety of senses subordinate to these main distinctions. And this is represented by them as a peculiar excellence of the Sacred Writings, characteristic of their Divine origin. Thus Bellarmine says, " Est enim Scripturæ divinæ proprium, *quia Deum habet auctorem*, ut sæpenumero contineat duos sensus, literalem, sive historicum, et spiritualem, sive mysticum. *Literalis* est, quem verba immediate proferunt; *Spiritualis* est, qui alio refertur, quam ad id quod verba immediate significant. . . . Porro literalis est duplex; alius *simplex*, qui consistit in proprietate verborum, alius *figuratus*, quo verba transferuntur a naturali significatione ad alienam. Et hujus tot sunt genera, quot sunt genera figurarum. . . . Spiritualis autem sensus a recentioribus Theologis distinguitur triplex, *allegoricus, tropologicus, anagogicus*. Allegoricum vocant, cum verba Scripturæ, præter literalem sensum, significant aliquid in N. T. quod ad Christum vel Ecclesiam pertineat... Tropologicum appellant, cum verba aut facta referuntur ad aliquid significandum, quod pertineat ad mores... Anagogicum vocant, cum verba aut facta referuntur ad significandam vitam æternam.... Ex his sensibus literalis invenitur in omni sententia, tam veteris quam novi Testamenti. Nec est improbabile, interdum *plures literales in eadem sententia* reperiri." *De Verbo Dei*, lib. iii. cap. 3. In this last sentence is contained the point in controversy; for, respecting the specific subdivisions of the literal and spiritual sense, here laid down, there is no solid ground of objection; instances of each kind being frequent in Scripture. But to affirm that these different senses may concur in one and the same passage of Scripture, so as to admit of various interpretations, is a position which has been strenuously resisted by Protestant writers, as highly derogatory to Scripture, and affording a pretext for the grossest misinterpretation. " Hoc ipsum est," says Glassius, " quod potissimum in Pontificiis reprehendimus. Unicum enim cujuslibet loci sensum esse literalem, infra probatum dabitur. Romanenses vero, dum varietatem sensuum literalium introducunt, Scripturæ claritatem et certitudinem, quantum in ipsis est, elidere satagunt." *Philol. Sacr.* lib. ii. part. i. tr. 1. sect. 2. art. 1.

That the admission of a spiritual or mystical sense in certain passages of Scripture, superadded to the literal, gives no countenance to this position of the Romanists, is evident from the definition already given of it, that it is " a sense founded, not on a transfer of *words* from one signification to another, but on the entire application of the *matter* itself to a different subject." And whether such a sense is to be superadded, or not, to any particular text, must be collected from its context, or from such other parts of Scripture as have reference to it. So that, as Dr. Waterland observes, " the difference may be accommodated by the help of a single *distinction*, viz. between the meaning of *words*, and the meaning of *things*; or by saying, that the

APPENDIX. 341

words of Scripture in such case express such a *thing*, and that *thing* represents or signifies *another thing*. The *words* properly bear but *one sense*, and that one sense is the *literal* one; but the *thing* expressed by the letter, is further expressive of something sublime and spiritual. Thus, for example, the *words* relating to Jonah carry but one meaning, the *literal* meaning, expressing such a *fact*; but then that *fact* expresses, prefigures, or typifies, *another fact* of a higher and more important nature. . . . In this way of settling the forms of speaking, (for that is all,) the same *one sense* of Scripture texts is maintained against the *Romanists*; and the contending parties of *Protestants* may obtain all that they really aim at." *General Preface to Script. Vindicated*, pp. vii. viii. See this point largely discussed in Glassius, as above; also in Turretin, de S. S. Interpr. part. i. cap. 4. and in Aug. Pfeifferi Herm. Sacr. cap. iii. §. 1—10.

P. 187. l. 14. *Repugnant to the evidence of our senses*, &c.] It is on this ground, and not merely on the *incomprehensibility* of the mystery, (as the Romanists would charge upon us,) that the doctrine of Transubstantiation is rejected by Protestants. Turretin observes, " Nullum dogma, quo posito tota religio corruit, admittendum, est. Si admittatur transubstantiatio, sensibus credi non potest; si sensibus non credatur, corruunt argumenta ex miraculis Christi et ejus resurrectione ducta pro religionis Christianæ veritate." Again, " Atque hæc est Augustini circa corporis Christi manducationem regula: Cum enim hoc præceptum ad literam acceptum impium quidpiam imperare videtur, hinc non ad literam, sed figurate intelligendum esse concludit." *De S. S. Interpr.* p. 394, 258.

Ibid. l. 24. *That he did not intend his words to be understood in their literal sense.*] " If," says Dr. Felton, " they will have these words of the Institution to be literally understood, they must first settle the construction of the pronoun, *This* is my Body. If it relates to the Bread, it must, according to several of their own writers, be taken *figuratively*: This Bread is my Body, or the sign of my Body. If the pronoun referreth literally to the Body, then it is an absurd tautology, and affirms nothing at all, but that this

z 3

Body is my Body. The pronoun must refer either to the Bread or to the Body: if to the Bread, then something is distinctly affirmed of it, This Bread is my Body; and the predicate cannot destroy the subject, that it shall be no longer Bread: and when it cannot be *literally* understood, it must be *figuratively* taken, and explained by the Sign, or Communion of the Body of Christ. They ought next to shew, why the words are not to be literally understood in the second instance, as well as in the first, and affirm, that the *Cup* is as really the *Blood*, or the New Testament in the Blood, as the Bread is the real and very Body of Christ." *L. M. Lect.* pref. p. xii.

P. 187. l. 25. *And this is further evident from the conduct of the Disciples themselves.*] " In locorum expositione attendendum est ad effectum, quem certa verba natura sua parere debuerunt, si certo modo intellecta sint: si vero effectum illum non pepererint, quem verba certo sensu accepta parere debuerunt, id magno indicio est, ea verba eo sensu accepta non esse. Exemplum in transubstantiatione; nam certe, si verba Christi eo sensu intellecta fuissent ab Apostolis, maximum in iis stuporem creare debuissent, quod tamen contigisse non videmus." *Turretin de S. S. Interpr.* pp. 393, 394. To account for the different conduct of the Apostles on this and on the former occasion, when our Lord spake of the necessity of eating his flesh and drinking his blood, it may be observed, that as our Lord, in that memorable discourse, John vi. 51—66, spake of giving his Body and his Blood as a thing *future*, and did not immediately accompany the declaration with any outward sign or token by which the mystical sense of the expressions might be made evident, it is the less surprising that they should *then* have understood the words in their literal sense, and have taken offence accordingly: but when our Lord in this instance spake to them in the *present* tense, " Take, eat, this *is* my Body," and when they saw the material Bread and the living Body both before their eyes unchanged, they had no choice; there was no room for the gross literal apprehension of the terms, and they were constrained to receive them in their figurative and symbolical sense.

APPENDIX. 343

P. 188. l. 16. *The Socinian, always solicitous to divest Christianity of every thing mysterious.*] The connection between this Sacrament and the doctrine of our Lord's *Atonement* sufficiently explains the solicitude of the Socinian that it should not be interpreted in any higher sense. The two Sacraments have been greatly instrumental in preserving entire the fundamental Articles of the Christian Faith. This has been shewn by Dr. Waterland, in his Charge on the doctrinal Use of the Christian Sacraments, 8vo. Lond. 1736. He remarks of Socinus, that " after a thousand subtleties brought to elude plain Scripture, he was yet sensible that he should prevail nothing, unless, together with the doctrine of the Trinity, he could discard the *two Sacraments* also, or render them *contemptible*. Baptism was a standing monument of the *Personality* and *equal* Divinity of the *Father, Son,* and *Holy Ghost ;* and the other Sacrament was an abiding memorial of the *merits* (though no *creature* can *merit*) of our Lord's Obedience and Sufferings. And both together were lasting attestations, all the way down, from the very infancy of the Church, of the secret workings, the heavenly graces and influences of the *Holy Spirit* upon the faithful receivers. The *Form* of *Baptism* stood most directly in his way. As to the *Eucharist,* if he could but reduce it to a bare *Commemoration* of an absent friend, there would be nothing left in it to create him much trouble." p. 33—35. The low estimation in which Sacraments, as such, are held by Socinians, is largely discussed in Hoornbeck's Socin. Confut. tom. iii. p. 220—248. Stapfer thus concisely states the true ground of their depreciation of both: " Cum porro Sacramenta in hunc præcipue finem sint instituta, ut divinam gratiam, per sacrificium Christi partam, fœderatis obsignarent, et veluti arrhæ et pignora iis essent; Sociniani autem negent rem signatam, scilicet, quod per Christi obedientiam et sanguinis effusionem, sive per passiones ejus et mortem, omnibus fidelibus parta sit remissio peccatorum et jus ad vitam æternam ; hinc illis etiam omnis Sacramentorum usus fuit inventendus ; inde est, quod dicant, ritus illos symbolicos, quos Sacramenta vocamus, tantum habendos esse pro tesseris et notis externæ Christianismi professionis, adeoque eorum usum esse tantum depingere et significare gratiam, non autem obsignare." *Inst. Theol. Polem.* tom. iii. p. 392.

P. 188. l. 26. *The Fanatic. . . also alike depreciates their value.*] It is characteristic of all Enthusiasts to think meanly of Sacramental Institutions. Presuming that *vital* Christianity consists in certain inward feelings and convictions produced by the *immediate* agency of the Holy Spirit upon the heart and mind, they regard the Sacraments as little better than lifeless ceremonies, and stigmatize those who ascribe to them any instrumental efficiency as means of Grace, by the opprobrious appellation of *formalists*. Nor are they, in this respect, chargeable with inconsistency. For if it be true, that Grace can be communicated to the believer only by the *immediate* agency of the Holy Spirit, it will not be easy to shew the necessity or advantage of any instituted *means* of Grace whatever. That which is to be obtained, and can only be obtained, by the *immediate* act of God, cannot require, nor even admit, any *medium* of communication: and consequently, the Sacraments, losing that part of their essential character, will be regarded only as *signs* or *representations* of some spiritual benefits which either have been or are to be bestowed, without any external instrumentality. Thus, even by some who allow the Sacraments to be Christian Ordinances, Baptism is held to be nothing more than an *emblem* of that Regeneration or Conversion, which, if ever it really take place, is to be effected by some *subsequent* operation of the Spirit; and the Lord's Supper is received merely in acknowledgment of that assurance of pardon and sanctification which the Communicant is persuaded he has already received by the effectual working of the Holy Spirit within him, independently of the use of this, or any other outward ordinance. . . . Stapfer has remarked this of several fanatical sects:—
" Neque propterea *mediis Gratiæ externis* opus habent; unde non tantum Verbi Divini in hoc statu usum rejiciunt, sed de Sacramentis etiam contemtim loquuntur." And again, of Weigelius, the leader of one of those sects, " Uti

omnium *mediorum externorum* usum rejiciebat, ita etiam Sacramentorum usum summopere contemnebat. Quisquis enim essentialiter cum Deo aut Christo ita unitus est, ut Deus ipse subjective omnia in eo operetur, is omnino externis mediis haudquaquam opus habet." *Inst. Theol. Polem.* tom. iv. pp. 345, 360.

P. 189. l. 16. *The sense of the words of the Institution is undoubtedly mystical.*] " These expressions," says Dr. Felton, (speaking of St. Paul's account of the Institution, 1 Cor. x. 16. and xi. 23—26. together with those of the Evangelists,) " are to be understood in a figurative, symbolical, and commemorative sense, so that the Bread and the Cup are a real Communion of his Body and Blood. The outward part, or visible sign of this Sacrament, is, as our Church Catechism teacheth, Bread and Wine; the inward part, or thing signified, is the body and blood of Christ, which is verily and indeed taken and received, in all their real and spiritual effects, by the Faithful. This is the real Presence, which we hold. He is so present, as to annex the very benefits of his Body and Blood to our Communion of the Bread and Wine, which are now made the spiritual food and nourishment of our souls; that as He loved us and gave Himself for us, we might ever be partakers of, and give thanks unto Him for his unspeakable gift." *L. M. Lect.* pref. pp. x. xi.

P. 190. l. 14. *It is in vain to reason* a priori *for its total rejection.*] The argument *a priori* is, however, much more strongly in favour of this mode of communicating spiritual truth, than against it. The object of Revelation being to make known things which " eye hath not seen, nor ear heard, nor have entered into the heart of man to conceive," it seems hardly possible, that the human mind should be capable of apprehending them, but through the medium of figurative language or mystical representations. This is well illustrated by Dr. John Clarke, in his Enquiry into the Origin of Evil. " The foundation of Religion and Virtue being laid in the mind and heart, the secret dispositions and genuine acts of which are invisible, and known only to a man's self; therefore the powers and operations of the mind can only be expressed in figurative terms, and signified by external symbols. The motives also and inducements to practice are spiritual; such as affect men in a way of moral influence, and not of natural efficiency; the principal of which are drawn from the consideration of a Future State: and consequently *these* likewise must be represented by Allegories and Similitudes, taken from things most known and familiar here. And thus we find in Scripture the state of Religion illustrated by all the beautiful images that we can conceive; in which natural unity, order, and harmony consist, as regulated by the strictest and most exact rules of discipline, taken from those observed in the best ordered temporal governments. In the interpretation of places, in which any of these images are contained, the principal regard is to be had to the figurative or spiritual, and not to the literal sense of the words. From not attending to which have arisen absurd doctrines and inferences, which weak men have endeavoured to establish as Scripture-truths; whereas, in the other method of explication, the things are plain and easy to every one's capacity, make the deepest and most lasting impressions upon their minds, and have the greatest influence upon their practice. Of this nature are all the rites and ceremonies prescribed to the Jews, with relation to the external form of religious worship; every one of which was intended to shew the obligation, or recommend the practice of some moral duty, and was esteemed of no further use than as it produced that effect. And the same may be applied to the rewards and punishments peculiar to the Christian Dispensation, which regard a future state. The rewards are set forth by such things as the generality of men take their greatest delight, and place their highest satisfaction of this life in; and the punishments are such as are inflicted by human laws upon the worst of malefactors: but they can neither of them be understood in the *strictly literal* sense, but only by way of analogy, and corresponding in the general nature and intention of the thing, though very different in kind." *Boyle's Lect.* vol. iii. p. 229. ed. fol. 1739.

P. 191. l. 27. *In determining the extent of this species of*

Interpretation.] " Hic vero (ut in more positum est mortalibus ad extrema propendere) alii *excessu,* alii *defectu,* peccant: quorum *illi* sensus arcanos et mysticos ubique fere locorum acri studio venantur, nimiumque allegoriis, satis sæpe contortis, indulgent; *hi* angustissimis terminis sensum mysticum circumscribunt, inque perpaucis scripturæ locis eum agnoscunt; prout nimirum quisquis vel natura adfectus est, vel studiis a prima juventute excultus, vel prout magnorum virorum auctoritatibus ducitur." *Rambachii de Sensus Mystici Criteriis,* §. iii. pp. 8, 9.

P. 191. last line. *Some would confine it to the expositions given by our Lord and his Apostles.*] Rambachius censures this as restricting it within too narrow limits, and charges it upon Socinian interpreters, as one of their known characteristics. Ibid. §. vii. pp. 24, 25.

P. 192. l. 2. *Others regard those expositions as ensamples only of what we are to apply universally to the Sacred Writings.*] Rambachius inclines to carry these expositions to a considerable extent. "Sufficit, quod a viris θεοπνεύστοις clavem acceperimus, qua ad mysticum plurimorum locorum sensum recludendum feliciter uti et possumus et debemus." Ibid. §. viii. p. 27. In this he accords with Witsius, who argues upon St. Paul's intimation, that there were other figurative services enjoined in the Old Testament, requiring a mystical interpretation, of which he "could not then speak particularly," Heb. ix. 5. And doubtless, there are types and symbolical representations, as well as prophecies in the Old Testament, relating to Christ, and applicable to the Christian Dispensation, of which the Apostles have not left particular expositions. Too much caution, however, can hardly be used in extending the rule.

Ibid. l. 15. *The best Writers on the subject seem to be agreed.*] Glassius, in his Philologia Sacra, lays down certain general and special rules respecting the literal sense of Scripture. The *general* Rules are these:—" Canon 1. Sensus literalis Scripturæ textuum non parvi pendendus, sed maxime in pretio habendus, et solicite eruendus est. 2. Unus tantum est cujusque tum vocis, tum contextus Biblici, literalis sensus. 3. Quilibet Scripturæ locus sensum literalem admittit. 4. Sensus Scripturæ literalis a verbis Scripturæ nequaquam est separandus. 5. Sensus literalis præcipue est argumentativus, non tamen excluso mystico."—The *special* Rules are as follow :—"1. Sensus literalis proprius arcte tenendus, nisi in fidei articulos aut charitatis præcepta palam et vere incurrat, et simul evidenter ex eodem vel aliis locis figuratus sermo detegatur ac probetur. 2. Præsertim ubicunque articulus fidei ex professo traditur, ibi urgendus est sensus literalis proprius, sive τὸ ῥητόν. 3. Verba quæ continent primam cultus novi vel fœderis institutionem, et recentem præceptionem, sine tropis, sensu literali proprio sunt accipienda, nisi evidentissima tropi alicujus adsit explicatio. 4. Declaratio et demonstratio tropici sensus debet esse evidens, ac sufficiens." Lib. ii. part. ii. tr. 2. sect. 1. p. 263—288.

Chladenius, after proposing similar rules, remarks, "Unde graviter errare necesse est, 1. *Judæos* et *Muhamedanos*, quorum innumeræ fabulæ et mendacia Talmudica, ex Scripturæ vaticiniis et oraculis ad literam sumtis, quæ tamen figurate accipienda erant, paulatim enasci potuerant. 2. *Chiliastas* et *Fanaticos* qui *aurea secula, Apocatastasin* et *Chiliasmum* ex vaticiniis, juxta intentionem Dei nonnisi figurate intelligendis, proprie tamen explicatis, effingunt, et Judaica fere captant somnia, vicissim vero Christi historiam in figuras et tropos convertunt. Vide exemplum rei in Barclaio, Apol. p. 85. thes. vi. Ita Fanatici phrases *radicandi, fundandi, illuminandi, introeundi, implendi,* in actibus gratiæ Spiritus S. describendis adhibitas, plerumque sensu literæ sumendas existimant. . . 4. *Pontificios,* qui *in tropis quærunt quod in iis nunquam est reconditum ;* ita τὸ ποιμαίνειν, Joh. xxi. 17. de dominio a Papa affectato; *Solem et Lunam,* in Creationis historia, de Imperio sacro et civili, ridicule satis exponunt. 5. *Socinianos,* qui, ut divinitatem Salvatoris Jesu Christi infringant, tropos formant, ubi non sunt, et *filium Dei* ejusque *generationem, dominium,* et alia, per *meram tropologiam* et improprie exponunt." *Inst. Exeg.* p. 215—217. See also J. E. Pfeifferi Inst. Herm. Sacr. p. 432—443. and 740—752. Turretin de S. S. Interpr. p. 140—144. and p. 390—393. Rambachii de Sens. Myst. Criteriis, p. 29—65.

APPENDIX. 349

P. 194. l. 22. *Whatever is generally necessary to Salvation.*] " *Omnis fidei articulus in Scripturis alicubi ex professo propriis et perspicuis verbis est expositus*, quæ illius articuli propria quasi sedes et domicilium est. *Nihil est obscure dictum in Scripturis quod spectet ad fidem, vel mores, quod non planissime dictum sit in aliis locis*. Si igitur in tali Scripturæ textu versemur, in quo fidei articulus aliquis ex professo traditur, ibi ut ne latum unguem a verborum proprietate divelli nos patiamur, conveniens est." *Glassii Philol. Sacr.* lib. ii. part. i. tr. 2. sect. 1. p. 286.

P. 195. l. 13. *Parables.*] Glassius has largely treated on the subject of Parables. The following are among his chief rules for their interpretation. " Canon 3. In parabolis, si integre accipientur, tria sunt: *radix, cortex, et medulla sive fructus. Radix* est scopus, in quem tendit parabola. *Cortex* est similitudo sensibilis quæ adhibetur, et *suo sensu literali* constat. *Medulla* seu fructus est *sensus parabolæ mysticus*, seu ipsa res, ad quam parabolæ fit accommodatio, seu quæ per similitudinem propositam significatur. 4. In explicatione et applicatione parabolarum legitime instituenda, primo omnium attendendus est dicentis scopus. 5. In parabolis non est opus nimia cura in singulis verbis anxium esse, neque in singulis partibus adaptatio et accommodatio ad rem spiritualem nimis ἀκριβῶς quærenda est. 6. Theologia parabolica non est argumentativa. Canon hic in Theologorum scholis tritissimus est. Intelligendus autem de parabolicis expositionibus et accommodationibus non *innatis*, quæ in ipsa Scriptura habentur (illæ enim certas pariunt demonstrationes, perinde ac alia quæ ῥητῶς in sacris literis habentur) sed *illatis*, et quidem *externis* et *alienis*, quando vel a scopo, vel a fidei analogia et orthodoxia disceditur. 8. Cum frequenter dicitur simile est regnum cœlorum huic vel illæ rei, &c. non oportet ex hoc intelligere, similitudinem sumtam in omnibus suis partibus convenire regni cœlorum mysteriis: cum sufficiat illam servire in ea regni cœlorum parte aut conditione, propter quam declarandam erat assumta. Sic in quadam parabola Christus comparatur *furi*, Luc. xii. 39. sed in illo tantum *quod ut ille venit hora qua non putatur, ita Christus venturus est qua hora non putamus*.

Sic Luc. xvi. imitandus proponitur *villicus iniquitatis*, non in omnibus, sed in solertia, eaque non in omni materia, sed in tali de qua hoc loco sermo est. 9. Non omnes parabolæ eodem modo concludunt, sed diversis. Quædam nimirum a *simili*, ut septem illæ parabolæ Matt. xiii. et multæ aliæ: aliæ vero per locum *a dissimili*, ut est parabola *de iniquo judice qui nec Deum timebat, nec homines reverebatur; et de amico petente tres panes; et de villico iniquitatis.*" *Philol. Sacr.* lib. ii. part. i. tr. 2. sect. 5. p. 336—350. See also Aug. Pfeifferi Herm. Sacr. cap. iii. §. 13. p. 635. J. E. Pfeifferi Inst. Herm. Sacr. cap. xiii. p. 753—773. Turretin de S. S. Interpr. part. ii. cap. 2. §. 14. and Waterland's Gen. Pref. to Script. Vindic. p. ix—xi.

P. 197. l. 27. *Types.*] "Deus per omniscientiam futura omnia cognoscit, per summam vero sapientiam res ita conformare potest, ut altera alteram similitudine sua referat; et quum ens tale, quod similitudine sua refert alterum, *imago* audiat, præsentia Deus ita conformare potest, ut imagines evadant futurorum. Res præsens, quam rei futuræ imaginem esse Deus voluit, *typus* appellatur; unde facile patet ad typum requiri, ut non sit fictum quid, sed revera exhibitum; ut sit imago rei alterius; ut ex voluntate atque intentione divina idem sit; atque ut res illa cujus imago est, non præterita, non præsens, sed futura sit." *J. E. Pfeifferi Inst. Herm. Sacr.* cap. xiv. p. 730—795. See also Aug. Pfeifferi Herm. Sacr. cap. iii. §. 12. p. 635. Waterland's Gen. Pref. to Script. Vindic. p. xiv—xvi. Jenkins's Reasonableness of Christianity, vol. ii. ch. 7. and 15. and an elaborate Discourse by Bp. Lavington, on the Nature and Use of a Type, 8vo. Lond. 1724. Glassius, in his Philologia Sacra, has given a series of Canons of Typical Interpretation, drawn up with great accuracy and precision. But they require the accompanying illustrations to make them clearly intelligible.

P. 200. l. 5. *Allegory.*] Almost all the authors above referred to treat of Allegories as distinct from Types and Parables. To them, therefore, I must again direct the reader who is desirous of fuller information. The whole subject, however, of figurative and mystical interpretation has been recently discussed, with his usual perspicuity and judgment, by Dr. Marsh, in his Lectures, part iii. lect. 17, 18.

P. 200. l. 24. *Symbols.*] Dr. Waterland expresses a doubt, whether *symbolical* language should be referred to *figurative* or to *mystical* construction; but inclines to the *latter;* considering a Symbol to be a kind of *simile*, and therefore more resembling a *parable* than a *metaphor*. An example, he observes, will best shew its meaning. "We read in Isaiah, that *all the host of heaven shall be dissolved.* Now, the *host of heaven* literally signifies sun, moon, and stars: but sun, moon, and stars *symbolically* signify the *princes* and *nobles,* (Civil and Ecclesiastical,) forming any state or polity. So then, the *dissolving the host of heaven* symbolically means the dissolving the whole frame and constitution of such civil and ecclesiastical state. This kind of construction nearly resembles the *parable*, where the *literal meaning* is but the *shell* or *shadow*, and the *mystical* is the thing intended: the one is but the *image*, as it were, while the other is the *truth* represented by it, or veiled under it." Again;—"I distinguish a *type* from a *symbol*, in this respect, that a *type* is some *real* fact or thing, whereas a *symbol* is rather fictitious than real." *Gen. Pref. to Script. Vindic.* p. xi—xiv. Bishop Hurd's definition is clear and accurate. " By Symbols I mean certain representative marks, rather than express pictures; or if pictures, such as were at the same time *characters*, and, besides presenting to the eye the resemblance of a particular object, suggested a general idea to the mind. As when a *horn* was made to denote *strength*, an *eye* and *sceptre, majesty*, and in numberless such instances; where the picture was not drawn to express merely the thing itself, but something else, which was, or was conceived to be, analogous to it. This more complex and ingenious form of picture-writing was much practised by the Egyptians, and is that which we know by the name of Hieroglyphics." *Warburton Lect.* Serm. ix. p. 288. ed. 8vo. 1722. See also Dr. Felton's L. M. Lect. p. 207—211. and Lancaster's Symbolical Dictionary, prefixed to his Abridgment of Daubuz on the Revelation, 4to. Lond. 1730.

P. 202. l. 18. *Two distinguished Writers of this class,*

in the last century.] Collins, in his Grounds and Reasons of the Christian Religion, and the Scheme of Literal Prophecy considered; and Woolston, in his Discourses on the Miracles of our Saviour. See Leland's View of the Deistical Writers, vol. i. letters 7, 8. Similar attempts have been made in our own times, by Volney and other French Infidel Writers, and by Sir William Drummond, in his Oedipus Judaicus, to entirely explain away the principal historical facts of Scripture; attempts calculated to impose upon the superficial and unwary by an ostentatious display of learning, but which have been successfully repelled by Christian advocates of sounder learning and better principles.

P. 206. l. 1. *From such corrupt sources some Christian Commentators appear to have unguardedly drawn their supplies.*] " Præcipue harum partium sectatores, qui hoc vitio laborant, sunt 1. *Antiquissimi Judæorum doctores,* maxime qui ex schola Alexandrina prodierunt, ubi morbus ille allegoricus quam maxime grassabatur; speciatim in scriptis *Philonis,* inque *Midraschim* et *Rabboth* veterum Hebræorum: in quibus ceterum illud laudandum est, quod Messiam, scripturæ nucleum, quæsiverunt, quamvis loco sæpe satis alieno. 2. Multi *patres Ecclesiæ,* maxime qui Origenem ducem in scriptura sacra interpretanda sectati sunt. 3. *Pontificii* interpretes, interque illos præcipue *doctores scholastici.* 4. *Mystici impuriores* et paradoxis speculationibus, arcanæ sapientiæ speciem mentientibus, dediti, ex Paracelsi maxime atque Bohmii schola. 5. Multi Jo. Cocceii asseclæ, luxuriante ingenio in multiplicandis interpretationibus typicis atque allegoricis abrepti. 6. Nonnulli ex ipso philosophorum recentiorum ordine, ut Thomas Burnetius, aliique." *Rambachii de Sens. Mystic. Criteriis,* §. iii. pp. 9, 10.

Ibid. l. 27. *Spiritual improvements, as they are sometimes called,* &c.] Dr. Waterland observes of the allegorical comments of the Fathers, that very often they were " not so properly *Interpretations,* (for they generally admitted a *literal* Interpretation besides of the same Texts,) as a kind of moral or spiritual *uses* or *improvements* raised upon the Texts, for the practical edification of the people. The design seems to have been much the same (only employed upon a nobler subject) with what several pious persons have attempted, in endeavouring to turn every common incident of life, every thing they hear, read, or see, to some spiritual improvement, by apposite reflections or meditations." Of this he afterwards remarks, " Whether such spiritual uses were really intended in such place by the Sacred Penman, or no, yet if the words might be but aptly accommodated thereto, and were but pertinently and soberly applied, and the Analogy of Faith preserved, a good end was answered thereby, and true *doctrine* at least kept, if not true Interpretation." Again ; " which ends [the *improving* their *morals* and *elevating* their *affections*] might be, in a good measure, answered by apposite meditations on the Text, though they should not be *true* Interpretations. And it was that consideration chiefly, as I conceive, which made the *Fathers* take the more freedom in *moralizing* and *spiritualizing* (if I may so speak) the *Letter* of Sacred Writ." *Import. of the Trinity*, p. 437, 510—515. where these sentiments are confirmed and illustrated by quotations from St. Augustin.

That no such applications, however, of Scripture are to be received as properly *expositions* of the Sacred Word, is evident. " Repeto id," says Glassius, " quod supra inculcatum fuit, quando de sensu Scripturæ mystico hic agitur, intelligi tantummodo eum, quem Scriptura ipsa, sui ipsius interpres, dilucide commonstrat. De reliquis autem, vel *allegoricis*, vel *typicis*, vel *parabolicis* interpretationibus, quæ ab interpretum pendent arbitrio, verum illud Hieronymi in 2. com. super Matth. *Pius hic sensus: sed nunquam parabola aut dubia ænigmatum intelligentia potest ad autoritatem dogmatum quicquam proficere.* Et Bellarm. de Verbo Dei, lib. iii. c. 3. *quod sensus mystici* [sc. Scripturæ manifesta explicatione destituti et ab interpretibus illati] *licet ædificent cum non sunt contra fidem aut bonos mores, tamen non constet an sint a Spiritu Sancto intenti.* Et hoc in sensus mystici enucleatione diligenter observandum." *Philol. Sacr.* ut supr. p. 290. See also Turretin de S. S. Interpr. part. i. cap. iv. p. 144—152.

P. 208. l. 5. *What errors too in religious opinions may not receive a plausible appearance by the aid of a mode of Interpretation so lax and flexible in itself,* &c.] The abuse of *figurative* interpretation is not peculiar to mystics and fanatics. The *Socinians*, who would arrogate to themselves, almost exclusively, the character of *rational* Christians, often discover a strong propensity to figurative and even mystical expositions of Scripture, when they find it impossible to adapt the *literal* sense to their own hypotheses. Dr. Edwards, in his Preservative against Socinianism, has shewn this in several instances. " When we produce," says he, " the plain words and expressions of Scripture, if those words contain a doctrine that is repugnant to their reason, they say, in this case it is lawful to *wrest* and *pervert* them to another meaning, quite contrary to what the natural construction of them would direct us to. From the *natural* you may fly to a *figurative* construction; and if *ordinary* figures will not serve the turn, you may call in to your assistance *tropos inusitatos,* any the most uncommon and unusual *tropes,* and thereby compel them to comply with your conceptions. If they are to be credited, such a *figurative and mystical meaning* is couched under the *plainest expressions,* as render the Scripture the most *obscure and mystical book* in the whole world. Now, if it be a fault (as they seem to think) that our religion as to some parts of it is *mystical,* these men must be inexcusable in laying it to our charge, because they themselves must come under the same and a much heavier condemnation. For, by making a *figurative* and *obscure* meaning to lie hid under the *plainest* and *easiest* expressions of Scripture, they are found to be the promoters of a *mystical incomprehensible* sort of Divinity, which none can unfold but themselves. Thus, in their exposition of John viii. 58. *Verily, verily, I say unto you, Before Abraham was, I am,* πρὶν 'Αβραὰμ γενέσθαι, ἐγὼ εἰμί. First, they have perverted the word *Abraham* from being a *proper name* to be an *Appellative,* so that, according to them, it doth not denote the *person of Abraham,* but rather the *privilege and blessing* that was denoted by the change of his name from *Abram* to *Abraham*; viz. that he should be *the Father of many nations*. Now if you enquire of them whether it is ever taken in any part of the Bible, otherwise than to denote the *person of Abraham;* they must answer in the negative. And yet quite contrary to the *constant use of the word*, both in this chapter and all other parts of the Bible, as also against the *reason and design of the place*, it must be wrested and turned to a *metaphorical signification*, because otherwise we should here find a plain and uncontrollable declaration of our Saviour's *preexistence*, and that will lead us to a belief of his *Divine Nature*, which must not be allowed, whatever becomes of the Scriptures which affirm it; and therefore you may *quantamcunque vim adhibere,* use any the greatest force to oblige them to speak otherwise. But, secondly, the word γενέσθαι is altered from denoting the *substantial* formation and *existence* of *Abraham*, into an *accidental* and *metaphorical* mutation, whereby he was made not *a man*, but *the Father of many nations*. And the like alteration hath the verb εἰμὶ undergone, by which our Saviour designed to signify his *real and substantial existence;* but they have made it to denote *his office*, viz. that of being the *Messiah*, or the Redeemer of the world. So that whereas the literal construction of the words would lead us to this plain truth, that before *Abraham* was born or did exist, our Saviour had a being and did exist, and therefore it was no wonder that he should see him; by their figurative distorting of the words they have extracted this unexpected meaning, that before *Abram can be Abraham*, that is, *the Father of many nations,* ἐγὼ εἰμὶ, *I*, saith Jesus, *must be the Saviour and light of the world.*" Part iv. p. 70—106. where much more occurs to the same purpose; fully justifying the author's observation, that " by directing men to the Scriptures for instruction, if a Socinian is to be their guide, you only bring them into a *labyrinth*, out of which no care, no endeavours can extricate them."

In like manner Bishop Horsley observes, of the Unitarian doctrine, " if ever it should be clearly proved to have been the sense of the Sacred Writers; the just conclusion will be, that of all writers they have been the most unnecessarily and the most wilfully obscure. The Unitarians themselves pretend not that their doctrine is to be found in the plain literal sense of Holy Writ: on the contrary, they take the greatest pains to explain away the literal meaning. They pretend that the Sacred Writers delight in certain metaphors and images, which, however unnatural and obscure they may seem at this day, are supposed to have been of the genius of the eastern languages, and of consequence familiar to the first Christians; who, in the greater part, were of Jewish extraction. By the help of these supposed metaphors, the Unitarian expositors contrive to purge the Scripture of every thing which they disapprove, and make it the oracle, not of God's wisdom, but of their own fancies." *Tracts in Controv. with Priestley*, pp. 103, 104. In another part of the work, after exposing a false criticism of Dr. Priestley's on a passage of Clemens Romanus, he subjoins, " But language is no key to unlock the mind of a Socinian." p. 120. *note.*

With reference to this subject, Dr. Waterland observes, that " most of the *abuses*, with regard to the interpreting of Scripture, when traced up to their fountain-head, will appear to have been owing to this, that some will *fancy* the plain and obvious sense *unreasonable* or *absurd*, when it really is not; and will thereupon obtrude their own *surmises, conjectures,* and *prejudices,* upon the Word of God. For, having taken their own *conceits* for certain *truths,* and having determined beforehand, that the *letter* of Scripture shall give way to them, they will of course rack and torture Scripture, as far as wit, learning, or invention can assist them, in order to contrive some construction or other, which may but seem to favour their preconceived opinions; unless they choose rather to reject or adulterate the texts which make against them, or to devise new Scriptures to serve the purpose. Add to this, that the art of *torturing* plain words has been advanced to great perfection in these latter ages, since the revival of learning and sciences; and especially since the *Socinians* and *Romanists* have taken almost incredible pains to make themselves complete masters in that way. There is nothing now almost, but what some or other will attempt, if there be occasion, to drag over into the service of any cause, and to wrest to what sense they please, though ever so contrary to the words themselves, or to the known intention of the authors or compilers. The ancient Misbelievers most of them were young practitioners in comparison: for they commonly *rejected or adulterated* the Scriptures which they did not like; not understanding, or however not trusting to *qualifying* interpretations, which might steal away the *sense*, without injuring the *letter*." Import. of the Trinity, p. 362—364.

P. 213. l. 7. *Nevertheless, let not the dry and spiritless Critic,* &c.] Ὅμως δὲ μέσην χωροῦντες ἡμεῖς, τῶν τε πάντη παχυτέρων τὴν διάνοιαν, καὶ τῶν ἄγαν θεωρητικῶν τε καὶ ἀνηγμένων, ἵνα μήτε παντελῶς ἀργοὶ καὶ ἀκίνητοι μένωμεν, μήτε περιεργότεροι τοῦ δέοντος ὦμεν, καὶ τῶν προκειμένων ἔκπτωτοι καὶ ἀλλότριοι, (τὸ μὲν γὰρ Ἰουδαϊκόν πως καὶ ταπεινὸν, τὸ δὲ ὀνειροκριτικὸν, καὶ ὁμοίως ἀμφότερα κατεγνωσμένα,) οὕτω περὶ τούτων διαλεξόμεθα κατὰ τὸ ἡμῖν ἐφικτόν· καὶ οὐ λίαν ἔκτοπον, οὐδὲ τοῖς πολλοῖς καταγέλαστον. Greg. Nazianz. Orat. 42. tom. i. p. 684. ed. Paris. 1630.

SERMON VIII.

P. 217. l. 8. *But the more obvious application of the text to the Universal Church,* &c.] " By *Church* here is not meant the Church of Ephesus alone; but the whole Catholic Church, the pillar and ground of the truth; to whose Officers and Governors the Gospel is committed; wherein it is taught, preached, and practised; and to which belongs the promise of indefectibility. And the collecting into Churches, and the subordination, hath been, and still is, the great means of preserving Religion in the whole." *Bp. Fell in locum.*——" If," says Dr. Hammond on this text, " the truth of the Gospel had been scattered abroad by preaching to single men, and those men never compacted together into a Society, under the government of Bishops, or Stewards, &c. such as Timothy was, to whom was delivered by St. Paul that παρακαταθήκη, 1 Tim. vi. 20. a *depositum*, or *body of sound doctrine*, to be kept as a standard in the Church, by which all other doctrines were to be measured and judged; if, I say, such a summary of Faith had not been delivered to all Christians that came in, in any place, to the Apostle's preaching, and if there had not been some Steward to keep it, then had there wanted an eminent means to sustain and uphold this truth of the Gospel thus preached unto men. But by the gathering of single converted Christians into assemblies or Churches, and designing Governors in those Churches, and entrusting this *depositum*, or *form of wholesome doctrine*, to their keeping, it comes to pass that the Christian Truth is sustained and held up: and so this *house of God* is affirmed to be *the pillar and basis of Truth*, or that pillar on a *basis* by which Truth is supported. According to which it is, that Christ is said to have *given not only Apostles*, and *Prophets*, and *Evangelists, but also Pastors and Teachers*, that is, the Bishops in the Church, (known indifferently by those two titles,) εἰς καταρτισμὸν τῶν ἁγίων, for *the compacting of the Saints* into a Church, εἰς οἰκοδομὴν, *for the building up of the body of Christ*, confirming and continuing them in all truth, Eph. iv. 14. *that we should be no longer like children carried about with every wind of doctrine*, &c. And so again, when Heresies came into the Church in the first ages, it is every where apparent, by Ignatius's Epistles, that the only way of avoiding error and danger was to adhere to the Bishop in communion and doctrine, and whosoever departed from him, and that *form of wholesome words* kept by him, ἔφθαρται, was supposed to be corrupted."

P. 218. l. 2. *The Visible Church here on earth.*] Respecting the great distinction between the Visible and Invisible Church, on which most of the Controversies concerning its Divine Institution principally depend, see Dr. Rogers's Discourse on the subject, 8vo. Lond. 1719, and a Review of that Discourse, published soon afterwards, and entering more largely into a discussion of the controverted points; both of them masterly Treatises. An author of more modern date, thoroughly conversant with the subject, well observes, " The necessary distinction between the earthly or visible state of Christ's kingdom, and its heavenly or invisible state, is too often overlooked, especially by those who teach that Christ is the only Head of his Church. It may with equal reason be maintained, that the Almighty Creator is the only Head of all civil Society: and, in a certain sense, both positions are true. But if our Lord had designed for the Church no head but himself, the invisible one, we can upon no reasonable ground account for his visible system of religious worship, for his visible means of grace, and for his visible ministry to administer those means; a ministry endowed with large visible powers; and among others, that of perpetuating a succession to the end of the world." *Sikes's Discourse on Parochial Communion*, p. 130. 8vo. 1812.

P. 219. l. 21. *The design of the Christian Church, both with respect to its first institution and the means ordained for its perpetuity.*] For a full account of every point relating to the primitive Constitution of the Christian Church, the reader is referred to Archbishop Potter's Treatise on Church-Government, which has long been esteemed a standard of authority. A more concise but very clear and satisfactory view of the subject will be found in Mr. Sikes's work just referred to, ch. i. p. 12—125.

P. 222. l. 27. *The Church itself has proved a successful instrument, in the hands of Providence, both of transmitting the unadulterated word of God, and of promulgating and maintaining its fundamental Truths*, &c.] It must never be forgotten, that although the Scripture is, to all who are in possession of it, the sole infallible guide to religious Truth; yet from the *Church* we have received that precious deposit; and through the channel of her instruction, the general knowledge of Christian truth has been communicated to mankind. Thus far the preservation of Christianity may be said to have been made dependent on the preservation of the Church; and the Divine Author of both to have ordained the latter in subservience to the former, for the good of his creatures. Nor is this attributing any undue influence to the Church, as if she might propound a Rule of Faith of her own devising, to be implicitly received on her authority; since it represents her only as a competent witness of the authenticity of the Sacred Oracles, and a faithful guardian of the truths they contain. How those Oracles could have been otherwise transmitted to us, with unexceptionable evidence of their Divine original; or how the sum and substance of their essential doctrines could have been so diffusively and so uniformly spread over the civilized world, as the harmony of the several confessions of the Faith proves it to have been, if no such means had been instituted for the purpose; it is for the sceptical to explain. It is sufficient for those who accept and duly appreciate the benefit, to discern and gratefully to acknowledge the hand of Providence, both in the formation of this vast design, and in the course of its operation through so many successive ages.

P. 223. l. 24. *It can hardly be disputed that this form of Ecclesiastical Polity has so generally prevailed*, &c.] Dr. Bennet, after examining many of the arguments alleged by Separatists against the necessity of Episcopal Communion, produces a remarkable passage from a Dissenting Writer, cautioning his brethren against precipitate or intemperate censure of the advocates of Episcopacy. It purports to be an extract from the work of a Dr. Bryan, entitled, "Dwelling with God," and is as follows.—" All that I desire of you is only this, that laying aside all passion, you will but pause and ponder what is alleged to give satisfaction to this objection; which may cool at least the fierceness of your spirits, and abate the desperate prejudice you have conceived against the government and worship established in these churches. Touching the exercise of Ecclesiastical Government in general, you know it is not of absolute necessity to the Constitution of a Church. And as to the Government of the Churches by Bishops, (speaking of it only as they are superior to Presbyters, without meddling with the extent of their dioceses, &c.) when you find so much written with so much confidence, that Episcopacy is the true, ancient, Apostolical Government of the Christian Church; that it was received in profession and practice in all ages, and is so far Divine, that Bishops were in the very time of the Apostles;

APPENDIX. 361

that they were ordained and appointed by the Apostles themselves; that there was an approved succession of them in the Apostolical Churches; that in all the following ages all the Churches in the world were governed by them for more than fifteen hundred years, without any opposition, save by the Arian Aerius, who was therefore cried down as an Heretic by the ancient Fathers; that the first reformed Protestant Churches cast not off Episcopacy with any averseness to the order, as appears by the history of the Augustan Confession, to which Calvin himself signed; that some of these Churches were governed by Superintendants, the same with Bishops; that there was long since a challenge made to them that have any averseness to the Degree or Order, in these words, *We require you to find out but one Church on the face of the earth, that hath not been ordered by Episcopal regimen*, which, to this day, as they say, is not answered:—These allegations may, methinks, so far allay your heat, as to restrain your thoughts and tongues from passing so sore a censure upon the government, that it is devilish and Anti-Christian, till you can solidly absolve all these arguments." *Discourse of Schism*, ch. xxix. pp. 124, 125. 8vo. 1718.

P. 224. l. 11. *According to the interpretation of a distinguished Commentator.*] See Dr. Hammond on the Text, as above quoted.

Ibid. l. 25. *Those only ought to be considered as sanctioned by Church-authority*, &c.] " Hoc unum præmonemus, judicium primarum Ecclesiarum de necessitate hujus alteriusve alicujus nostræ religionis articuli, nobis seris nepotibus haud alia certiori ratione constare posse, quam primo consulendo Catholicorum Patrum et celebriorum in Ecclesiis illis Doctorum scripta et monimenta, quæ extant; ut inde, quid illi hac de quæstione senserint, cognoscamus: deinde perscrutando Historiam Ecclesiasticam de iis qui in primis sæculis Jesu Christi Domini nostri Divinitatem negarunt; ut intelligamus, cujusmodi in ipsos sententiam tulerint illorum temporum Ecclesiæ; utrum in communione sua eosdem retinuerint, an rejecerint, ut a corpore Christi alienos. Est quidem et tertia ratio dignoscendi, quæ dogmata primæva Ecclesia pro creditu necessariis habuerit, nempe ex Symbolis et Fidei confessionibus, quas ab iis, qui communione sua frui vellent, exigebat." *Bulli Judic. Eccl. Cathol.* introd. p. 5. ed. fol. Lond. 1703.

It is in full reliance on this only sure test of conformity to the primitive Faith, that our Church repels the charges of Heresy and Schism continually brought against her by the Church of Rome. " Ita isti," says Bp. Jewell, " nos calumniantur esse Hæreticos, ab Ecclesia et Christi communione discessisse: non quod ista vera esse credant, neque enim id illis curæ est; sed quod ea hominibus imperitis possint aliqua forte ratione videri vera. Nos enim discessimus, non, ut Hæretici solent, ab Ecclesia Christi, sed, quod omnes boni debent, a malorum hominum et hypocritarum contagione. Hic tamen isti mirifice triumphant, Illam esse Ecclesiam; Illam esse sponsam Christi; Illam esse columnam veritatis; Illam esse arcam Noe, extra quam nulla salus sperari possit: nos vero discessionem fecisse; Christi tunicam lacerasse; a corpore Christi avulsos esse, et a fide Catholica defecisse. Cumque nihil relinquant indictum, quod in nos, quamvis falso et calumniose, dici possit, hoc tamen unum non possunt dicere, nos vel a verbo Dei, vel ab Apostolis Christi, vel a primitiva Ecclesia descivisse. Atqui nos Christi et Apostolorum et sanctorum Patrum primitivam Ecclesiam, semper judicavimus esse Catholicam; nec eam dubitamus arcam Noe, sponsam Christi, columnam et firmamentum veritatis appellare; aut in ea omnem salutis nostræ rationem collocare. Odiosum quidem est a societate cui assueveris discedere, maxime vero illorum hominum, qui quamvis non sint, tamen videantur saltem, atque appellentur Christiani. Et certe nos istorum Ecclesiam, qualiscunque tandem ea nunc est, vel nominis ipsius causa, vel quod in ea Evangelium Jesu Christi aliquando vere ac pure illustratum fuerit, non ita contemnimus; nec ab ea nisi necessario et perinviti discessionem fecissemus. Sed quid si in Ecclesia Dei idolum excitetur, et desolatio illa quam Christus futuram prædixit stet palam in loco Sancti? Quid si arcam Noe prædo aliquis aut pirata occupet? Certe isti quoties Ecclesiam nobis prædicant, seipsos solos eam faciunt; et omnes illos titulos sibi ipsis adscribunt; atque ita triumphant, ut olim qui clamabant, Templum Domini, Templum Domini, aut ut Pharisæi et Scribæ, cum jactarent se esse filios Abrahami." *Apologia Eccles. Anglic.* §. 79, 80, 81.

P. 225. l. 13. *Individuals, or congregations of individuals, may have tainted large portions of the Christian community with pestilential heresies.*] The abettors of heresy, both in ancient and modern times, have usually shewn some solicitude not to be considered as cut off from communion with the Church, or as renouncing the primitive Faith. But in the writings of the early Fathers, we find it almost invariably insisted upon, that the Church Catholic utterly disclaimed the opinions maintained by the Heresiarchs with whom they contended: and in modern times the labours of Bishop Bull, Waterland, Horsley, and others engaged in similar controversies, have been directed to prove that all such errors as relate to *fundamental* articles, at least, of the Christian Faith, whatever antiquity they may pretend to, or to whatever extent they may have prevailed, have been unsanctioned, discountenanced, disclaimed, and rejected by the Church itself. This, however, must be understood to relate only to great *essential* truths, and taken in their *general* acceptation, as laid down in Creeds and other public Confessions of Faith; not according to particular expositions of them by individuals, however distinguished by their adherence to the Church, nor with respect to differences upon lesser points, where no fundamental article is impugned. See Berriman's L. M. Lect. Serm. i.

P. 226. l. 9. *Arianism.*] Bp. Bull has clearly shewn, that the Arian heresy was not only directly at variance with the Nicene Creed, but that it was virtually disclaimed by the Church in the judgment it passed upon other heresies similar to it, and before it. " Namque apertissimum est, commemoratos Hæreticos ab Ecclesia damnatos fuisse ob causam, quæ ipsis cum Arianis fuit, nempe quod Servatorem nostrum Deum esse negarent. Respice quæ in hoc capite de Theodoto, Artemone, et Paulo Samosateno ex Veteribus observavimus; et videbis eorum omnium hæresin in eo a S. Patribus constitutam fuisse; non quod Christum inferiorem quam revera erat creaturam, sed quod meram creaturam omnino statuerent, neque verum Deum agnoscerent." Again: " Doctores Catholici ante Arium, utcunque alias in quæstione de Filii Divinitate illorum nonnulli vel incautius, vel obscurius nonnunquam locuti fuerint, tamen uno quasi ore, Filium Dei ita ex Deo Patre genitum esse fatebantur, ut ex ipsa ejus essentia natus, adeoque Deus revera ipse fuerit: quod in nostra Nicenæ Fidei defensione per totam sectionem secundam fusissime demonstratum est. Frustra igitur gloriabantur Ariani se ab antiquo Fidei Canone minime recessisse; siquidem regulæ illius verba tantum, non verum atque inde ab initio receptum in Ecclesia sensum tenuere." *Judic. Eccl. Cathol.* cap. ii. §. 9. p. 29. cap. vi. §. 21. p. 59.

P. 227. l. 26. *Did the Church in primitive times yield one iota of its essential doctrine,* &c.] Bishop Bull has proved that several articles in the Nicene Creed, and in the Creeds of still earlier date, were specially inserted in opposition to certain tenets maintained by the Gnostics: and he remarks, that the article respecting *one Catholic Church* was evidently intended to form a line of distinction between those who adhered to the primitive Apostolic Faith and those self-constituted communities of professed believers who departed from it. " Recte igitur Valesius, (in not. in lib. vii. Hist. Eccl. Eus. c. x. p. 256.) *Apparet hoc cognomen Ecclesiæ inditum esse circa primam Apostolorum successionem, cum hæreses multis in locis exortæ, veram Christi fidem et Apostolorum traditionem subvertere conarentur. Tunc enim, ut vera et genuina Christi Ecclesia ab adulterinis Hæreticorum cœtibus distingueretur,* CATHOLICÆ, *cognomen soli orthodoxorum Ecclesiæ attributum est.* Verum illud porro notandum est, Gnosticos, qui maxime in prima Apostolorum διαδοκῇ hæreses suas disseminarunt, plerosque omnes eo arrogantiæ atque impudentiæ pervenisse, ut jactitarent, purum et sincerum Evangelium in suis tantum conventiculis doceri, se solos Dei mysteria veramque salutis obtinendæ rationem invenisse et scivisse; unde et Gnosticorum nomen sibi fecerunt: illam vero doctrinam, quam ab Apostolis traditam Ecclesia Catholica acceperat atque amplexa erat, falsam in plerisque atque adulterinam

APPENDIX. 365

fuisse.... Adversus hos impios Dogmatistas Ecclesiæ filii omnes illius ævi meritissimo jure tenebantur profiteri, se credidisse in *unam Catholicam Ecclesiam,* hoc est, se doctrinæ et fidei illi voluisse constanter adhærescere, quæ juxta S. Scripturas, in Ecclesiis Apostolicis ubique gentium, ab Episcopis et Doctoribus uno quasi ore prædicaretur." *Jud. Ecc. Cathol.* cap. vi. §. 14. p. 54.

P. 230. l. 10. *The Athanasian Creed,* &c.] Several other heresies besides those here mentioned appear to have been had in view by the author or compiler of this Creed. "Whoever wrote this Creed," says Dr. Hey, "he meant nothing more than to *collect* things said in various Catholic writers, against the various *heresies* subsisting, and to *simplify* and *arrange* the expressions, so as to form a confession of Faith the most concise, orderly, and comprehensive possible. Not with any view of *explaining* any mysterious truths, but with the sole design of *rejecting* hurtful or heretical *errors*." This is fully proved by Dr. Hey, in his discussion of this Creed. See his Divinity Lect. vol. iii. p. 93—119. and his Visitation Sermon, 8vo. 1790. See also a Sermon on the subject by Dr. Horbery, Wheatley's L. M. Lect. 8vo. 1738, and Waterland's Critical Hist. of the Athanasian Creed, 8vo. 1723 and 1728.

P. 231. l. 23. *By the confession of her adversaries, the Church of England is eminent in this respect.*] Dr. Puller observes, "If the scattered concessions which have been made by our adversaries at sundry times and upon divers occasions, should be gathered together, there is scarce any judgment, or practice, or constitution of our Church, but hath been acknowledged, by some or other of them, as reasonable and moderate. He quotes one remarkable instance of such concession from a publication, entitled, a Conference between a Protestant and a Papist, 1673; in which the author, speaking of the Church of England, says, *I believe her Moderation hath preserved what may one day yet much help to close the breach betwixt us. We observe that she, and peradventure she alone, has preserved the face of a continued mission, and uninterrupted ordination. Then in doctrines, her Moderation is great: in those of greatest*

concern she has expressed herself very warily. In Discipline, she preserves the government by Bishops: but above all, we prize her aversion from Fanaticism, and that wild error of the private spirit, with which it is impossible to deal: from this absurdity the Church of England desires to keep herself free: she holds indeed, that Scripture is the rule of controversy; but she holds withal, that it is not of private interpretation: for she is for Vincentius's method."
See Puller's Moderation of the Church of England, ch. iii. pp. 39, 40.

P. 232. l. 8. *She avoids with equal care the error of those,* &c.] If the venerable and judicious Hooker may be allowed to speak the sentiments of our Church, there can be no doubt of her desire neither to elevate authority of any kind above that of the Sacred Word, nor to depreciate the value of human reason and human learning as subsidiary to its right interpretation. " The whole drift," he observes, " of the Scripture of God, what is it, but only to teach Theology? Theology, what is it, but the science of things Divine? What science can be attained unto, without the help of natural Discourse and Reason? *Judge you of that which I speak*, saith the Apostle. In vain it were to speak any thing of God, but that by Reason men are able somewhat to judge of that they hear, and by Discourse to discern how consonant it is to truth. Scripture, indeed, teacheth things above nature, things which our reason by itself could not reach unto. Yet those things also we believe, knowing by reason, that the Scripture is the Word of God. ... Wherefore if I believe the Gospel, yet is reason of singular use, for that it confirmeth me in this my belief the more: if I do not as yet believe, nevertheless, to bring me into the number of believers except reason did somewhat help, and were an instrument which God doth use unto such purposes, what should it boot to dispute with infidels or godless persons for their conversion and persuasion in that point? Neither can I think that when grave and learned men do sometimes hold that of this principle there is no proof but by the testimony of the Spirit, which assureth our hearts therein, it is their meaning to exclude utterly all force which any kind of reason may have in that behalf; but I rather incline to interpret such their speeches, as if they had more expressly set down, that other motives and inducements, be they never so strong and consonant unto reason, are notwithstanding ineffectual of themselves to work Faith concerning this principle, if the special grace of the Holy Ghost concur not to the enlightening of our minds." Again;—" Exclude the use of natural Reasoning about the sense of Holy Scripture, concerning the Articles of our Faith; and then that the Scripture doth concern the Articles of our Faith, who can assure us? That which by right exposition buildeth up Christian faith, being misconstrued breedeth error: between true and false construction, the difference Reason must shew." *Eccl. Polity*, b. iii. §. 8. See also Puller's Moderat. of Ch. of England, ch. iv. and v.

P. 233. l. 16. *She omits not to testify her deference to the judgment of the Church Catholic.*] Dr. Puller refers to several instances in the Canons and other public documents of our Church, where this reverence for antiquity in matters both of doctrine and discipline is strongly marked; and he observes, "the reverence of the Church of England to the ancient Fathers, as it is most regular and well governed, so is it most uniform and constant; whereas nothing is more ordinary with the Romanists, than when they are pressed and urged by the authority of the ancient Fathers against them, to depreciate their testimonies, and add some scurvy, false insinuations concerning them; as hath been often observed of Baronius, Bellarmine, Stapleton, and others. Whereas the constant reverence of the Church of England to the ancient Fathers is such, that the Romanists cannot but acknowledge it very often, as De Cressy (Exomolog. pp. 102, 135.) saith, *Indeed the Protestants in England make honourable mention of the Fathers. They profess greater reverence to antiquity than any other sect whatsoever.*" See, as above, ch. v. p. 90.

Bp. Jewell thus ably vindicates our Church in this respect. " Nos quidem, uti diximus, de mutanda religione nihil temere aut insolenter, nihil nisi cunctanter, et magna cum deliberatione fecimus: neque id unquam animum induxissemus facere, nisi nos et manifesta atque indubitata voluntas Dei nobis in sacrosanctis Scripturis patefacta, et salutis nostræ ratio coegisset. Etsi enim discessimus ab illa Ecclesia, quam isti appellant Catholicam, et ea re nobis apud illos, qui judicare non possunt, invidiam faciunt, tamen id satis est nobis, satisque esse debet homini prudenti, et pio, et de æterna vita cogitanti, nos ab ea Ecclesia discessisse, quæ errare potuerit; quam Christus, qui errare non potest, tanto ante prædixerat erraturam; quamque nos ipsi oculis perspicue videbamus a sanctis Patribus, ab Apostolis, a Christo ipso, a primitiva et Catholica Ecclesia discessisse. Accessimus autem, quantum maxime potuimus ad Ecclesiam Apostolorum et veterum Catholicorum Episcoporum et Patrum, quam scimus adhuc fuisse integram, utque Tertullianus ait, incorruptam virginem, nulla dum Idololatria, nec errore gravi ac publico contaminatam: nec tantum doctrinam nostram, sed etiam Sacramenta, precumque publicarum formam, ad illorum ritus et instituta direximus: utque Christum ipsum, et omnes fere pios fecisse scimus, religionem ab istis turpiter neglectam et depravatam ad originem, et ad primordia revocavimus. Inde enim putavimus instaurationem petendam esse, unde prima Religionis initia ducta essent." *Apol. Ecc. Ang.* §. 150.

P. 234. l. 5. *Homilies.*] The declared purpose for which the Homilies were drawn up sufficiently indicates the care of our Church, that the Scriptures should not be indiscreetly or unlearnedly handled, either by the Laity or Clergy. They are commended in the thirty-fifth Article, not only as "containing a godly and wholesome doctrine," but also as "*necessary for those times;*" times, when even the Clergy in general, just emerging from the darkness of Popery, and distracted by intricate and perplexing controversies among many conflicting parties, were but ill qualified for the work of public instruction. This is especially adverted to in the Preface, as it was published in the year 1562, where the reason for directing them to be read in Churches is stated to be, that the people might "both learn their duty towards God, their Prince, and their neighbours, according to the mind of the Holy Ghost, expressed in the Scriptures, and

APPENDIX. 369

also to avoid the manifold enormities which heretofore by *false doctrine* have crept into the Church of God;" and because that " all they which are appointed Ministers *have not the gift of preaching sufficiently to instruct the people.*" Therefore, for "the quieting of their consciences in the chief and principal points of Christian Religion," and " to expel and drive away as well corrupt, vicious, and ungodly living, as also erroneous and poisoned doctrines tending to superstition and idolatry," this book was set forth. Hence it is manifest that our Reformers considered the interpretation of Scripture as a work not to be confided to unskilful hands; nor would they suffer unlettered or meanly educated persons to hazard the experiment. Accordingly, in the second part of the first Homily on the reading of Holy Scripture, the people are admonished that they should " take upon them to expound it no farther than they could plainly understand it. For, as St. Augustine saith, the knowledge of Holy Scripture is a great, large, and a high place; but the door is very low, so that the high and arrogant man cannot run in; but he must stoop low, and humble himself, that shall enter into it. Presumption and arrogancy are the mother of all error; and humility needeth to fear no error. For humility will only search to know the truth; it will search and will bring together one place with another, and where it cannot find out the meaning, it will pray, it will ask of others that know, and will not presumptuously and rashly define any thing which it knoweth not." These admonitions, with much more immediately following to the same purpose, though they give great encouragement to modest and pious readers to search the Scriptures for their own edification, yet clearly shew that our Church entirely discountenances the notion that such edification is attainable without competent instruction in the use of them, and without a willingness to receive instruction from those who are set over them for that purpose.

P. 234. l. 16. *As a faithful Expositor of God's word, her caution and judgment are evinced,* &c.] Our Church shews also the importance she attaches to a judicious *collation* of Scripture, by the rich supply of *marginal references* in her authorized versions of the Bible. These serve to exemplify the good effect of searching for passages parallel either in verbal expression, or in general signification, or in matters of historical fact, and points of Faith and Practice. Probably no Church is so well provided as ours with these helps to Scriptural knowledge.

P. 235. l. 3. *Accuses us of having merely a negative Religion.*] It is remarked by Bp. Bramhall, that the Romanists " call our Religion a negative Religion, because in all the controversies between us and them, we maintain the negative; that is, we go as far as we dare or can, with warrant from Holy Scripture and the primitive Church, and leave them in their excesses, or those inventions which they themselves have added. But in the mean while, they forget that we maintain all those Articles and truths which are contained in any of the ancient Creeds of the Church; which I hope are more than negative." *Protestant Ordination defended.* See his Works, folio, p. 1018.

Ibid. l. 13. *She teaches in her seventh Article*, &c.] In the Reformatio Legum, there is an Article more particularly noticing the opposite errors which have prevailed respecting the Jewish and Christian Dispensations, and expressly disclaiming them. *De Hæresibus*, cap. iv. p. 9. ed. 4to. Lond. 1641.

P. 236. l. 3. *Her three last Articles.*] These also are considerably enlarged upon, with a special view to the errors of the Anabaptists, in the Reformatio Legum, de Hæres. c. xiii. xiv. xv.

Ibid. l. 19. *Her doctrine of the Sacraments.*] The nature of the Sacraments is thus stated in the Reformatio Legum. " Magna quoque temeritas illorum est, qui Sacramenta sic extenuant, ut ea pro nudis signis, et externis tantum indiciis capi velint, quibus, tanquam notis, hominum Christianorum religio possit a cæteris internosci; nec animadvertunt quantum sit scelus, hæc sancta instituta inania et vacua reddere. Quæ cum inter nos dispertiuntur, ut divini Spiritus fides confirmetur, erigitur conscientia, promissio etiam veniæ peccatorum per Christum facta intrinsecus exhibetur, extrinsecus vero istis Sacramentis quasi Sigillo quodam consignatur. Præterea verbo Dei quod intercedit, et Symbolorum adhibitorum naturis, erudiuntur fideles de pretio nostræ redemptionis per Christum comparatæ, Spiritus sanctus et gratia in mentibus fidelium ulterius instillatur, tum etiam fœdus quod per Christum inter Deum et nos ictum est corroboratur, ut nobis ille proprius sit Deus, nos illi peculiaris populus; et astringimus nos ipsos ad peccatorum abolitionem, et integritatem vitæ suscipiendam. Quæ si recte ponderentur, necesse est ut obmutescat illorum calumnia, qui Sacramentorum inopem volunt et nudam naturam relinquere."—*De Hæresibus*, c. xvii.

P. 239. l. 10. *Hence she has been regarded as the fit medium of reconciliation between other Churches.*] Dr. Puller takes notice of the wholesome advice given by King James to the English Divines who were to attend the Synod of Dort, that "*in case of main opposition between any overmuch addicted to their own opinions, their endeavours should be that certain propositions be moderately laid down, which may tend for the mitigation of heat on both sides.*" Dr. P. then adds, "the same is already performed in our constitution for a general accommodation of controversy: neither will any, I hope, have the worse opinion of our Church, because *Grotius* thought *the Church of* England *a right medium of reconciliation:* [See Bp. Bramhall's Vind. pp. 22, 23.] whose pacificatory design Mr. Baxter took to be one of the most blessed noble works that any man can be employed in." *Moder. of Ch. of Eng.* ch. xiv. pp. 396, 397.

Projects of a general union between foreign Protestant Churches and our own, and of bringing back the Separatists in this country to communion with our national Church, have, in former times, often occupied the attention of great and good men, tenacious of sound principles, yet desirous, from the purest motives of Christian Charity, to effect an external agreement in essential Truth, leaving lesser differences to remain unmolested. Little hope, however, can be entertained of effecting these purposes, without a sacrifice, on one side or the other, of principle, or, at least, of conscientious scruple. Nor does the broader basis of modern liberality give a reasonable assurance of better success. The strength and permanency of union depends upon *consistency*, at least, if not *identity* of principle and of sentiment, in the parties who are to coalesce. But how that consistency is to be obtained by an association of opposite and discordant opinions, it is not easy to conceive: nor does it seem probable, that any such union would be effected, but upon a principle (if such it may be called) of entire *indifference to the truth*. After all, will not the peace and harmony of the whole Christian community, even of those who separate from the Church as well as of those who adhere to it, be better secured by an upright and conscientious maintenance, among every denomination of Christians, of their own fixed and sincere persuasions? Is this integrity of conduct in any wise inconsistent with the pure benevolence and forbearance of the Christian character? Does not the honest assertion, on either side, of what is deemed to be the truth, lay the surest foundation of mutual respect and good-will?

But upon the importance of upholding Church-Unity as the best safeguard of Religion itself, let us hear the sentiments of one of our most excellent Divines.—" It has been pretended," says he, "that the laws of *Charity* and *Benevolence* are sufficient provisions for all the union that Christ ever intended among his Disciples. But these unite us only as *men*, and not as *Christians*. These duties are indeed prescribed to us by the Gospel with greater accuracy and refinement, than by any other Institution; but still they are but a more correct edition of the common rules of *humanity*. Something more is required to unite and distinguish us as *Christians*, viz. such a profession of *Faith*, a participation in such *Ordinances*, and the observation of those *Laws* which embody us as a *visible Society:* and without these I presume that the Church of Christ will quickly become *invisible* in a sense that will imply its utter destruction. It is evident that all the designs which have been formed against Christianity, since its first Institution, have endeavoured its subversion as a *visible Society*. And that the present enemies of the Gospel among us pursue the same maxims appears from the applause and triumph with which they receive all notions, which tend to dissolve the external polity of the Church, and withdraw men's respect from those *offices* and *administrations*, without which it cannot subsist. They are contented that the duties which flow from our *internal* relation to Christ, and belong to us as members of his *invisible* Church, should be pressed and recommended, provided the submission we owe to those *whom He has appointed to rule over us*, be left out of the catalogue, and all those Laws, Duties, and Offices, which incorporate and unite us as a *visible Society*, be exposed as *priestcraft* and *imposture;* because they see plainly that these principles will so effectually assist them in subverting the Church as a *visible Society*, that not even a single Congregation can be formed upon them. And they are very well satisfied, that if they can once dissolve those ties which unite us together as a *visible* Church, our *invisible* Church will give them no trouble, but expire of itself." *Dr. Rogers on the Visible and Invisible Church*, part iv. ch. ii. p. 121, 122.

THE END.